A Treasury of
Biblical Quotations

A Treasury of
Biblical Quotations

Edited by
Lester V. Berrey

DOVER PUBLICATIONS, INC.
Mineola, New York

Copyright

Copyright © 1948, 1976 by Lester V. Berrey
All rights reserved under Pan American and International Copyright
Conventions.

Published in the United Kingdom by David & Charles, Brunel House, Forde
Close, Newton Abbot, Devon TQ12 4PU.

Bibliographical Note

This Dover edition, first published in 2002, is an unabridged reprint of the first
edition, published by Doubleday & Co., Garden City, New York, in 1948.

Library of Congress Cataloging-in-Publication Data

A treasury of biblical quotations / edited by Lester V. Berrey.
    p. cm.
Originally published: Garden City, N.Y. : Doubleday, 1948.
Includes bibliographical references and index.
ISBN 0-486-42503-7 (pbk.)
    1. Bible—Quotations. I. Berrey, Lester V., 1907-.

BS391.3 .T74 2002
220.5'2036—dc21

             2002031297

Manufactured in the United States of America
Dover Publications, Inc., 31 East 2nd Street, Mineola, N.Y. 11501

Dedicated to

MY MOTHER AND FATHER

Preface

A TREASURY OF BIBLICAL QUOTATIONS is a thesaurus of the significant pointed passages of Scripture topically classified and so organized for ready reference that students, ministers, teachers, writers, speakers, and all who seek the desired verse, the pertinent passage, the comforting or instructive Scripture on any subject may find it quickly and easily. It is designed for the layman for the pleasures and rewards of stimulating and inspirational reading, and especially for its great usefulness as a tool for the Bible student, as a constantly employed direct reference work. It is a book which will, it is planned, facilitate the inquirer's approach to the Bible by affording ready access to its treasures and heighten his appreciation of it by an analysis of its significance.

Its preparation was inspired by the obvious deficiencies of such pioneer classifications of Scripture as have hitherto been available and have consequently passed into general disuse. With but slight modifications, they followed Matthew Talbot's inadequate method of presentation of over a century ago, in which selected passages of length were grouped, as they could, under general headings. They were consequently a partial and an indiscriminate analysis of matter without regard to particular application, rather than a thorough classification of pertinent verses. Nor has the opposite extreme been considered a virtue, in which the number of groupings has been extended to include numerous synonymous or nearly identical subjects, with a representative selection of passages under each, so that, in the end, one must turn to them all to find a full display, only to discover a promiscuous duplication of content insufficiently recorded. Neither should worth be measured by magnitude, in a classification of *everything* found in the Scriptures, which, while of value to the student in quest of extended passages, sacrifices pertinence of application, in search of which the reader must wade through a mass of irrelevant matter.

The present work is intended to supply the modern need for a topical presentation of Scripture, constructed on the same plan as popular collections of literary quotations, embracing the widest possible range of practical subjects and providing a comprehensive display of significant passages, with space-devouring overclassification and overlapping avoided by an extensive utilization of cross references. The object was not to develop religious subjects only, but to furnish all those which may be of service to every requirement and to all those who desire to consult the Bible.

The result is a thoroughly up-to-date reference work for modern needs and modern demands.

In constructing the following system of classification, the chief aim has been the basic one of obtaining the greatest amount of practical utility. The plan is simple. Subjects are arranged in alphabetical order, and, under each subject, the verses appear in their Biblical sequence. Wide scope is given to each classification, and duplication has been avoided, by an elaborate system of cross references to kindred and antithetical groups of categories. These follow immediately after the heading and are listed in their order of approximation in significance to the subject or cross-reference heading, rather than alphabetically. A complete listing of subjects and cross references is provided in the Subject Index at the back of the book, as well as in the text.

The categories have evolved out of the natural connotations of the verses, not arbitrarily imposed according to a preconceived plan. Thus will one find the essential topics represented, and the basic-synonym cross references to them. The dimensions of the sections are in proportion to the Biblical emphasis and to the relative importance and utility of subjects.

Theological bias has been avoided. The texts have not been selected and classified to sustain any sectarian acceptance. Passages variously interpreted are so cited, without reference to the personal views of the compiler.

The King James version has been quoted throughout.

The Books of the Bible

THE OLD TESTAMENT

Genesis
Exodus
Leviticus
Numbers
Deuteronomy
Joshua
Judges
Ruth
1 Samuel
2 Samuel
1 Kings
2 Kings
1 Chronicles
2 Chronicles
Ezra
Nehemiah
Esther
Job
Psalms
Proverbs

Ecclesiastes
Song of Solomon
Isaiah
Jeremiah
Lamentations
Ezekiel
Daniel
Hosea
Joel
Amos
Obadiah
Jonah
Micah
Nahum
Habakkuk
Zephaniah
Haggai
Zechariah
Malachi

THE NEW TESTAMENT

Matthew
Mark
Luke
John
Acts
Romans
1 Corinthians
2 Corinthians
Galatians
Ephesians
Philippians
Colossians
1 Thessalonians
2 Thessalonians

1 Timothy
2 Timothy
Titus
Philemon
Hebrews
James
1 Peter
2 Peter
1 John
2 John
3 John
Jude
Revelation

Abbreviations

Chron.	– Chronicles	Lam.	– Lamentations
Col.	– Colossians	Lev.	– Leviticus
Cor.	– Corinthians	Mal.	– Malachi
Dan.	– Daniel	Matt.	– Matthew
Deut.	– Deuteronomy	Mic.	– Micah
Eccl.	– Ecclesiastes	Nah.	– Nahum
Eph.	– Ephesians	Neh.	– Nehemiah
Esth.	– Esther	Num.	– Numbers
Ex.	– Exodus	Obad.	– Obadiah
Ezek.	– Ezekiel	Pet.	– Peter
Gal.	– Galatians	Phil.	– Philippians
Gen.	– Genesis	Philem.	– Philemon
Hab.	– Habakkuk	Prov.	– Proverbs
Hag.	– Haggai	Psa.	– Psalms
Heb.	– Hebrews	Rev.	– Revelation
Hos.	– Hosea	Rom.	– Romans
Isa.	– Isaiah	Sam.	– Samuel
Jas.	– James	S. of S.	– Song of Solomon
Jer.	– Jeremiah	Thess.	– Thessalonians
Jon.	– Jonah	Tim.	– Timothy
Josh.	– Joshua	Tit.	– Titus
Judg.	– Judges	Zech.	– Zechariah
Kin.	– Kings	Zeph.	– Zephaniah

A Treasury of
Biblical Quotations

A

Abasement, see HUMILITY

ABILITY; see also STRENGTH, TALENT

If so be the Lord will be with me, then I shall be able to drive them out. —Jos. 14:12

If ye have faith as a grain of mustard seed . . . nothing shall be impossible unto you.
—MATT. 17:20

With men this is impossible; but with God all things are possible.
—MATT. 19:26

The spirit indeed is willing, but the flesh is weak. —MATT. 26:41

All things are possible to him that believeth. —MARK 9:23

She hath done what she could.
—MARK 14:8

Many . . . will seek to enter in, and shall not be able.
—LUKE 13:24

To will is present with me; but how to perform that which is good I find not. —ROM. 7:18

I have fed you with milk, and not with meat: for hitherto ye were not able to bear it, neither yet now are ye able. —1 COR. 3:2

God is faithful, who will not suffer you to be tempted above that ye are able; but will with the temptation also make a way to escape, that ye may be able to bear it.
—1 COR. 10:13

I can do all things through Christ which strengtheneth me.
—PHIL. 4:13

I thank Christ Jesus our Lord, who hath enabled me.
—1 TIM. 1:12

As every man hath received the gift, even so minister the same one to another. —1 PET. 4:10

If any man minister, let him do it as of the ability which God giveth. —PET. 4:11

ABSENCE

The Lord watch between me and thee, when we are absent one from another. —GEN. 31:49

Absent in body, but present in spirit. —1 COR. 5:3

Whilst we are at home in the body, we are absent from the Lord.
—2 COR. 5:6

Wherefore we labour, that, whether present or absent, we may be accepted of him. —2 COR. 5:9

As ye have always obeyed, not as in my presence only, but now much more in my absence, work out your own salvation with fear and trembling. —PHIL. 2:12

Absolution, see REMISSION, FOR-GIVENESS

ABSTINENCE; see also TEMPER-ANCE, RENUNCIATION, INTOXICA-TION

Drink not wine nor strong drink, and eat not any unclean thing.
—JUDG. 13:4

Wine is a mocker, strong drink is raging: and whosoever is deceived thereby is not wise. —PROV. 20:1

Be not among winebibbers.
—PROV. 23:20

Look not thou upon the wine when it is red, when it giveth his colour in the cup, when it moveth itself aright. At the last it biteth like a serpent, and stingeth like an adder. —PROV. 23:31, 32

It is good neither to eat flesh, nor to drink wine, nor any thing whereby thy brother stumbleth.
—ROM. 14:21

Be not drunk with wine, wherein is excess. —EPH. 5:18

Touch not; taste not; handle not.
—COL. 2:21

Abstain from fleshly lusts, which war against the soul. —1 PET. 2:11

Abuse, see HARM, MALICE, OP-PRESSION, PERSECUTION

ACCOMPLISHMENT

God saw every thing that he had made, and, behold, it was very good. —GEN. 1:31

The desire accomplished is sweet to the soul. —PROV. 13:19

The Lord will do great things.
—JOEL 2:21

Which of you, intending to build a tower, sitteth not down first, and counteth the cost, whether he have sufficient to finish it?—LUKE 14:28

My meat is to do the will of him that sent me, and to finish his work. —JOHN 4:34

I have glorified thee on the earth: I have finished the work which thou gavest me to do. —JOHN 17:4

Now therefore perform the doing of it; that as there was a readiness to will, so there may be a perform-ance also out of that which ye have.
—2 COR. 8:11

I have not run in vain, neither laboured in vain. —PHIL. 2:16

I have fought a good fight, I have finished my course, I have kept the faith. —2 TIM. 4:7

Let us go on unto perfection.
—HEB. 6:1

The effectual fervent prayer of a righteous man availeth much.
—JAS. 5:16

Accord, see HARMONY

Accountability, see RESPONSIBILITY

ACCUSATION; see also JUDG-MENT, CENSURE

Thou shalt not raise a false re-port: put not thine hand with the wicked to be an unrighteous witness.
—EX. 23:1

Blessed are ye, when men shall revile you, and persecute you, and shall say all manner of evil against you falsely, for my sake.
—MATT. 5:11

Do violence to no man, neither accuse any falsely. —LUKE 3:14

Woman, where are those thine accusers? hath no man con-demned thee? —JOHN 8:10

Acquittal, see FORGIVENESS, REMISSION

Action, see INDUSTRY, WORKS

Admonition, see COUNSEL, REPROOF

Adoration, see REVERENCE, WORSHIP, PRAISE

Adulation, see FLATTERY, PRAISE

ADULTERY

Thou shalt not commit adultery.
—EX. 20:14

Thou shalt not lie carnally with thy neighbour's wife, to defile thyself with her.   —LEV. 18:20

I made a covenant with mine eyes; why then should I think upon a maid?   —JOB 31:1

The lips of a strange woman drop as an honeycomb, and her mouth is smoother than oil: But her end is bitter as wormwood, sharp as a two-edged sword. Her feet go down to death; her steps take hold on hell.
—PROV. 5:3–5

Can a man take fire in his bosom, and his clothes not be burned? Can one go upon hot coals, and his feet not be burned? So he that goeth in to his neighbour's wife: whosoever toucheth her shall not be innocent.
—PROV. 6:27–29

Whoso committeth adultery with a woman lacketh understanding: he that doeth it destroyeth his own soul.   —PROV. 6:32

The mouth of strange women is a deep pit: he that is abhorred of the Lord shall fall therein.
—PROV. 22:14

A whore is a deep ditch; and a strange woman is a narrow pit.
—PROV. 23:27

He that keepeth company with harlots spendeth his substance.
—PROV. 29:3

There be three things which are too wonderful for me, yea, four which I know not: The way of an eagle in the air; the way of a serpent upon a rock; the way of a ship in the midst of the sea; and the way of a man with a maid.
—PROV. 30:18, 19

Give not thy strength unto women, nor thy ways to that which destroyeth kings.   —PROV. 31:3

Whosoever looketh on a woman to lust after her hath committed adultery with her already in his heart.   —MATT. 5:28

Out of the heart proceed evil thoughts, adulteries, fornications.
—MATT. 15:19

Let us walk honestly, as in the day; not in rioting and drunkenness, not in chambering and wantonness.
—ROM. 13:13

Flee fornication. Every sin that a man doeth is without the body; but he that committeth fornication sinneth against his own body.
—1 COR. 6:18

The works of the flesh are manifest, which are these; Adultery, fornication, uncleanness, lasciviousness.   —GAL. 5:19

Fornication, and all uncleanness, let it not be once named among you.   —EPH. 5:3

Mortify therefore your members which are upon the earth; fornication, uncleanness, inordinate affection, evil concupiscence.
—COL. 3:5

Whoremongers, and adulterers, God will judge. —HEB. 13:4

Adversity, see AFFLICTION, TROUBLE

Advice, see COUNSEL, INSTRUCTION

Affection, see LOVE

AFFLICTION; see also SORROW, SUFFERING, TROUBLE, CHASTENING

In my distress I called upon the Lord, and cried to my God: and he did hear my voice out of his temple. —2 SAM. 22:7

The afflicted people thou wilt save: but thine eyes are upon the haughty, that thou mayest bring them down. —2 SAM. 22:28

To him that is afflicted pity should be shewed from his friend. —JOB. 6:14

If they be bound in fetters, and be holden in cords of affliction; Then he sheweth them their work, and their transgressions that they have exceeded. He openeth also their ear to discipline, and commandeth that they return from iniquity. —JOB 36:8–10

He delivereth the poor in his affliction, and openeth their ears in oppression. —JOB 36:15

Thou hast enlarged me when I was in distress. —PSA. 4:1

Yea, though I walk through the valley of the shadow of death, I will fear no evil: for thou art with me; thy rod and thy staff they comfort me. —PSA. 23:4

Many are the afflictions of the righteous: but the Lord delivereth him out of them all. —PSA. 34:19

Cast thy burden upon the Lord, and he shall sustain thee; he shall never suffer the righteous to be moved. —PSA. 55:22

The Lord heareth the poor, and despiseth not his prisoners. —PSA. 69:33

My flesh and my heart faileth: but God is the strength of my heart, and my portion for ever. —PSA. 73:26

Like as a father pitieth his children, so the Lord pitieth them that fear him. For he knoweth our frame; he remembereth that we are dust. —PSA. 103:13, 14

Fools, because of their transgression, and because of their iniquities, are afflicted. —PSA. 107:17

This is my comfort in my affliction: for thy word hath quickened me. —PSA. 119:50

Before I was afflicted I went astray: but now have I kept thy word. —PSA. 119:67

It is good for me that I have been afflicted; that I might learn thy statues. —PSA. 119:71

Trouble and anguish have taken hold on me: yet thy commandments are my delights. —PSA. 119:143

In the day when I cried thou answeredst me, and strengthenedst me with strength in my soul. —PSA. 138:3

I know that the Lord will maintain the cause of the afflicted, and the right of the poor.—PSA. 140:12

The Lord upholdeth all that fall, and raiseth up all those that be bowed down. —PSA. 145:14

All the days of the afflicted are evil: but he that is of a merry heart hath a continual feast.

—Prov. 15:15

The spirit of a man will sustain his infirmity; but a wounded spirit who can bear? —Prov. 18:14

If thou faint in the day of adversity, thy strength is small.

—Prov. 24:10

Thou hast been a strength to the poor, a strength to the needy in his distress, a refuge from the storm, a shadow from the heat. —Isa. 25:4

Like as a woman with child, that draweth near the time of her delivery, is in pain, and crieth out in her pangs; so have we been in thy sight, O Lord. —Isa. 26:17

Sing, O heavens; and be joyful, O earth; and break forth into singing, O mountains: for the Lord hath comforted his people, and will have mercy upon his afflicted.

—Isa. 49:13

O thou afflicted, tossed with tempest, and not comforted, behold, I will lay thy stones with fair colours, and lay thy foundations with sapphire. —Isa. 54:11

Remembering mine afflictions and my misery, the wormwood and the gall. My soul hath them still in remembrance, and is humbled in me. —Lam. 3:19, 20

It is of the Lord's mercies that we are consumed, because his compassions fail not. —Lam. 3:22

Come, and let us return unto the Lord: for he hath torn, and he will heal us: he hath smitten, and he will bind us up. —Hos. 6:1

Blessed are they that mourn: for they shall be comforted. . . . Blessed are they which are persecuted for righteousness' sake: for theirs is the kingdom of heaven. Blessed are ye, when men shall revile you, and persecute you, and shall say all manner of evil against you falsely, for my sake. Rejoice, and be exceeding glad: for great is your reward in heaven: for so persecuted they the prophets which were before you.

—Matt. 5:4, 10–12

Come unto me, all ye that labour and are heavy laden, and I will give you rest. —Matt. 11:28

O my Father, if it be possible, let this cup pass from me: nevertheless, not as I will, but as thou wilt.

—Matt. 26:39

These things I have spoken unto you, that in me ye might have peace. In the world ye shall have tribulation; but be of good cheer; I have overcome the world.

—John 16:33

We must through much tribulation enter into the kingdom of God.

—Acts 14:22

We glory in tribulations also; knowing that tribulation worketh patience: And patience, experience; and experience, hope.

—Rom. 5:3, 4

We know that all things work together for good to them that love God, to them who are the called according to his purpose.

—Rom. 8:28

Who shall separate us from the love of Christ? shall tribulation, or distress, or persecution?

—Rom. 8:35

Though our outward man perish, yet the inward man is renewed day by day. For our light affliction, which is but for a moment, worketh for us a far more exceeding and eternal weight of glory.
—2 COR. 4:16, 17

I take pleasure in infirmities, in reproaches, in necessities, in persecutions, in distresses for Christ's sake: for when I am weak, then am I strong. —2 COR. 12:10

Bear ye one another's burdens, and so fulfil the law of Christ.
—GAL. 6:2

Unto you it is given in the behalf of Christ, not only to believe on him, but also to suffer for his sake.
—PHIL. 1:29

Endure hardness, as a good soldier of Jesus Christ.—2 TIM. 2:3

If we suffer, we shall also reign with him. —2 TIM. 2:12

Watch thou in all things, endure afflictions. —2 TIM. 4:5

The Lord is my helper, and I will not fear what man shall do unto me. —HEB. 13:6

Pure religion and undefiled before God and the Father is this, To visit the fatherless and widows in their affliction, and to keep himself unspotted from the world.
—JAS. 1:27

Take, my brethren, the prophets, who have spoken in the name of the Lord, for an example of suffering affliction, and of patience. Behold, we count them happy which endure. Ye have heard of the patience of Job, and have seen the end of the Lord; that the Lord is very pitiful, and of tender mercy.
—JAS. 5:10, 11

Is any among you afflicted? let him pray. —JAS. 5:13

What glory is it, if, when ye be buffeted for your faults, ye shall take it patiently? but if, when ye do well, and suffer for it, ye take it patiently, this is acceptable with God. —1 PET. 2:20

Resist stedfast in the faith, knowing that the same afflictions are accomplished in your brethren that are in the world. —1 PET. 5:9

AGE

Thou shalt rise up before the hoary head, and honour the face of the old man. —LEV. 19:32

With the ancient is wisdom; and in length of days understanding.
—JOB. 12:2

Days should speak, and multitude of years should teach wisdom.
—JOB 32:7

He asked life of thee, and thou gavest it him, even length of days for ever and ever. —PSA. 21:44

I have been young, and now am old; yet have I not seen the righteous forsaken. —PSA. 37:25

Mine age is as nothing before thee. —PSA. 39:5

We spend our years as a tale that is told. —PSA. 90:9

So teach us to number our days, that we may apply our hearts unto wisdom. —PSA. 90:12

The fear of the Lord prolongeth days. —PROV. 10:27

The hoary head is a crown of glory, if it be found in the way of righteousness. —PROV. 16:31

If a man beget an hundred children, and live many years, so that the days of his years be many, and his soul be not filled with good, and also that he have no burial; I say that an untimely birth is better than he. —Eccl. 6:3

We all do fade as a leaf.
—Isa. 64:6

No man also having drunk old wine straightway desireth new.
—Luke 5:39

Old things are passed away; behold all things are become new.
—2 Cor. 5:17

Rebuke not an elder, but intreat him as a father. —1 Tim. 5:1

Aged men be sober, grave, temperate, sound in faith, in charity, in patience. —Tit. 2:2

Agreement, see Harmony

Aid, see Help, Service, Giving

Ailment, see Affliction, Infirmity, Healing

Alms, see Giving

Altruism, see Charity, Giving, Kindness, Unselfishness, Help, Service

AMBITION; see also Aspiration, Pride

Let us make us a name.
—Gen. 11:4

The Lord preserveth the faithful, and plentifully rewardeth the proud doer. —Psa. 31:23

He that is greedy of gain troubleth his own house.
—Prov. 15:27

Better is it to be of an humble spirit with the lowly, than to divide the spoil with the proud.
—Prov. 16:19

Labour not to be rich . . . Wilt thou set thine eyes upon that which is not? for riches certainly make themselves wings; they fly away as an eagle toward heaven.
—Prov. 23:4,5

Better it is that it be said unto thee, Come up hither; than that thou shouldest be put lower in the presence of the prince whom thine eyes have seen. —Prov. 25:7

All things are full of labour; man cannot utter it: the eye is not satisfied with seeing, nor the ear filled with hearing. —Eccl. 1:8

There is one alone, and there is not a second; yea, he hath neither child nor brother: yet is there no end of all his labour; neither is his eye satisfied with riches; neither saith he, For whom do I labour, and bereave my soul of good?
—Eccl. 4:8

He that loveth silver shall not be satisfied with silver; nor he that loveth abundance with increase: this is also vanity. When goods increase, they are increased that eat them; and what good is there to the owners thereof, saving the beholding of them with their eyes?
—Eccl. 5:10, 11

Seekest thou great things for thyself? seek them not. —Jer. 45:5

Though thou exalt thyself as the eagle, and though thou set thy nest among the stars, thence will I bring thee down, saith the Lord.
—Obad. 4

Ye have sown much, and bring in little; ye eat, but ye have not enough; ye drink, but ye are not filled with drink; ye clothe you, but there is none warm; and he that earneth wages earneth wages to put it into a bag with holes.

—HAG. 1:6

What is a man profited, if he shall gain the whole world, and lose his own soul? —MATT. 16:26

The last shall be first, and the first last. —MATT. 20:16

He that is greatest among you shall be your servant. And whosoever shall exalt himself shall be abased; and he that shall humble himself shall be exalted.

—MATT. 23:11, 12

If any man desire to be first, the same shall be last of all, and servant of all. —MARK 9:35

Whosoever will be great among you, shall be your minister: and whosoever of you will be the chiefest, shall be servant of all.

—MARK 10:43, 44

How can ye believe, which receive honour one of another, and seek not the honour that cometh from God only? —JOHN 5:44

Labour not for the meat which perisheth, but for that meat which endureth unto everlasting life.

—JOHN 6: 27

Covet earnestly the best gifts.

—1 COR. 12:31

Set your affection on things above, not on things on the earth.

—COL. 3:2

All that is in the world, the lust of the flesh, and the lust of the eyes, and the pride of life, is not of the Father, but is of the world.

—1 JOHN 2:16

Amusement, see PLEASURE
ANGER

Wrath killeth the foolish man and envy slayeth the silly one.

—JOB 5:2

Cease from anger, and forsake wrath: fret not thyself in any wise to do evil. —PSA. 37:8

A fool's wrath is presently known: but a prudent man covereth shame. —PROV. 12:16

He that is soon angry dealeth foolishly. —PROV. 14:17

A soft answer turneth away wrath: but grievous words stir up anger. —PROV. 15:1

A wrathful man stirreth up strife: but he that is slow to anger appeaseth strife. —PROV. 15:18

He that is slow to anger is better than the mighty; and he that ruleth his spirit than he that taketh a city.

—PROV. 16:32

The discretion of a man deferreth his anger; and it is his glory to pass over a transgression.

—PROV. 19:11

A man of great wrath shall suffer punishment: for if thou deliver him, yet thou must do it again.

—PROV. 19:19

Proud and haughty scorner is his name, who dealeth in proud wrath.

—PROV. 21:24

Make no friendship with an angry man, and with a furious man thou shalt not go: Lest thou learn his ways, and get a snare to thy soul. —PROV. 22:24, 25

He that hath no rule over his own spirit is like a city that is broken down, and without walls.
—PROV. 25:28

A stone is heavy, and the sand weighty; but a fool's wrath is heavier than them both.
—PROV. 27:3

Scornful men bring a city into a snare; but wise men turn away wrath.   —PROV. 29:8

If a wise man contendeth with a foolish man, whether he rage or laugh, there is no rest.
—PROV. 29:9

He that is slow to wrath is of great understanding.—PROV. 14:29

An angry man stirreth up strife, and a furious man aboundeth in transgression.   —PROV. 29:22

Surely the churning of milk bringeth forth butter, and the wringing of the nose bringeth forth blood: so the forcing of wrath bringeth forth strife.—PROV. 30:33

Be not hasty in thy spirit to be angry: for anger resteth in the bosom of fools.   —ECCL. 7:9

The works of the flesh are manifest . . . hatred, variance, emulations, wrath.   —GAL. 5:19, 20

Be ye angry, and sin not: let not the sun go down upon your wrath.
—EPH. 4:6

Let all bitterness, and wrath, and anger, and clamour, and evil speaking, be put away from you, with all malice.   —EPH. 4:31

Let every man be swift to hear, slow to speak, slow to wrath: For the wrath of man worketh not the righteousness of God.
—JAS. 1:19, 20

Anguish, see SORROW, SUFFERING

Animosity, see ANGER, CONTENTION, ENMITY, HATRED, MALICE, RETALIATION

Anticipation, see EXPECTATION, HOPE

ANXIETY; see also CARE, COURAGE

Fear ye not, stand still, and see the salvation of the Lord.
—EX. 14:13

Yea, though I walk through the valley of the shadow of death, I will fear no evil: for thou art with me; thy rod and thy staff they comfort me.   —PSA. 23:4

I sought the Lord, and he heard me, and delivered me from all my fears.   —PSA. 34:4

Fret not thyself because of evildoers.   —PSA. 37:1

Why art thou cast down, O my soul? and why art thou disquieted within me? hope in God.
—PSA. 43:5

Behold, God is my salvation: I will trust, and not be afraid.
—ISA. 12:2

The Lord shall give thee rest from thy sorrow, and from thy fear.   —ISA. 14:3

Fear thou not; for I am with thee.   —ISA. 41:10

Fear not; for thou shalt not be ashamed: neither be thou confounded; for thou shalt not be put to shame.   —ISA. 54:4

Take no thought for your life, what ye shall eat, or what ye shall drink; nor yet for your body, what ye shall put on. Is not the life more than meat, and the body than raiment?   —MATT. 6:25

Which of you by taking thought can add one cubit unto his stature? —MATT. 6:27

Take therefore no thought for the morrow: for the morrow shall take thought for the things of itself. Sufficient unto the day is the evil thereof. —MATT. 6:34

Let not your heart be troubled: ye believe in God, believe also in me. —JOHN 14:1

Peace I leave with you, my peace I give unto you: not as the world giveth, give I unto you. Let not your heart be troubled, neither let it be afraid. —JOHN 14:27

In nothing be anxious. —PHIL. 4:6

God hath not given us the spirit of fear; but of power, and of love, and of a sound mind.—2 TIM. 1:7

Perfect love casteth out fear. —1 JOHN 4:18

Apathy, see HALFHEARTEDNESS

Apostasy, see BACKSLIDING

APPEARANCE; see also HYPOC-
RISY

Man looketh on the outward appearance, but the Lord looketh on the heart. —1 SAM. 16:7

There is a way that seemeth right unto a man, but the end thereof are the ways of death.—PROV. 16:25

Ye are like unto whited sepulchres, which indeed appear beautiful outward, but are within full of dead men's bones. —MATT. 23:27

Judge not according to the appearance. —JOHN 7:24

If any man among you seem to be religious . . . but deceiveth his own heart, this man's religion is vain. —JAS. 1:26

Apprehension, see ANXIETY, COUR-
AGE

Ardor, see ZEAL

Arrogance see PRIDE, CONCEIT, BOASTING

ASPIRATION; see also DESIRE, HOPE, AMBITION

This is the generation of them that seek him. —PSA. 24:6

Lift up your heads, O ye gates; even lift them up, ye everlasting doors; and the King of glory shall come in. —PSA. 24:9

Unto thee, O Lord, do I lift up my soul. —PSA. 25:1

Truly my soul waiteth upon God. —PSA. 62:1

My soul, wait thou only upon God; for my expectation is from him. —PSA. 62:5

With my whole heart have I sought thee. —PSA. 119:10

I will lift up mine eyes unto the hills, from whence cometh my help. —PSA. 121:1

Mine eyes are unto thee, O God the Lord. —PSA. 141:8

Lift up your eyes on high. —ISA. 40:26

Let us lift up our heart with our hands unto God in the heavens. —LAM. 3:41

We would see Jesus. —JOHN 12:21

Forgetting those things which are behind, and reaching forth unto those things which are before, I press toward the mark. —PHIL. 3:13, 14

Seek those things which are above. —COL. 3:1

Set your affection on things above. —Col. 3:2

Asssistance, see Help, Service, Giving

Assurance, see Faith

Astonishment, see Wonder

Atheism, see Infidelity, Unbelief

Atonement, see Redemption, Reconciliation

AVARICE; see also Wealth

Thou shalt not covet thy neighbour's house, thou shalt not covet thy neighbour's wife, nor his manservant, nor his maidservant, nor his ox, nor his ass, nor any thing that is thy neighbour's.

—Ex. 20:17

The wicked boasteth of his heart's desire, and blesseth the covetous, whom the Lord abhorreth.

—Psa. 10:3

Incline my heart unto thy testimonies, and not to covetousness.

—Psa. 119:36

He that is greedy of gain troubleth his own house.—Prov. 15:27

Better is a little with righteousness than great revenues without right. —Prov. 16:8

The desire of the slothful killeth him; for his hands refuse to labour. He coveteth greedily all the day long: but the righteous giveth and spareth not. —Prov. 21:25, 26

Give me neither poverty nor riches; feed me with food covenient for me: Lest I be full, and deny thee, and say, Who is the Lord?

—Prov. 30:8, 9

All things are full of labour; man cannot utter it: the eye is not satisfied with seeing, nor the ear filled with hearing. —Eccl. 1:8

There is one alone, and there is not a second; yea, he hath neither child nor brother: yet is there no end of all his labour; neither is his eye satisfied with riches; neither saith he, For whom do I labour, and bereave my soul of good?

—Eccl. 4:8

He that loveth silver shall not be satisfied with silver; nor he that loveth abundance with increase: this is also vanity. When goods increase, they are increased that eat them: and what good is there to the owners thereof, saving the beholding of them with their eyes?

—Eccl. 5:10, 11

Woe unto them that join house to house, that lay field to field, till there be no place, that they may be placed alone in the midst of the earth! —Isa. 5:8

Yea, they are greedy dogs which can never have enough, and they are shepherds that cannot understand: they all look to their own way, every one for his gain, from his quarter. —Isa. 56:11

From the least of them even unto the greatest of them every one is given to covetousness.—Jer. 6:13

As the partridge sitteth on eggs, and hatcheth them not; so he that getteth riches, and not by right, shall leave them in the midst of his days, and at his end shall be a fool.

—Jer. 17:11

O thou that dwellest upon many waters, abundant in treasures, thine end is come, and the measure of thy covetousness. —Jer. 51:13

Woe to him that increaseth that which is not his! —Hab. 2:6

Woe to him that coveteth an evil covetousness to his house, that he may set his nest on high, that he may be delivered from the power of evil! —HAB. 2:9

Ye have sown much, and bring in little; ye eat, but ye have not enough; ye drink, but ye are not filled with drink; ye clothe you, but there is none warm; and he that earneth wages earneth wages to put it into a bag with holes.—HAG. 1:6

What is a man profited, if he shall gain the whole world, and lose his own soul? —MATT. 16:26

Take heed, and beware of covetousness: for a man's life consisteth not in the abundance of the things which he possesseth.—LUKE 12:15

Labour not for the meat which perisheth, but for that meat which endureth unto everlasting life.
—JOHN 6:27

Set your affection on things above, not on things on the earth.
—COL. 3:2

Mortify therefore your members which are upon the earth . . . and covetousness, which is idolatry.
—COL. 3:5

They that will be rich fall into temptation and a snare, and into many foolish and hurtful lusts, which drown men in destruction and perdition. —1 TIM. 6:9

The love of money is the root of all evil. —1 TIM. 6:10

Men shall be lovers of their own selves, covetous. —2 TIM. 3:2

Let your conversation be without covetousness; and be content with such things as ye have.—HEB. 13:5

Ye lust, and have not; ye kill, and desire to have, and cannot obtain.
—JAS. 4:2

Aversion, see HATRED

Awe, see REVERENCE, WONDER

B

Backbiting, see SLANDER

BACKSLIDING

Take heed to thyself, and keep thy soul diligently, lest thou forget the things which thine eyes have seen, and lest they depart from thy heart all the days of thy life.

—DEUT. 4:9

Beware that thou forget not the Lord thy God, in not keeping his commandments, and his judgments, and his statutes.   —DEUT. 8:11

Of the Rock that begat thee thou art unmindful, and hast forgotten God that formed thee.

—DEUT. 32:18

The Lord your God is gracious and merciful, and will not turn away his face from you, if ye return unto him. —2 CHRON. 30:9

Hold up my goings in thy paths, that my footsteps slip not.

—PSA. 17:5

The backslider in heart shall be filled with his own ways.

—PROV. 14:14

A just man falleth seven times and riseth up again; but the wicked shall fall into mischief.

—PROV. 24:16

As a dog returneth to his vomit, so a fool returneth to his folly.

—PROV. 26:11

Let the wicked forsake his way, and the unrighteous man his thoughts: and let him return unto the Lord.   —ISA. 55:7

My people have committed two evils; they have forsaken me the fountain of living waters, and hewed them out cisterns, broken cisterns, that can hold no water.

—JER. 2:13

I had planted thee a noble vine, wholly a right seed: how then art thou turned into the degenerate plant of a strange vine unto me?

—JER. 2:21

They have turned their back unto me, and not their face: but in the time of their trouble they will say, Arise, and save us.   —JER. 2:27

Turn, O backsliding children, saith the Lord.   —JER. 3:14

My people hath been lost sheep: their shepherds have caused them to go astray, they have turned them away on the mountains: they have gone from mountain to hill, they have forgotten their resting place.

—JER. 50:6

Let us search and try our ways, and turn again to the Lord.

—LAM. 3:40

Come, and let us return unto the Lord: for he hath torn, and he will heal us; he hath smitten, and he will bind us up.   —HOS. 6:1

Return unto me, and I will return unto you, saith the Lord of hosts. —MAL. 3:7

If the salt have lost his savour, wherewith shall it be salted? it is thenceforth good for nothing, but to be cast out, and to be trodden under foot of men.—MATT. 5:13

No man, having put his hand to the plough, and looking back, is fit for the kingdom of God.

—LUKE 9:62

He that is not with me is against me: and he that gathereth not with me scattereth. —LUKE 11:23

Remember Lot's wife.

—LUKE 17:32

Let him that thinketh he standeth take heed lest he fall.

—1 COR. 10:12

The Lord your God is gracious and merciful, and will not turn away his face from you, if ye return unto him. —2 CHRON. 30:9

After that ye have known God, or rather are known of God, how turn ye again to the weak and beggarly elements, whereunto ye desire again to be in bondage?

—GAL. 4:9

Ye did run well; who did hinder you that ye should not obey the truth? —GAL. 5:7

If any man draw back, my soul shall have no pleasure in him.

—HEB. 10:38

Bad Companions, see COMPANIONS, EVIL

Badness, see EVIL, SIN, IMPERFECTION

BAPTISM

Go ye therefore, and teach all nations, baptizing them in the name of the Father, and of the Son, and of the Holy Ghost. —MATT. 28:19

He that believeth and is baptized shall be saved. —MARK 16:16

Except a man be born of water and of the Spirit, he cannot enter into the kingdom of God.

—JOHN 3:5

Repent, and be baptized every one of you in the name of Jesus Christ for the remission of sins.

—ACTS 2:38

Arise, and be baptized, and wash away thy sins, calling on the name of the Lord. —ACTS 22:16

Know ye not, that so many of us as were baptized into Jesus Christ were baptized into his death? Therefore we are buried with him by baptism into death: that like as Christ was raised up from the dead by the glory of the Father, even so we also should walk in newness of life.

—ROM. 6:3, 4

By one Spirit are we all baptized into one body, whether we be Jews or Gentiles, whether we be bond or free; and have been all made to drink into one Spirit.

—1 COR. 12:13

As many of you as have been baptized into Christ have put on Christ. —GAL. 3:27

One Lord, one faith, one baptism.

—EPH. 4:5

Beatitudes, see BLESSED

BEAUTY

Worship the Lord in the beauty of holiness. —1 CHRON. 16:29

Deck thyself now with majesty and excellency; and array thyself with glory and beauty. —JOB 40:10

When thou with rebukes dost correct man for iniquity, thou makest his beauty to consume away like a moth: surely every man is vanity. —Psa. 39:11

Thou art fairer than the children of men: grace is poured into thy lips. —Psa. 45:2

Let the beauty of the Lord our God be upon us. —Psa. 90:17

He will beautify the meek with salvation. —Psa. 149:4

Lust not after her beauty in thine heart; neither let her take thee with her eyelids. —Prov. 6:25

As a jewel of gold in a swine's snout, so is a fair woman which is without discretion. —Prov. 11:22

Favour is deceitful, and beauty is vain. —Prov. 31:30

He hath made every thing beautiful in his time. —Eccl. 3:11

Behold, thou art fair, my love; behold, thou art fair.
—S. of S. 1:15

Beauty is a fading flower.
—Isa. 28:1

Thine eyes shall see the king in his beauty. —Isa. 33:17

How beautiful upon the mountains are the feet of him that bringeth good tidings. —Isa. 52:7

Thou art unto them as a very lovely song of one that hath a pleasant voice. —Ezek. 33:32

How great is his goodness, and how great is his beauty!
—Zech. 9:17

Consider the lilies of the field, how they grow; they toil not, neither do they spin: And yet I say unto you, That even Solomon in all his glory was not arrayed like one of these. —Matt. 6:28, 29

How beautiful are the feet of them that preach the gospel of peace, and bring glad tidings of good things. —Rom. 10:15

Whatsoever things are lovely . . . think on these things. —Phil. 4:8

BEHAVIOR

Be of good courage, and let us behave ourselves valiantly.
—1 Chron. 19:13

Walk in the fear of our God.
—Neh. 5:9

I will behave myself wisely in a perfect way. —Psa. 101:2

Walk in the way of good men, and keep the paths of righteousness. —Prov. 2:20

A man of understanding walketh uprightly. —Prov. 15:21

Whatsoever ye would that men should do to you, do ye even so to them. —Matt. 7:12

Walk not after the flesh, but after the Spirit. —Rom. 8:4

Let not . . . your good be evil spoken of. —Rom. 14:16

Take heed lest by any means this liberty of yours become a stumblingblock to them that are weak.
—1 Cor. 8:9

If meat make my brother to offend, I will eat no flesh while the world standeth, lest I make my brother to offend. —1 Cor. 8:13

Whether . . . ye eat, or drink, or whatsoever ye do, do all to the glory of God. —1 Cor. 10:31

Charity . . . doth not behave itself unseemly. —1 Cor. 13:5

Evil communications corrupt good manners. —1 Cor. 15:33

Let all your things be done with charity.   —1 COR. 16:14

Walk not as other Gentiles walk, in the vanity of their mind.
—EPH. 4:17

Let your conversation be as it becometh the gospel of Christ.
—PHIL. 1:27

Be thou an example of the believers, in word, in conversation, in charity, in spirit, in faith, in purity.
—1 TIM. 4:12

With well doing . . . put to silence the ignorance of foolish men.
—1 PET. 2:15

Be courteous.   —1 PET. 3:8

Follow not that which is evil, but that which is good.   —3 JOHN 11

Belief, see FAITH

BENEDICTION

The Lord watch between me and thee, when we are absent one from another.   —GEN. 31:49

The Lord bless thee, and keep thee: The Lord make his face shine upon thee, and be gracious unto thee: The Lord lift up his countenance upon thee, and give thee peace.   —NUM. 6:24–26

The Lord God of your fathers make you a thousand times so many more as ye are, and bless you, as he hath promised you!
—DEUT. 1:11

Let the beauty of the Lord our God be upon us.   —PSA. 90:17

Now the God of patience and consolation grant you to be likeminded one toward another according to Christ Jesus: That ye may with one mind and one mouth glorify God, even the Father of our Lord Jesus Christ. —ROM. 15:5, 6

Now the God of hope fill you with all joy and peace in believing, that ye may abound in hope, through the power of the Holy Ghost.   —ROM. 15:13

Now the God of peace be with you all.   —ROM. 15:33

The grace of our Lord Jesus Christ be with you. —ROM. 16:20

Grace be unto you, and peace, from God our Father, and from the Lord Jesus Christ.   —1 COR. 1:3

The grace of the Lord Jesus Christ, and the love of God, and the communion of the Holy Ghost, be with you all.   —2 COR. 13:14

Brethren, the grace of our Lord Jesus Christ be with your spirit.
—GAL. 6:18

Peace be to the brethren, and love with faith, from God the Father and the Lord Jesus Christ. Grace be with all them that love our Lord Jesus Christ in sincerity.
—EPH. 6:23, 24

Now the Lord of peace himself give you peace always by all means. The Lord be with you all.
—2 THESS. 3:16

The Lord Jesus Christ be with thy spirit. Grace be with you.
—2 TIM. 4:22

Now the God of peace, that brought again from the dead our Lord Jesus, that great shepherd of the sheep, through the blood of the everlasting covenant, Make you perfect in every good work to do his will, working in you that which is wellpleasing in his sight, through Jesus Christ; to whom be glory for ever and ever. Amen.
—HEB. 13:20, 21

Grace unto you, and peace, be multiplied. —1 PET. 1:2

But the God of all grace, who hath called us unto his eternal glory by Christ Jesus, after that ye have suffered a while, make you perfect, stablish, strengthen, settle you. To him be glory and dominion for ever and ever. Amen. —1 PET. 5:10, 11

Peace be with you all that are in Christ Jesus. —1 PET. 5:14

Grace and peace be multiplied unto you through the knowledge of God, and of Jesus our Lord.
—2 PET. 1:2

Grace be with you, mercy, and peace, from God the Father, and from the Lord Jesus Christ, the Son of the Father, in truth and love.
—2 JOHN 1:3

Beloved, I wish above all things that thou mayest prosper and be in health, even as thy soul prospereth.
—3 JOHN 1:2

Mercy unto you, and peace, and love, be multiplied. —JUDE 1:2

The grace of our Lord Jesus Christ be with you all. Amen.
—REV. 22:21

Benefit, see BLESSING, HELP, SERVICE, GIVING, GOODNESS, KINDNESS

Benevolence, see CHARITY, GIVING, KINDNESS, LOVE, MERCY, FORGIVENESS, TOLERANCE, UNSELFISHNESS, HELP, SERVICE.

Bereavement, see COMFORT, DEATH, MOURNING, SORROW

Betterment, see IMPROVEMENT

Bible, see SCRIPTURE

BIGOTRY; see also HYPOCRISY, SELF-RIGHTEOUSNESS

The Egyptians might not eat bread with the Hebrews; for that is an abomination unto the Egyptians.
—GEN. 43:32

Wherefore . . . lift ye up yourselves above the congregation of the Lord? —NUM. 16:3

He that is void of wisdom despiseth his neighbour. —PROV. 11:12

The way of a fool is right in his own eyes: but he that hearkeneth unto counsel is wise. —PROV. 12:15

Seest thou a man wise in his own conceit? there is more hope of a fool than of him. —PROV. 26:12

Why eateth your Master with publicans and sinners?
—MATT. 9:11

Go not into the way of the Gentiles, and into any city of the Samaritans enter ye not.
—MATT 10:5

Take heed and beware of the leaven of the Pharisees and of the Sadducees. —MARK 8:15

Ye blind guides, which strain at a gnat, and swallow a camel.
—MATT. 23:24

How is it that he eateth and drinketh with publicans and sinners?
—MARK 2:16

The sabbath was made for man, and not man for the sabbath.
—MARK 2:27

They brought young children to him, that he should touch them: and his disciples rebuked those that brought them. —MARK 10:13

They all murmured, saying, That he was gone to be guest with a man that is a sinner. —LUKE 19:7

The Jews have no dealings with the Samaritans. —JOHN 4:9

God hath shewed me that I should not call any man common or unclean. —Acts 10:28

Birth (Spiritual), see REGENERATION

Blame, see ACCUSATION, CENSURE, JUDGMENT, REPROOF

Blasphemy, see IRREVERENCE

BLESSED

Blessed is the man that walketh not in the counsel of the ungodly, nor standeth in the way of sinners, nor sitteth in the seat of the scornful. —PSA. 1:1

Blessed are all they that put their trust in him. —PSA. 2:12

Blessed is he whose transgression is forgiven, whose sin is covered.

—PSA. 32:1

Blessed is the man unto whom the Lord imputeth not iniquity, and in whose spirit there is no guile.

—PSA. 32:2

O taste and see that the Lord is good: blessed is the man that trusteth in him. —PSA. 34:8

Blessed is the man that maketh the Lord his trust. —PSA. 40:4

Blessed is he that considereth the poor: the Lord will deliver him in time of trouble. —PSA. 41:1

Blessed is the man whose strength is in thee. —PSA. 84:5

Blessed is the man that trusteth in thee. —PSA. 84:12

Blessed is the man whom thou chastenest, O Lord, and teachest him out of thy law. —PSA. 94:12

Blessed are they that keep judgment, and he that doeth righteousness at all times. —PSA. 106:3

Blessed is the man that feareth the Lord, that delighteth greatly in his commandments. —PSA. 112:1

Blessed are the undefiled in the way, who walk in the law of the Lord. —PSA. 119:1

Blessed are they that keep his testimonies, and that seek him with the whole heart. —PSA. 119:2

Hearken unto me, O ye children: for blessed are they that keep my ways. —PROV. 8:32

Blessed are the poor in spirit: for theirs is the kingdom of heaven. Blessed are they that mourn: for they shall be comforted. Blessed are the meek: for they shall inherit the earth. Blessed are they which do hunger and thirst after righteousness: for they shall be filled. Blessed are the merciful: for they shall obtain mercy. Blessed are the pure in heart: for they shall see God. Blessed are the peacemakers: for they shall be called the children of God. Blessed are they which are persecuted for righteousness' sake: for theirs is the kingdom of heaven. Blessed are ye, when men shall revile you, and persecute you, and shall say all manner of evil against you falsely, for my sake.

—MATT. 5:3–10

Blessed are they that hear the word of God, and keep it.

—LUKE 11:28

Blessed are they whose iniquities are forgiven, and whose sins are covered. —ROM. 4:7

Blessed are they that do his commandments. —ROM. 22:14

Blessed is the man that endureth temptation: for when he is tried, he shall receive the crown of life. —JAS. 1:12

BLESSING; see also BENEDICTION, PRAISE, PRAYER

The Almighty . . . shall bless thee with blessings of heaven above, blessings of the deep that lieth under. —GEN. 49:25

He whom thou blessest is blessed. —NUM. 22:6

The Lord thy God blesseth thee, as he promised thee. —DEUT. 15:6

The Lord hath blessed his people. —2 CHRON. 31:10

Stand up and bless the Lord your God for ever and ever. —NEH. 9:5

Salvation belongeth unto the Lord: thy blessing is upon thy people. —PSA. 3:8

For thou, Lord, wilt bless the righteous: with favour wilt thou compass him as with a shield. —PSA. 5:12

Thou preparest a table before me in the presence of mine enemies: thou anointest my head with oil; my cup runneth over. —PSA. 23:5

He that hath clean hands, and a pure heart . . . shall receive the blessing from the Lord, and righteousness from the God of his salvation. —PSA. 24:4, 5

The Lord will give strength unto his people: the Lord will bless his people with peace. —PSA. 29:11

The earth is full of the goodness of the Lord. —PSA. 33:5

God be merciful unto us, and bless us; and cause his face to shine upon us. —PSA. 67:1

God shall bless us; and all the ends of the earth shall fear him. —PSA. 67:7

Blessed be the Lord, who daily loadeth us with benefits. —PSA. 68:19

Men shall be blessed in him; all nations shall call him blessed. —PSA. 72:17

No good thing will he withhold from them that walk uprightly. —PSA. 84:11

Bless the Lord, O my soul, and forget not all his benefits. —PSA. 103:2

He will bless them that fear the Lord, both small and great. —PSA. 115:13

Thou openest thine hand, and satisfiest the desire of every living thing. —PSA. 145:16

Blessings are upon the head of the just. —PROV. 10:6

The blessing of the Lord, it maketh rich, and he addeth no sorrow with it. —PROV. 10:22

A faithful man shall abound with blessings. —PROV. 28:20

Every man should eat and drink, and enjoy the good of all his labour, it is the gift of God. —ECCL. 3:13

There shall be showers of blessing. —EZEK. 34:26

Seek ye first the kingdom of God, and his righteousness; and all these things shall be added unto you. —MATT. 6:33

Eye hath not seen, nor ear heard, neither have entered into the heart of man, the things which God hath prepared for them that love him. —1 COR. 2:9

Blessed be the Father of our Lord Jesus Christ, who hath blessed us with all spiritual blessings.

—EPH. 1:3

The earth which drinketh in the rain that cometh oft upon it, and bringeth forth herbs meet for them by whom it is dressed, receiveth blessing from God. —HEB. 6:7

Blessing I will bless thee, and multiplying I will multiply thee.

—HEB. 6:14

Every good gift and every perfect gift is from above. —JAS. 1:17

Blindness, see IGNORANCE, INCOMPREHENSION

BOASTING; see also CONCEIT, PRIDE

Talk no more so exceeding proudly; let not arrogancy come out of your mouth: for the Lord is a God of knowledge, and by him actions are weighed.

—1 SAM. 2:3

Let not him that girdeth on his harness boast himself as he that putteth it off. —1 KIN. 20:11

Why boastest thou thyself in mischief, O mighty man? the goodness of God endureth continually.

—PSA. 52:1

He that is despised, and hath a servant, is better than he that honoureth himself, and lacketh bread.

—PROV. 12:9

Most men will proclaim every one his own goodness; but a faithful man who can find?—PROV. 20:6

Whoso boasteth himself of a false gift is like clouds and wind without rain. —PROV. 25:14

For men to search their own glory is not glory. —PROV. 25:27

Boast not thyself of to morrow; for thou knowest not what a day may bring forth. —PROV. 27:1

Let another man praise thee, and not thine own mouth; a stranger, and not thine own lips.

—PROV. 27:2

Shall the ax boast itself against him that heweth therewith? or shall the saw magnify itself against him that shaketh it? as if the rod should shake itself against them that lift it up, or as if the staff should lift up itself, as if it were no wood. —ISA. 10:15

Where is boasting then? It is excluded. By what law? of works? Nay: but by the law of faith.

—ROM. 3:27

No flesh should glory in his presence. —1 COR. 1:29

Who maketh thee to differ from another? and what hast thou that thou didst not receive? now if thou didst receive it, why dost thou glory, as if thou hadst not received it?

—1 COR. 4:7

Not he that commendeth himself is approved, but whom the Lord commendeth. —2 COR. 10:18

BODY

The Lord God formed man of the dust of the ground, and breathed into his nostrils the breath of life; and man became a living soul.

—GEN. 2:7

Dust thou art, and unto dust shalt thou return. —GEN. 3:19

Houses of clay, whose foundation is the dust. —JOB 4:19

He remembered that they were but flesh. —Psa. 78:39

He knoweth our frame; he remembereth that we are dust.
—Psa. 103:14

I am fearfully and wonderfully made. —Psa. 139:14

All are of the dust, and all turn to dust again. —Eccl. 3:20

All flesh is grass. —Isa. 4:6

Take no thought of your life, what ye shall eat, or what ye shall drink; nor yet for your body, what ye shall put on. Is not the life more than meat, and the body than raiment? —Matt. 6:25

Fear not them which kill the body, but are not able to kill the soul. —Matt. 10:28

The spirit indeed is willing, but the flesh is weak. —Matt. 26:41

It is the spirit that quickeneth; the flesh profiteth nothing.
—John 6:63

With the mind I myself serve the law of God; but with the flesh the law of sin. —Rom. 7:25

Ye are not in the flesh, but in the Spirit, if so be that the Spirit of God dwell in you. —Rom. 8:9

If ye through the Spirit do mortify the deeds of the body, ye shall live. —Rom. 8:13

The natural man receiveth not the things of the Spirit of God.
—1 Cor. 2:14

Know ye not that ye are the temple of God, and that the Spirit of God dwelleth in you?
—1 Cor. 3:16

The temple of God is holy, which temple ye are. —1 Cor. 3:17

Know ye not that your bodies are the members of Christ?
—1 Cor. 6:15

Know ye not that your body is the temple of the Holy Ghost which is in you, which ye have of God, and ye are not your own?
—1 Cor. 6:19

Glorify God in your body, and in your spirit, which are God's.
—1 Cor. 6:20

Now ye are the body of Christ.
—1 Cor. 12:27

Our earthly house. —2 Cor. 5:1

Whilst we are at home in the body, we are absent from the Lord.
—2 Cor. 5:6

The flesh lusteth against the Spirit, and the Spirit against the flesh. —Gal. 5:17

There is one body, and one Spirit. —Eph. 4:4

Christ shall be magnified in my body, whether it be by life, or by death. —Phil. 1:20

The body without the spirit is dead. —Jas. 2:26

Boldness, see Courage

BORROWING · and **LENDING**

If thou lend money to any of my people that is poor by thee, thou shalt not be to him as an usurer, neither shalt thou lay upon him usury. —Ex. 22:25

Thou shalt not lend upon usury to thy brother; usury of money, usury of victuals, usury of any thing that is lent upon usury.
—Deut. 23:19

The wicked borroweth, and payeth not again. —Psa. 37:21

A good man sheweth favour, and lendeth: he will guide his affairs with discretion. —Psa. 112:5

He that hath pity upon the poor lendeth unto the Lord; and that which he hath given will he pay him again. —Prov. 19:17

The rich ruleth over the poor, and the borrower is servant to the lender. —Prov. 22:7

He that by usury and unjust gain increaseth his substance, he shall gather it for him that will pity the poor. —Prov. 28:8

He that hath not given forth upon usury, neither hath taken any increase, that hath withdrawn his hand from iniquity, hath executed true judgment between man and man. —Ezek. 18:8

Give to him that asketh thee, and from him that would borrow of thee turn not thou away.

—Matt. 5:42

If ye lend to them of whom ye hope to receive, what thank have ye? —Luke 6:34

Bragging, see Boasting

Bravery, see Courage

BRIBERY

Thou shalt take no gift: for the gift blindeth the wise, and perverteth the words of the righteous.

—Ex. 23:8

Gather not my soul with sinners, nor my life with bloody men: In whose hands is mischief, and their right hand is full of bribes.

—Psa. 26:9, 10

A wicked man taketh a gift out of the bosom to pervert the ways of judgment. —Prov. 17:23

A man's gift maketh room for him, and bringeth him before great men. —Prov. 18:16

A gift in secret pacifieth anger: and a reward in the bosom strong wrath. —Prov. 21:14

A gift destroyeth the heart.

—Eccl. 7:7

Woe unto them . . . which justify the wicked for reward.

—Isa. 5:22,23

BROTHERHOOD; see also Friendship, Love

Let there be no strife, I pray thee, between me and thee . . . for we be brethren. —Gen. 13:8

Thou shalt open thy hand wide unto thy brother. —Deut. 15:11

Behold, how good and how pleasant it is for brethren to dwell together in unity! —Psa. 133:1

A friend loveth at all times, and a brother is born for adversity.

—Prov. 17:17

Can two walk together, except they be agreed? —Amos 3:3

Let none of you imagine evil against his brother in your heart.

—Zech. 7:10

Have we not all one father? hath not one God created us?

—Mal. 2:10

He stretched forth his hand toward his disciples, and said, Behold my mother and my brethren!

—Matt. 12:49

One is your Master, even Christ; and all ye are brethren.

—Matt. 23:8

Inasmuch as ye have done it unto one of the least of these my brethren, ye have done it unto me.

—Matt. 25:40

Strengthen thy brethren.
—LUKE 22:32

A new commandment I give unto you, That ye love one another; as I have loved you, that ye also love one another. —JOHN 13:34

Sirs, ye are brethren.
—ACTS. 7:26

Be kindly affectioned one to another with brotherly love; in honour preferring one another.
—ROM. 12:10

Bear ye one another's burdens, and so fulfil the law of Christ.
—GAL. 6:2

We are members one of another. —EPH. 4:25

Be likeminded, having the same love, being of one accord, of one mind. —PHIL. 2:2

Let us consider one another to provoke unto love and to good works. —HEB. 10:24

Let brotherly love continue.
—HEB. 13:1

Love one another with a pure heart fervently. —1 PET. 1:22

Love the brotherhood.
—1 PET. 2:17

Be ye all of one mind, having compassion one of another, love as brethren, be pitiful, be courteous.
—1 PET. 3:8

Add ; . . to godliness brotherly kindness; and to brotherly kindness charity. —2 PET. 1:5, 7

If we walk in the light, as he is in the light, we have fellowship one with another. —1 JOHN 1:7

He that loveth his brother abideth in the light, and there is none occasion of stumbling in him.
—1 JOHN 2:10

He that loveth not his brother abideth in death. —1 JOHN 3:14

Love one another, as he gave us commandment. —1 JOHN 3:23

Burden, see CARE

Busybody, see GOSSIP, MEDDLING

C

CALLING; see also MINISTRY, ORDINATION

The Lord hath anointed me to preach good tidings. —ISA. 61:1

Follow me, and I will make you fishers of men. —MATT. 4:19

Many be called, but few chosen, —MATT. 20:16

The harvest truly is great, but the labourers are few: pray ye therefore the Lord of the harvest, that he would send forth labourers into his harvest. —LUKE 10:2

Ye have not chosen me, but I have chosen you, and ordained you, that ye should go and bring forth fruit, and that your fruit should remain. —JOHN 15:16

Whom he did predestinate, them he also called: and whom he called, them he also justified; and whom he justified, them he also glorified. —ROM. 8:30

God is faithful, by whom ye were called unto the fellowship of his Son Jesus Christ our Lord. —1 COR. 1:9

Not many wise men after the flesh, not many mighty, not many noble, are called. —1COR. 1:26

Every man hath his proper gift of God, one after this manner, and another after that. —COR. 7:7

Let every man abide in the same calling wherein he was called. —1 COR. 7:20

Walk worthy of the vocation wherewith ye are called. —EPH. 4:1

Ye are called in one hope of your calling. —EPH. 4:4

He gave some, apostles; and some, prophets; and some, evangelists; and some, pastors and teachers. —EPH. 4:11

I press toward the mark for the prize of the high calling of God in Christ Jesus. —PHIL. 3:14

Walk worthy of God, who hath called you unto his kingdom and glory. —1 THESS. 2:12

No man taketh his honour unto himself, but he that is called of God. —HEB. 5:4

Candor, see SINCERITY, IMPARTIALITY

Cant, see HYPOCRISY

Capability, see ABILITY

CARE; see also AFFLICTION, ANXIETY, TROUBLE, PRESERVATION, PROTECTION, PROVIDENCE

Cast thy burden upon the Lord, and he shall sustain thee: he shall never suffer the righteous to be moved. —PSA. 55:22

In the multitude of my thoughts within me thy comforts delight my soul.   —Psa. 94:19

My soul melteth for heaviness.   —Psa. 119:28

Heaviness in the heart of man maketh it stoop: but a good word maketh it glad.   —Prov. 12:25

Come unto me, all ye that labour and are heavy laden, and I will give you rest.   —Matt. 11:28

Take my yoke upon you.   —Matt. 11:19

My yoke is easy, and my burden is light.   —Matt. 11:30

The cares of this world . . . choke the word, and it becometh unfruitful.   —Mark 4:19

Take heed to yourselves, lest at any time your hearts be overcharged with surfeiting.   —Luke 21:34

Bear ye one another's burdens.   —Gal. 6:2

Every man shall bear his own burden.   —Gal. 6:5

Be careful for nothing.   —Phil. 4:6

Humble yourselves therefore under the mighty hand of God . . . casting all your care upon him; for he careth for you.—1 Pet. 5:6, 7

Carnality, see Adultery, Licentiousness, Lust, Worldliness

Caution, see Prudence

CELIBACY

There are some eunuchs, which were so born from their mother's womb: and there are some eunuchs which were made eunuchs of men: and there be eunuchs, which have made themselves eunuchs for the kingdom of heaven's sake.   —Matt. 19:12

It is better to marry than to burn.   —1 Cor. 7:9

He that is unmarried careth for the things that belong to the Lord, how he may please the Lord: But he that is married careth for the things that are of the world, how he may please his wife.   —1 Cor. 7:32, 33

He that standeth stedfast in his heart, having no necessity, but hath power over his own will, and hath so decreed in his heart that he will keep his virgin, doeth well.   —1 Cor. 7:37

CENSURE; see also Accusation, Reproof

Let them be turned back for a reward of their shame that say, Aha, aha.   —Psa. 70:3

Blessed are ye, when men shall revile you, and persecute you, and shall say all manner of evil against you falsely, for my sake.   —Matt. 5:11

Judge not, that ye be not judged.   —Matt. 7:1

Why beholdest thou the mote that is in thy brother's eye, but considerest not the beam that is in thine own eye?   —Matt. 7:3

Do violence to no man, neither accuse any falsely.   —Luke 3:14

Judge not, and ye shall not be judged: condemn not, and ye shall not be condemned: forgive, and ye shall be forgiven.   —Luke 6:37

Judge not according to the appearance, but judge righteous judgment. —JOHN 7:24

Thou art inexcusable, O man, whosoever thou are that judgest: for wherein thou judgest another, thou condemnest thyself; for thou that judgest doest the same things. —ROM. 2:1

Who art thou that repliest against God? Shall the thing formed say to him that formed it, Why hast thou made me thus? —ROM. 9:20

Speak evil of no man. —TIT. 3:2

Speak not evil one of another. —JAS. 4:11

CHARITY; see also GIVING, LOVE, MERCY, KINDNESS, FORGIVENESS, JUDGMENT, TOLERANCE, UNSELF-ISHNESS, HELP, SERVICE

Withhold not good from them to whom it is due, when it is in the power of thine hand to do it. —PROV. 3:27

As ye would that men should do to you, do ye also to them likewise. —LUKE 6:31

Knowledge puffeth up, but charity edifieth. —1 COR. 8:1

Though I speak with the tongues of men and of angels, and have not charity, I am become as sounding brass, or a tinkling cymbal. And though I have the gift of prophecy, and understand all mysteries, and all knowledge; and though I have all faith, so that I could remove mountains, and have not charity, I am nothing. And though I bestow all my goods to feed the poor, and though I give my body to be burned, and have not charity, it profiteth me nothing. —1 COR. 13:1–3

Charity suffereth long, and is kind; charity envieth not; charity vaunteth not itself, is not puffed up, Doth not behave itself unseemly, seeketh not her own, is not easily provoked, thinketh no evil; Rejoiceth not in iniquity, but rejoiceth in the truth; Beareth all things, believeth all things, hopeth all things, endureth all things. —1 COR. 13:4–7

And now abideth faith, hope, charity, these three; but the greatest of these is charity. —COR. 13:13

Follow after charity, and desire spiritual gifts. —1 COR. 14:1

Let all your things be done with charity. —1 COR. 16:14

Be ye kind one to another, tenderhearted, forgiving one another, even as God for Christ's sake hath forgiven you. —EPH. 4:32

Put on . . . bowels of mercies, kindness, humbleness of mind, meekness, longsuffering; Forbearing one another, and forgiving one another, if any man have a quarrel against any: even as Christ forgave you, so also do ye. And above all these things put on charity, which is the bond of perfectness. —COL. 3:12–14

The end of the commandment is charity out of a pure heart, and of a good conscience, and of faith unfeigned. —1 TIM. 1:5

Be thou an example of the believers, in word, in conversation, in charity. —1 TIM. 4:12

Follow righteousness, faith, charity, peace, with them that call on the Lord out of a pure heart.
—2 Tim. 2:22

Speak evil of no man.
—Tit. 3:2

Let us consider one another to provoke unto love and good works.
—Heb. 10:24

Pure religion and undefiled before God and the Father is this. To visit the fatherless and widows in their affliction, and to keep himself unspotted from the world.
—Jas. 1:27

Speak not evil one of another.
—Jas. 4:11

Be ye all of one mind, having compassion one of another, love as brethren, be pitiful, be courteous.
—1 Pet. 3:8

Above all things have fervent charity among yourselves: for charity shall cover the multitude of sins.
—1 Pet. 4:8

Add . . . to godliness brotherly kindness; and to brotherly kindness charity.
—2 Pet. 1:5, 7

CHASTENING

As a man chasteneth his son, so the Lord thy God chasteneth thee.
—Deut. 8:5

Happy is the man whom God correcteth: therefore despise not thou the chastening of the Almighty.
—Job 5:17

He knoweth the way that I take: when he hath tried me, I shall come forth as gold.
—Job 23:10

Surely it is meet to be said unto God, I have borne chastisement, I will not offend any more: That which I see not teach thou me: if I have done iniquity, I will do no more.
—Job 34:31, 32

Thou, O God, hast proved us: thou hast tried us, as silver is tried.
—Psa. 66:10

Blessed is the man whom thou chastenest, O Lord, and teachest him out of thy law.
—Psa. 94:12

Before I was afflicted I went astray: but now have I kept thy word.
—Psa. 119:67

It is good for me that I have been afflicted; that I might learn thy statutes.
—Psa. 119:71

My son, despise not the chastening of the Lord; neither be weary of his correction: For whom the Lord loveth he correcteth; even as a father the son in whom he delighteth.
—Prov. 3:11, 12

The fining pot is for silver, and the furnace for gold: but the Lord trieth the hearts.
—Prov. 17:3

I will turn my hand upon thee, and purely purge away thy dross, and take away all thy tin.
—Isa. 1:25

Behold, I have refined thee, but not with silver; I have chosen thee in the furnace of affliction.
—Isa. 48:10

I will bring the third part through the fire, and will refine them as silver is refined, and will try them as gold is tried.
—Zech. 13:9

Despise not thou the chastening of the Lord, nor faint when thou art rebuked of him: For whom the Lord loveth he chasteneth, and scourgeth every son whom he receiveth.
—Heb. 12:5, 6

No chastening for the present seemeth to be joyous, but grievous: nevertheless afterward it yieldeth the peaceable fruit of righteousness unto them which are exercised thereby. —HEB. 12:11

As many as I love, I rebuke and chasten. —REV. 3:19

Chastisement, see CHASTENING

CHASTITY; see also ADULTERY

I made a covenant with mine eyes; why then should I think upon a maid? —JOB. 31:1

Lust not after her beauty in thine heart; neither let her take thee with her eyelids. —PROV. 6:25

Give not thy strength unto women, nor thy ways to that which destroyeth kings. —PROV. 31:3

It is good for man not to touch a woman. Nevertheless, to avoid fornication, let every man have his own wife, and let every woman have her own husband.
—1 COR. 7:1, 2

It is better to marry than to burn.
—1 COR. 7:9

He that standeth stedfast in his heart, having no necessity, but hath power over his own will, and hath so decreed in his heart that he will keep his virgin, doeth well.
—1 COR. 7:37

Cheating, see DECEIT

CHEERFULNESS; see also CONTENTMENT, JOY, PLEASURE, REJOICING

A merry heart maketh a cheerful countenance. —PROV. 15:13

He that is of a merry heart hath a continual feast. —PROV. 15:15

The light of the eyes rejoiceth the heart: and a good report maketh the bones fat. —PROV. 15:30

A merry heart doeth good like a medicine. —PROV. 17:22

As the crackling of thorns under a pot, so is the laughter of a fool.
—ECCL. 7:6

A man hath no better thing under the sun, than to eat, and to drink, and to be merry. —ECCL. 8:15

Go thy way, eat thy bread with joy, and drink thy wine with a merry heart. —ECCL. 9:7

A feast is made for laugher, and wine maketh merry: but money answereth all things. —ECCL. 10:19

Be of good cheer; it is I; be not afraid. —MATT. 14:27

God loveth a cheerful giver.
—2 COR. 9:7

CHILDREN; see also INSTRUCTION, PARENTS

Lo, children are an heritage of the Lord: and the fruit of the womb is his reward. —PSA. 127:3

As arrows are in the hand of a mighty man; so are children of the youth. Happy is the man that hath his quiver full of them.
—PSA. 127:4, 5

A wise son maketh a glad father: but a foolish son is the heaviness of his mother.
—PROV. 10:1

A wise son heareth his father's instruction. —PROV. 13:1

A good man leaveth an inheritance to his children's children.
—PROV. 13:22

Children's children are the crown of old men; and the glory of children are their fathers.

—Prov. 17:6

A foolish son is a grief to his father, and bitterness to her that bare him. —Prov. 17:25

A just man walketh in his integrity: his children are blessed after him. —Prov. 20:7

Train up a child in the way he should go: and when he is old, he will not depart from it.

—Prov. 22:6

Remember now thy Creator in the days of thy youth, while the evil days come not, nor the years draw nigh, when thou shalt say, I have no pleasure in them. —Eccl. 12:1

It is good for a man that he bear the yoke in his youth.—Lam. 3:27

Except ye be converted, and become as little children, ye shall not enter into the kingdom of heaven.

—Matt. 18:3

Suffer little children, and forbid them not, to come unto me: for of such is the kingdom of heaven.

—Matt. 19:14

Out of the mouth of babes and sucklings thou hast perfected praise.

—Matt. 21:16

When I was a child, I spake as a child, I understood as a child, I thought as a child: but when I became a man, I put away childish things. —1 Cor. 13:11

CHOICE

I have set before you life and death, blessing and cursing: therefore choose life, that both thou and thy seed may live. —Deut. 30:19

Choose you this day whom ye will serve. —Josh. 24:15

How long halt ye between two opinions? if the Lord be God, follow him; but if Baal, then follow him. —1 Kin. 18:21

Let us choose to us judgment: let us know among ourselves what is good. —Job 34:4

A man's heart deviseth his way: but the Lord directeth his steps.

—Prov. 16:9

A good name is rather to be chosen than great riches, and loving favour than silver and gold.

—Prov. 22:1

Refuse the evil, and choose the good. Isa. 7:15

Ye have not chosen me, but I have chosen you, and ordained you, that ye should go and bring forth fruit. —John 15:16

CHRIST; see also Reconciliation, Redemption, Remission, Salvation

Behold, a virgin shall conceive, and bear a son, and shall call his name Immanuel. —Isa. 7:14

Jesus Christ, the son of David, the son of Abraham.—Matt. 1:1

Thou shalt call his name Jesus: for he shall save his people from their sins. —Matt. 1:21

Come unto me, all ye that labour and are heavy laden, and I will give you rest. —Matt. 11:28

I am meek and lowly in heart.

—Matt. 11:29

This is my beloved Son, in whom I am well pleased. —Matt. 17:5

The Son of man came not to be ministered unto, but to minister, and to give his life a ransom for many. —MATT. 20:28

One is your Master, even Christ; and all ye are brethren.
—MATT. 23:8

All power is given unto me.
—MATT. 28:18

Lo, I am with you always, even unto the end of the world.
—MATT. 28:20

He taught them as one that had authority. —MARK 1:22

The Son of man hath power on earth to forgive sins.—MARK 2:10

A friend of publicans and sinners. —LUKE 7:34

The Son of man is come to seek and to save that which was lost.
—LUKE 19:10

Art thou then the Son of God? And he said unto them, Ye say that I am. —LUKE 22:70

Without him was not any thing made that was made. —JOHN 1:3

The Word was made flesh, and dwelt among us . . . full of grace and truth. —JOHN 1:14

Behold the Lamb of God, which taketh away the sin of the world!
—JOHN 1:29

The Father . . . hath given him authority to execute judgment also, because he is the Son of man.
—JOHN 5:26, 27

I am the bread of life: he that cometh to me shall never hunger; and he that believeth on me shall never thirst. —JOHN 6:35

My doctrine is not mine, but his that sent me. —JOHN 7:16

I am the door: by me if any man enter in, he shall be saved.
—JOHN 10:9

I am the good shepherd.
—JOHN 10:11

Let not your heart be troubled: ye believe in God, believe also in me. —JOHN 14:1

I am the way, the truth, and the life. —JOHN 14:6

These are written, that ye might believe that Jesus is the Christ, the Son of God; and that believing ye might have life through his name. —JOHN 20:31

Jesus of Nazareth . . . who went about doing good. —ACTS 10:38

Christ is the end of the law for righteousness to every one that believeth. —ROM. 10:4

God was in Christ, reconciling the world unto himself.
—2 COR. 5:19

Christ . . . the head over all things to the church.
—EPH. 1:20, 22

Christ is all, and in all.
—COL. 3:11

There is . . . one mediator between God and men, the man Christ Jesus. —1 TIM. 2:5

Our Lord Jesus Christ . . . who is the blessed and only Potentate, the King of kings, and Lord of lords. —1 TIM. 6:14, 15

Jesus Christ, the same yesterday, and today, and for ever.
—HEB. 13:8

Jesus, that great shepherd of the sheep. —HEB. 13:20

Christ also suffered for us, leaving us an example, that ye should follow his steps.
—1 PET. 2:21

CHURCH

Mine house shall be called a house of prayer for all people.
—ISA. 56:7

Those that be planted in the house of the Lord shall flourish in the courts of our God.
—PSA. 92:13

Upon this rock I will build my church; and the gates of hell shall not prevail against it.
—MATT. 16:18

There shall be one fold, and one shepherd. —JOHN 10:16

We, being many, are one body in Christ, and every one members one of another. —ROM. 12:5

We being many are one bread, and one body: for we are all partakers of that one bread.
—1 COR. 10:17

As the body is one, and hath many members, and all the members of that one body, being many, are one body: so also is Christ.
—1 COR. 12:12

Now ye are the body of Christ, and members in particular.
—1 COR. 12:27

Ye are all the children of God by faith in Christ Jesus.—GAL. 3:26

There is neither Jew nor Greek, there is neither bond nor free, there is neither male nor female: for ye are all one in Christ Jesus.
—GAL. 3:28

The church, Which is his body, the fulness of him that filleth all in all. —EPH. 1:22, 23

Ye are . . . fellow-citizens with the saints, and of the household of God. —EPH. 2:19

In whom all the building fitly framed together groweth unto an holy temple in the Lord.
—EPH. 2:21

Unto him be glory in the church.
—EPH. 3:21

We are members one of another.
—EPH. 4:25

The church is subject unto Christ. —EPH. 5:24

We are members of his body.
—EPH. 5:30

He is the head of the body, the church. —COL. 1:18

Him that overcometh will I make a pillar in the temple of my God. —REV. 3:12

Civility, see KINDNESS

Cleansing, see PURIFICATION

Clemency, see FORGIVENESS, MERCY

Clergy, see MINISTRY

COMFORT; see also COURAGE, DEATH, SORROW

The eternal God is thy refuge, and underneath are the everlasting arms. —DEUT. 33:27

Naked came I out of my mother's womb, and naked shall I return thither: the Lord gave, and the Lord hath taken away; blessed be the name of the Lord.
—JOB 1:21

They that know thy name will put their trust in thee: for thou, Lord, hast not forsaken them that seek thee. —PSA. 9:10

Yea, though I walk through the valley of the shadow of death, I will fear no evil: for thou art with me; thy rod and thy staff they comfort me. —Psa. 23:4

Weeping may endure for a night, but joy cometh in the morning. —Psa. 30:5

God is our refuge and strength, a very present help in trouble. —Psa. 46:1

Cast thy burden upon the Lord, and he shall sustain thee; he shall never suffer the righteous to be moved. —Psa. 55:22

The Lord heareth the poor, and despiseth not his prisoners. —Psa. 69:33

My flesh and my heart faileth: but God is the strength of my heart, and my portion for ever. —Psa. 73:26

Thou, Lord, hast holpen me, and comforted me. —Psa. 86:17

In the multitude of my thoughts within me thy comforts delight my soul. —Psa. 94:19

This is my comfort in my affliction: for thy word hath quickened me. —Psa. 119:50

I remembered thy judgments of old, O Lord; and have comforted myself. —Psa. 119:55

Let, I pray thee, thy merciful kindness be for my comfort. —Psa. 119:76

In the day when I cried thou answeredst me, and strengthenedst me with strength in my soul. —Psa. 138:3

Though I walk in the midst of trouble, thou wilt revive me. —Psa. 138:7

I know that the Lord will maintain the cause of the afflicted, and the right of the poor. —Psa. 140:12

The Lord upholdeth all that fall, and raiseth up all those that be bowed down. —Psa. 145:14

He healeth the broken in heart, and bindeth up their wounds. —Psa. 147:3

Heaviness in the heart of man maketh it stoop: but a good word maketh it glad. —Prov. 12:25

Comfort ye, comfort ye my people, saith your God. —Isa. 40:1

Sing, O heavens; and be joyful, O earth; and break forth into singing, O mountains: for the Lord hath comforted his people, and will have mercy upon his afflicted. —Isa. 49:13

The Lord God will help me; therefore shall I not be confounded: therefore have I set my face like a flint, and I know that I shall not be ashamed. —Isa. 50:7

I, even I, am he that comforteth you: who art thou, that thou shouldest be afraid of a man that shall die, and of the son of man which shall be made as grass. —Isa. 51:12

As one whom his mother comforteth, so will I comfort you. —Isa. 66:13

Is there no balm in Gilead? —Jer. 8:22

Blessed are they that mourn: for they shall be comforted. —Matt. 5:4

Come unto me, all ye that labour and are heavy laden, and I will give you rest. —Matt. 11:28

Lo, I am with you alway, even unto the end of the world.
—MATT. 28:20

I will not leave you comfortless: I will come to you.—JOHN 14:18

Peace I leave with you, my peace I give unto you: not as the world giveth, give I unto you. Let not your heart be troubled, neither let it be afraid. —JOHN 14:27

Verily, verily, I say unto you, That ye shall weep and lament, but the world shall rejoice; and ye shall be sorrowful, but your sorrow shall be turned into joy. —JOHN 16:20

All things work together for good to them that love God, to them who are the called according to his purpose. —ROM. 8:28

Rejoice with them that do rejoice, and weep with them that weep. —ROM. 12:15

Whatsoever things were written aforetime were written for our learning, that we through patience and comfort of the Scriptures might have hope. —ROM. 15:4

Blessed be God, even the Father of our Lord Jesus Christ, the Father of mercies, and the God of all comfort; Who comforteth us in all our tribulation, that we may be able to comfort them which are in any trouble, by the comfort wherewith we ourselves are comforted of God. —2 COR. 1:3, 4

Comfort yourselves together, and edify one another.—1 THESS. 5:11

I will never leave thee, nor forsake thee. —HEB. 13:5

Commandments, see LAW

COMMERCE; see also WEALTH, BORROWING AND LENDING

They that go down to the sea in ships, that do business in great waters. —PSA. 107:23

Seest thou a man diligent in his business? He shall stand before kings. —PROV. 22:29

Buy the truth, and sell it not.
—PROV. 23:23

He that by usury and unjust gain increaseth his substance, he shall gather it for him that will pity the poor. —PROV. 28:8

He is a merchant, the balances of deceit are in his hand.—HOS. 12:7

He that had received the five talents went and traded with the same, and made them other five talents.
—MATT. 25:16

Make not my Father's house an house of merchandise.
—JOHN 2:16

Thy merchants were the great men of the earth. —REV. 18:23

Commiseration, see COMFORT

COMPANIONS, EVIL

Thou shalt not follow a multitude to do evil. —EX. 23:2

Blessed is the man that walketh not in the counsel of the ungodly, nor standeth in the way of sinners, nor sitteth in the seat of the scornful. —PSA. 1:1

I have not sat with vain persons, neither will I go in with dissemblers. I have hated the congregation of evildoers; and will not sit with the wicked. —PSA. 26:4, 5

I had rather be a doorkeeper in the house of my God, than to dwell in the tents of wickedness.
—PSA. 84:10

Depart from me, ye evildoers: for I will keep the commandments of my God. —Psa. 119:115

Incline not my heart to any evil thing, to practice wicked works with men that work iniquity.
—Psa. 141:4

My son, if sinners entice thee, consent thou not. If they say, Come with us . . . walk not thou in the way with them; refrain thy foot from their path.
—Prov. 1:10, 11, 15

Enter not into the path of the wicked, and go not in the way of evil men. —Prov. 4:14

He that followeth vain persons is void of understanding.
—Prov. 12:11

The righteous is more excellent than his neighbour: but the way of the wicked seduceth them.
—Prov. 12:26

He that walketh with wise men shall be wise: but a companion of fools shall be destroyed.
—Prov. 13:20

Go from the presence of a foolish man, when thou perceivest not in him the lips of knowledge.
—Prov. 14:7

A violent man enticeth his neighbour, and leadeth him into the way that is not good. —Prov. 16:29

Thorns and snares are in the way of the froward: he that doth keep his soul shall be far from them.
—Prov. 22:5

Make no friendship with an angry man; and with a furious man thou shalt not go: Lest thou learn his ways, and get a snare to thy soul. —Prov. 22:24, 25

Be not thou envious against evil men, neither desire to be with them.
—Prov. 24:1

He that is a companion of riotous men shameth his father.
—Prov. 28:7

One sinner destroyeth much good. —Eccl. 9:18

A little leaven leaveneth the whole lump. —1 Cor. 5:6

Evil communications corrupt good manners. —1 Cor. 15:33

Be ye not unequally yoked together with unbelievers: for what fellowship hath righteousness with unrighteousness? and what communion hath light with darkness?
—2 Cor. 6:14

Have no fellowship with the unfruitful works of darkness.
—Eph. 5:11

Companionship, see Brotherhood, Friendship, Companions, Evil

Compassion, see Mercy

Compensation, see Reward

COMPLAINT

Fret not thyself because of evildoers, neither be thou envious against the workers of iniquity.
—Psa. 37:1

The foolishness of man perverteth his way; and his heart fretteth against the Lord.—Prov. 19:3

The eyes of man are never satisfied. —Prov. 27:20

Wherefore doth a living man complain, a man for the punishment of his sins? —Lam. 3:39

Murmur not among yourselves.
—John 6:43

Who art thou that repliest against God? Shall the thing formed say to him that formed it, Why hast thou made me thus?   —ROM. 9:20

Do all things without murmurings and disputings. —PHIL. 2:14

Grudge not one against another.
    —JAS. 5:9

Comprehension, see UNDERSTANDING, INCOMPREHENSION

CONCEALMENT

Is there any secret thing with thee.   —JOB 15:11

Hide me under the shadow of thy wings.   —PSA. 17:8

Cleanse thou me from secret faults.   —PSA. 19:12

Thou art my hiding place; thou shalt preserve me from trouble.
    —PSA. 32:7

He knoweth the secrets of the heart.   —PSA. 44:21

He that dwelleth in the secret place of the most High shall abide under the shadow of the Almighty.
    —PSA. 91:1

Stolen waters are sweet, and bread eaten in secret is pleasant.
    —PROV. 9:17

A talebearer revealeth secrets: but he that is of a faithful spirit concealeth the matter.
    —PROV. 11:13

A prudent man concealeth knowledge.   —PROV. 12:23

A prudent man foreseeth the evil, and hideth himself. —PROV. 22:3

He that covereth his sins shall not prosper: but whoso confesseth and forsaketh them shall have mercy.   —PROV. 28:13

There is nothing covered, that shall not be revealed; neither hid, that shall not be known.
    —LUKE 12:2

Every one that doeth evil hateth the light, neither cometh to the light, lest his deeds should be reproved.   —JOHN 3:20

God shall judge the secrets of man.   —ROM. 2:16

Charity shall cover the multitude of sins.   —1 PET 4:8

CONCEIT; see also BOASTING, PRIDE

Be not wise in thine own eyes.
    —PROV. 3:5

The way of a fool is right in his own eyes: but he that hearkeneth unto counsel is wise. —PROV. 12:15

The rich man's wealth is his strong city, and as an high wall in his own conceit.   —PROV. 18:11

Most men will proclaim every one his own goodness: but a faithful man who can find? —PROV. 20:6

Cease from thine own wisdom.
    —PROV. 23:4

For men to search their own glory is not glory. —PROV. 25:27

Answer a fool according to his folly, lest he be wise in his own conceit.   —PROV. 26:5

Seest thou a man wise in his own conceit? there is more hope of a fool than of him.   —PROV. 26:12

The sluggard is wiser in his own conceit than seven men that can render a reason.   —PROV. 26:16

The rich man is wise in his own conceit; but the poor that hath understanding searcheth him out.
    —PROV. 28:11

He that trusteth in his own heart is a fool. —PROV. 28:26

Woe unto them that are wise in their own eyes, and prudent in their own sight! —ISA. 5:21

Let not the wise man glory in his wisdom, neither let the mighty man glory in his might, let not the rich man glory in his riches.—JER. 9:23

Professing themselves to be wise, they became fools. —ROM. 1:22

Mind not high things, but condescend to men of low estate. Be not wise in your own conceit. —ROM. 12:16

If any man among you seemeth to be wise in this world, let him become a fool, that he may be wise. —1 COR. 3:18

Knowledge puffeth up, but charity edifieth. —1 COR. 8:1

If any man think that he knoweth any thing, he knoweth nothing yet as he ought to know.—1 COR. 8:2

Let him that thinketh he standeth take heed lest he fall. —1 COR. 10:12

If a man think himself to be something, when he is nothing, he deceiveth himself. —GAL. 6:3

Concord, see HARMONY

Condemnation, see ACCUSATION, CENSURE, JUDGMENT, REPROOF

Condolence, see COMFORT

Conduct, see BEHAVIOR

CONFESSION

I have sinned greatly in that I have done: and now, I beseech thee, O Lord, take away the iniquity of thy servant; for I have done very foolishly. —2 SAM. 24:10

I have sinned; what shall I do unto thee, O thou preserver of men? —JOB 7:20

How many are mine iniquities and sins? make me to know my transgression and my sin. —JOB 13:23

If any say, I have sinned, and perverted that which was right, and it profited me not; He will deliver his soul from going into the pit, and his life shall see the light. —JOB 33:27, 28

Behold, I am vile; what shall I answer thee? I will lay mine hand upon my mouth. —JOB 40:4

I said, I will confess my transgression unto the Lord; and thou forgavest the iniquity of my sin. —PSA. 32:5

I will declare mine iniquity; I will be sorry for my sin. —PSA. 38:18

Lord, be merciful unto me: heal my soul; for I have sinned against thee. —PSA. 41:4

I acknowledge my transgressions: and my sin is ever before me. —PSA. 51:2

He that covereth his sins shall not prosper: but whoso confesseth and forsaketh them shall have mercy. —PROV. 28:13

Woe is me! for I am undone: because I am a man of unclean lips, and I dwell in the midst of a people of unclean lips. —ISA. 6:5

We are all as an unclean thing, and all our righteousnesses are as filthy rags; and we all do fade as a leaf; and our iniquities, like the wind, have taken us away. —ISA. 64:6

We lie down in our shame, and our confusion covereth us: for we have sinned against the Lord our God. —JER. 3:25

We acknowledge, O Lord, our wickedness, and the iniquity of our fathers: for we have sinned against thee. —JER. 14:7

Behold, O Lord; for I am in distress: my bowels are troubled; mine heart is turned within me; for I have grievously rebelled.
—LAM. 1:20

We have sinned, and have committed iniquity, and have done wickedly, and have rebelled, even by departing from thy precepts and from thy judgments. —DAN. 9:5

Father, I have sinned against heaven, and before thee.
—LUKE 15:18

God be merciful to me a sinner.
—LUKE 18:13

Confidence, see FAITH, HOPE

CONSCIENCE

As he thinketh in his heart, so is he. —PROV. 23:7

The wicked flee when no man pursueth: the righteous are bold as a lion. —PROV. 28:1

The light of the body is the eye: if therefore thine eye be single, thy whole body shall be full of light. But if thine eye be evil, thy whole body shall be full of darkness.
—MATT. 6:22, 23

Herein do I exercise myself, to have always a conscience void of offence toward God, and toward men. —ACTS 24:16

One man esteemeth one day above another: another esteemeth every day alike. Let every man be fully persuaded in his own mind.
—ROM. 14:5

There is nothing unclean of itself: but to him that esteemeth any thing to be unclean, to him it is unclean. —ROM. 14:14

Happy is he that condemneth not himself in that thing which he alloweth. —ROM. 14:22

When ye sin so against the brethren, and wound their weak conscience, ye sin against Christ.
—1 COR. 8:12

If we would judge ourselves, we should not be judged.
—1 COR. 11:31

The end of the commandment is charity out of a pure heart, and of a good conscience, and of faith unfeigned. —1 TIM. 1:5

Unto the pure all things are pure: but unto them that are defiled and unbelieving is nothing pure: but even their mind and conscience is defiled. —TIT. 1:15

Worshippers once purged should have no more conscience of sins.
—HEB. 10:2

Let us draw near with a true heart in full assurance of faith, having our hearts sprinkled from an evil conscience. —HEB. 10:22

We trust we have a good conscience, in all things willing to live honestly. —HEB. 13:18

If our heart condemn us, God is greater than our heart, and knoweth all things. Beloved, if our heart condemn us not, then have we confidence toward God.
—1 JOHN 3:20, 21

Consideration, see KINDNESS, UN-SELFISHNESS

Consolation, see COMFORT

CONSTANCY; see also FAITHFUL-NESS, PATIENCE, INSTABILITY

The righteous also shall hold on his way, and he that hath clean hands shall be stronger and stronger.
—JOB 17:9

Keep mercy and judgment, and wait on thy God continually.
—HOS. 12:6

He that shall endure unto the end, the same shall be saved.
—MATT. 24:13

If ye continue in my word, then are ye my disciples indeed.
—JOHN 8:31

Abide in me, and I in you.
—JOHN 15:4

As the Father hath loved me, so have I loved you: continue ye in my love.
—JOHN 15:9

With purpose of heart . . . cleave unto the Lord.
—ACTS 11:23

Continue in the grace of God.
—ACTS 13:43

Continue in the faith.
—ACTS 14:22

By patient continuance in well doing seek for glory and honour and immortality.
—ROM. 2:7

Be ye stedfast, unmoveable, always abounding in the work of the Lord.
—1 COR. 15:58

Watch ye, stand fast in the faith, quit you like men, be strong.
—1 COR. 16:13

Wherefore we labour, that, whether present or absent, we may be accepted of him.
—2 COR. 5:9

Stand fast therefore in the liberty wherewith Christ hath made us free, and be not entangled again with the yoke of bondage.
—GAL. 5:1

Let us not be weary in well doing: for in due season we shall reap, if we faint not.
—GAL. 6:9

Take unto you the whole armour of God, that ye may be able to withstand in the evil day, and having done all, to stand.
—EPH. 6:13

Stand fast in one spirit, with one mind striving together for the faith of the gospel.
—PHIL. 1:27

Stand fast in the Lord.
—PHIL. 4:1

Continue in the faith grounded and settled, and be not moved away from the hope of the gospel.
—COL. 1:23

Now we live, if ye stand fast in the Lord.
—1 THESS. 3:8

Prove all things; hold fast that which is good.
—1 THESS. 5:21

Stand fast, and hold the traditions which ye have been taught.
—2 THESS. 2:15

Be not weary in well doing.
—2 THESS. 3:13

Hold fast the form of sound words.
—2 TIM. 1:13

Endure hardness, as a good soldier of Jesus Christ.
—2 TIM. 2:3

Continue thou in the things which thou hast learned and hast been assured of, knowing of whom thou hast learned them.
—2 TIM. 3:14

Hold fast the confidence and the rejoicing of the hope firm unto the end.
—HEB. 3:6

We are made partakers with Christ, if we hold the beginning of our confidence stedfast unto the end. —HEB. 3:14

Let us go on unto perfection.
—HEB. 6:1

Let us hold fast the profession of our faith without wavering.
—HEB. 10:23

We count them happy which endure. —JAS. 5:11

Give diligence to make your calling and election sure: for if ye do these things, ye shall never fall.
—2 PET. 1:10

Be thou faithful unto death, and I will give thee a crown of life.
—REV. 2:10

Hold that fast which thou hast, that no man take thy crown.
—REV. 3:11

He that is righteous, let him be righteous still: and he that is holy, let him be holy still.—REV. 22:11

Contempt, see SCORN

CONTENTION; see also ANGER, ENMITY, WAR

Strive not with a man without cause, if he have done thee no harm. —PROV. 3:30

A naughty person, a wicked man, walketh with a froward mouth.
—PROV. 6:12

Hatred stirreth up strifes: but love covereth all sins.
—PROV. 10:12

Only by pride cometh contention: but with the well advised is wisdom. —PROV. 13:10

A wrathful man stirreth up strife: but he that is slow to anger appeaseth strife. —PROV. 15:18

A froward man soweth strife: and a whisperer separateth chief friends. —PROV. 16:28

Better is a dry morsel, and quietness therewith, than an house full of sacrifices with strife.
—PROV. 17:1

The beginning of strife is as when one letteth out water: therefore leave off contention, before it be meddled with. —PROV. 17:14

He loveth transgression that loveth strife: and he that exalteth his gate seeketh destruction.
—PROV. 17:19

A fools lips enter into contention, and his mouth calleth for strokes.
—PROV. 18:6

A brother offended is harder to be won than a strong city: and their contentions are like the bars of a castle. —PROV. 18:19

A foolish son is the calamity of his father: and the contentions of a wife are a continual dropping.
—PROV. 19:13

It is an honour for a man to cease from strife: but every fool will be meddling. —PROV. 20:3

It is better to dwell in the wilderness, than with a contentious and an angry woman. —PROV. 21:19

Cast out the scorner, and contention shall go out; yea, strife and reproach shall cease. —PROV. 22:10

Go not forth hastily to strive, lest thou know not what to do in the end thereof, when thy neighbour hath put thee to shame.
—PROV. 25:8

It is better to dwell in the corner of the housetop, than with a brawling woman and in a wide house.
—PROV. 25:24

He that passeth by, and meddleth with strife belonging not to him, is like one that taketh a dog by the ears.   —Prov. 26:17

As coals are to burning coals, and wood to fire; so is a contentious man to kindle strife.—Prov. 26:21

A continual dropping in a very rainy day and a contentious woman are alike.   —Prov. 27:15

He that is of a proud heart stirreth up strife.   —Prov. 28:25

An angry man stirreth up strife, and a furious man aboundeth in transgression.   —Prov. 29:22

Surely the churning of milk bringeth forth butter, and the wringing of the nose bringeth forth blood: so the forcing of wrath bringeth forth strife.—Prov.30:33

Agree with thine adversary quickly, whiles thou art in the way with him.   —Matt. 5:25

Whosoever shall smite thee on thy right cheek, turn to him the other also.   —Matt. 5:39

Every kingdom divided against itself is brought to desolation; and every city or house divided against itself shall not stand.—Matt. 12:25

If it be possible, as much as lieth in you, live peaceably with all men.
        —Rom. 12:18

If ye bite and devour one another, take heed that ye be not consumed one of another.—Gal. 5:15

Let nothing be done through strife or vainglory; but in lowliness of mind let each esteem other better than themselves.   —Phil. 2:3

Do all things without murmurings and disputings.   —Phil. 2:14

Foolish and unlearned questions avoid, knowing that they do gender strifes.   —2 Tim. 2:23

Where envying and strife is, there is confusion and every evil work.
        —Jas. 3:16

CONTENTMENT; see also Dis-
CONTENT

A little that a righteous man hath is better than the riches of many wicked.   —Psa. 37:16

A good man shall be satisfied from himself.   —Prov. 14:14

Better is a little with righteousness than great revenues without right.   —Prov. 16:8

Better is a dry morsel, and quietness therewith, than an house full of sacrifices with strife.
        —Prov. 17:1

The fear of the Lord tendeth to life: and he that hath it shall abide satisfied.   —Prov. 19:23

Give me neither poverty nor riches; feed me with food convenient for me.   —Prov. 30:8

There is nothing better for a man, than that he should eat and drink, and that he should make his soul enjoy good in his labour.
        —Eccl. 2:24

Better is an handful with quietness, than both the hands full with travail and vexation of spirit.
        —Eccl. 4:6

Contrition, see Remorse, Repentance

CONVERSION; see also Reformation, Regeneration, Repentance

I thought on my ways, and turned my feet unto thy testimonies.
        —Psa. 119:59

If the wicked will turn from all his sins that he hath committed, and keep all my statutes, and do that which is lawful and right, he shall surely live, he shall not die.
—EZEK. 18:21

Cast away from you all your transgression, whereby ye have transgressed; and make you a new heart and a new spirit.
—EZEK. 18:31

Turn yourselves, and live ye.
—EZEK. 18:32

It is time to seek the Lord, till he come and rain righteousness upon you. —HOS. 10:12

Turn thou to thy God: keep mercy and judgment, and wait on thy God continually. —HOS. 12:6

Turn to the Lord: say unto him, Take away all iniquity, and receive us graciously. —HOS. 14:2

Turn ye even to me with all your heart, and with fasting, and with weeping, and with mourning.
—JOEL 2:12

Ye were as a firebrand plucked out of the burning. —AMOS 4:11

Is not this a brand plucked out of the fire? —ZECH. 3:2

Except ye be converted, and become as little children, ye shall not enter into the kingdom of heaven.
—MATT. 18:3

I will arise and go to my father, and will say unto him, Father, I have sinned against heaven, and before thee. —LUKE 15:18

When thou art converted, strengthen thy brethren.
—LUKE 22:32

Repent ye therefore, and be converted, that your sins may be blotted out. —ACTS 3:19

Arise, and be baptized, and wash away thy sins, calling on the name of the Lord. —ACTS 22:16

Be ye reconciled to God.
—2 COR. 5:20

Without Christ . . . But now in Christ Jesus. —EPH. 2:12, 13

Awake thou that sleepest, and arise from the dead, and Christ shall give thee light. —EPH. 5:14

He which converteth the sinner from the error of his way shall save a soul from death, and shall hide a multitude of sins. —JAS. 5:20

Behold, I stand at the door and knock: if any man hear my voice, and open the door, I will come in to him, and will sup with him, and he with me. —REV. 3:20

Correction, see REPROOF, CHASTENING

Corruption, see EVIL, SIN, IMPERFECTION

COUNSEL; see also INSTRUCTION

A wise man will hear, and will increase learning; and a man of understanding shall attain unto wise counsels. —PROV. 1:5

Give instruction to a wise man and he will be yet wiser: teach a just man, and he will increase in learning. —PROV. 9:9

Where no counsel is, the people fall: but in the multitude of counsellors there is safety.—PROV. 11:14

The way of a fool is right in his own eyes: but he that hearkeneth unto counsel is wise.—PROV. 12:15

Only by pride cometh contention: but with the well advised is wisdom.   —Prov. 13:10

Without counsel purposes are disappointed: but in the multitude of counsellors they are established.   —Prov. 15:22

Hear counsel, and receive instruction; that thou mayest be wise in thy latter end.   —Prov. 19:20

Every purpose is established by counsel: and with good advice make war.   —Prov. 20:18

By wise counsel thou shalt make thy war: and in multitude of counsellors there is safety.—Prov. 24:6

Ointment and perfume rejoice the heart: so doth the sweetness of a man's friend by hearty counsel.   —Prov. 27:9

COURAGE; see also Anxiety

Fear ye not, stand still, and see the salvation of the Lord.
    —Ex. 14:13

Ye shall not be afraid of the face of man; for the judgment is God's.   —Deut. 1:17

Be strong and of good courage.   —Deut. 31:6

Be thou strong and very courageous.   —Josh. 1:7

Fear not: for they that be with us are more than they that be with them.   —2 Kin. 6:16

Yea, though I walk through the valley of the shadow of death, I will fear no evil: for thou art with me: thy rod and thy staff they comfort me.   —Psa. 23:4

The Lord is my light and my salvation; whom shall I fear? the Lord is the strength of my life; of whom shall I be afraid?
    —Psa. 27:1

Wait on the Lord: be of good courage, and he shall strengthen thine heart.   —Psa. 27:14

Be of good courage, and he shall strengthen your heart, all ye that hope in the Lord.   —Psa. 31:24

I sought the Lord, and he heard me, and delivered me from all my fears.   —Psa. 34:4

What time I am afraid, I will trust in thee.   —Psa. 56:3

I will not fear what flesh can do unto me.   —Psa. 56:4

The Lord is on my side; I will not fear: what can man do unto me?   —Psa. 118:6

Be not afraid of sudden fear . . . For the Lord shall be thy confidence.   —Prov. 3:25, 26

In the fear of the Lord is strong confidence: and his children shall have a place of refuge.
    —Prov. 14:26

The wicked flee when no man pursueth: but the righteous are bold as a lion.   Prov. 28:1

The fear of man bringeth a snare: but whoso putteth his trust in the Lord shall be safe.
    —Prov. 29:25

Behold, God is my salvation: I will trust, and not be afraid.
    —Isa. 12:2

Strengthen ye the weak hands, and confirm the feeble knees.
    —Isa. 35:3

Fear thou not; for I am with thee: be not dismayed; for I am thy God.   —Isa. 41:10

I, even I, am he that comforteth you: who art thou, that thou shouldest be afraid of a man that shall die, and of the son of man which shall be made as grass.
—Isa. 51:12

Fear not; for thou shalt not be ashamed: neither be thou confounded; for thou shalt not be put to shame.   —Isa. 54:4

Fear not them which kill the body, but are not able to kill the soul.   —Matt. 10:28

Be of good cheer; it is I; be not afraid.   —Matt. 14:27

Peace I leave with you, my grace I give unto you: not as the world giveth, give I unto you. Let not your heart be troubled, neither let it be afraid.   —John 14:27

If God be for us, who can be against us?   —Rom. 8:31

Watch ye, stand fast in the faith, quit you like men, be strong.
—1 Cor. 16:13

I can do all things through Christ that strengtheneth me.—Phil 4:13

God hath not given us the spirit of fear; but of power, and of love, and of a sound mind. —2 Tim. 1:7

The Lord is my helper, and I will not fear what man shall do unto me.   —Heb. 13:6

Perfect love casteth out fear.
—1 John 4:18

Courtesy, see Kindness

Covetousness, see Avarice

Cowardice, see Courage

CREATION

In the beginning God created the heaven and the earth. —Gen. 1:1

God created man in his own image, in the image of God created he him.   —Gen. 1:27

God saw every thing that he had made, and, behold, it was very good.   —Gen. 1:31

Thou hast made heaven, the heaven of heavens, with all their host, the earth, and all things that are therein, the seas, and all that is therein, and thou preservest them all.   —Neh. 9:6

He stretcheth out the north over the empty place, and hangeth the earth upon nothing. —Job 26:7

When I consider thy heavens, the work of thy fingers, the moon and the stars, which thou hast ordained; What is man, that thou art mindful of him?   —Psa. 8:3, 4

The heavens declare the glory of God; and the firmament sheweth his handywork.   —Psa. 19:1

By the word of the Lord were the heavens made; and all the host of them by the breath of his mouth.
—Psa. 33:6

Of old hast thou laid the foundation of the earth: and the heavens are the work of thy hands.
—Psa. 102:25

O Lord, how manifold are thy works! in wisdom hast thou made them all.   —Psa. 104:24

My help cometh from the Lord, which made heaven and earth.
—Psa. 121:2

The Lord by wisdom hath founded the earth; by understanding hath he established the heavens.
—Prov. 3:19

He hath made every thing beautiful in his time. —ECCL. 3:11

As thou knowest not what is the way of the spirit, nor how the bones do grow in the womb of her that is with child: even so thou knowest not the works of God who maketh all. —ECCL. 11:5

Lift up your eyes on high, and behold who hath created these things. —ISA. 40:26

I form the light, and create darkness: I make peace, and create evil: I the Lord do all these things. —ISA. 45:7

Of him, and through him, and to him, are all things. —ROM. 11:36

We are his workmanship. —EPH. 2:10

Credit, see BORROWING AND LENDING

Crime, see SIN, RETRIBUTION

Criticism, see CENSURE, REPROOF

Cruelty, see MALICE

Cupidity, see AVARICE

CURSE

Behold, I set before you this day a blessing and a curse. —DEUT. 11:26

The Lord thy God turned the curse into a blessing unto thee. —DEUT. 23:5

As he loved cursing, so let it come unto him: as he delighted not in blessing, so let it be far from him. —PSA. 109:17

Bless them that curse you. —MATT. 5:44

Christ hath redeemed us from the curse of the law. —GAL. 3:13

There shall be no more curse. —REV. 22:3

Cynicism, see PESSIMISM

D

Darkness, see IGNORANCE, LIGHT

DEATH; see also IMPERMANENCE, IMMORTALITY, COMFORT

Dust thou art, and unto dust shalt thou return. —GEN. 3:19

Let me die the death of the righteous, and let my last end be like his! —NUM. 23:10

Now he is dead, wherefore should I fast? can I bring him back again? I shall go to him, but he shall not return to me.
—2 SAM. 12:23

The Lord gave, and the Lord hath taken away; blessed be the name of the Lord. —JOB 1:21

There the wicked cease from troubling; and there the weary be at rest. There the prisoners rest together; they hear not the voice of the oppressor. The small and great are there; and the servant is free from his master. —JOB 3:17–19

As the cloud is consumed and vanisheth away: so he that goeth down to the grave shall come up no more. —JOB 7:9

All flesh shall perish together, and man shall turn again unto dust.
—JOB 34:15

Yea, though I walk through the valley of the shadow of death, I will fear no evil: for thou art with me; thy rod and thy staff they comfort me. —PSA. 23:4

Into thine hand I commit my spirit: thou hast redeemed me, O Lord God of truth. —PSA. 31:5

Lord, make me to know mine end, and the measure of my days, what it is; that I may know how frail I am. —PSA. 39:4

God will redeem my soul from the power of the grave: for he shall receive me. —PSA. 49:15

Unto God the Lord belong the issues from death. —PSA. 68:20

Thou shalt guide me with thy counsel, and afterward receive me to glory. —PSA. 73:24

Teach us to number our days, that we may apply our hearts unto wisdom. —PSA. 90:12

Precious in the sight of the Lord is the death of his saints.
—PSA. 116:15

There is a way which seemeth right unto a man, but the end thereof are the ways of death.
—PROV. 14:12

The righteous hath hope in his death. —PROV. 14:32

A good name is better than precious ointment; and the day of death than the day of one's birth.
—ECCL. 7:1

Then shall the dust return to the earth as it was; and the spirit shall return unto God who gave it.
—ECCL. 12:7

He will swallow up death in victory; and the Lord God will wipe away tears from off all faces.

—Isa. 25:8

Weep ye not for the dead, neither bemoan him: but weep sore for him that goeth away. —Jer. 22:10

Go thou thy way till the end be: for thou shalt rest, and stand in thy lot at the end of the days.

—Dan. 12:13

Fear not them which kill the body, but are not able to kill the soul. —Matt. 10:28

Lord, now lettest thou thy servant depart in peace, according to thy word. —Luke 2:29

I must work the works of him that sent me, while it is day: the night cometh, when no man can work. —John 9:4

Whether we live, we live unto the Lord; and whether we die, we die unto the Lord: whether we live therefore, or die, we are the Lord's.

—Rom. 14:8

This corruptible must put on incorruption, and this mortal must put on immortality. —1 Cor. 15:53

O death, where is thy sting? O grave, where is thy victory?

—1 Cor. 15:55

We know that if our earthly house of this tabernacle were dissolved, we have a building of God, an house not made with hands, eternal in the heavens.

—2 Cor. 5:1

I would not have you to be ignorant, brethren, concerning them which are asleep, that ye sorrow not, even as others which have no hope. —1 Thess. 4:13

We brought nothing into this world, and it is certain we can carry nothing out. —1 Tim. 6:7

It is appointed unto men once to die, but after this the judgment.

—Heb. 9:27

God shall wipe away all tears from their eyes; and there shall be no more death, neither sorrow, nor crying, neither shall there be any more pain: for the former things are passed away. —Rev. 21:4

Debt, see Borrowing and Lending

DECEIT; see also Falsehood, Flattery, Hypocrisy

Let not him that is deceived trust in vanity: for vanity shall be his recompence. —Job. 15:31

My lips shall not speak wickedness, nor my tongue utter deceit.

—Job 27:4

If I have walked with vanity, or if my foot hath hasted to deceit; Let me be weighed in an even balance, that God may know mine integrity. —Job 31:5, 6

The Lord will abhor the bloody and deceitful man. —Psa. 5:6

The workers of iniquity, which speak peace to their neighbours, but mischief is in their hearts.

—Psa. 28:3

Thou lovest all devouring words, O thou deceitful tongue.

—Psa. 52:4

He that worketh deceit shall not dwell within my house: he that telleth lies shall not tarry in my sight. —Psa. 101:7

Deliver my soul, O Lord, from lying lips, and from a deceitful tongue. —Psa. 120:2

Rid me, and deliver me from the hand of strange children, whose mouth speaketh vanity, and their right hand is a right hand of falsehood. —PSA. 144:11

A naughty person, a wicked man, walketh with a froward mouth. He winketh with his eyes, he speaketh with his feet, he teacheth with his fingers. —PROV. 6:12, 13

He that speaketh truth sheweth forth righteousness; but a false witness deceit. —PROV. 12:17

Deceit is in the heart of them that imagine evil. —PROV. 12:20

The folly of fools is deceit.
—PROV. 14:8

A true witness delivereth souls: but a deceitful witness speaketh lies.
—PROV. 14:25

Bread of deceit is sweet to a man; but afterwards his mouth shall be filled with gravel. —PROV. 20:17

Be not a witness against thy neighbour without cause; and deceive not with thy lips.
—PROV. 24:28

Confidence in an unfaithful man in time of trouble is like a broken tooth, and a foot out of joint.
—PROV. 25:19

As a mad man who casteth firebrands, arrows, and death, So is the man that deceiveth his neighbour, and saith, Am I not in sport?
—PROV. 26:18, 19

He that hateth dissembleth with his lips, and layeth up deceit within him. —PROV. 26:24

The heart is deceitful above all things, and desperately wicked: who can know it? —JER. 17:9

A double minded man is unstable in all his ways. —JAS. 1:8

Decision, see CHOICE, RESOLUTION, INDECISION

Deeds, see WORKS

Defect, see IMPERFECTION, WANT

Defence, see PROTECTION

Defilement, see EVIL, SIN, IMPERFECTION

Deity, see GOD

Dejection, see SADNESS, DESPAIR, SORROW, COMFORT

Delight, see JOY, PLEASURE, REJOICING

Denial, see REJECTION, RENUNCIATION, SACRIFICE, ABSTINENCE, TEMPERANCE

Dependability, see FAITHFULNESS

Depravity, see EVIL, SIN, IMPERFECTION

Derision, see SCORN

DESIRE; see also ASPIRATION, HOPE, AVARICE, LUST

Delight thyself also in the Lord; and he shall give thee the desires of thine heart. —PSA. 37:4

Lord, all my desire is before thee.
—PSA. 38:9

As the hart panteth after the water brooks, so panteth my soul after thee, O God. —PSA. 42:1

My soul thirsteth for God, for the living God. —PSA. 42:2

My soul thirsteth for thee, my flesh longeth for thee in a dry and thirsty land, where no water is.
—PSA. 63:1

There is none upon earth that I desire beside thee. —PSA. 73:25

My soul longeth, yea, even fainteth for the courts of the Lord: my
heart and my flesh crieth out for the
living God.   —Psa. 84:2

He satisfieth the longing soul, and
filleth the hungry soul with goodness.   —Psa. 107:9

My soul breaketh for the longing
that it hath unto thy judgments at
all times.   —Psa. 119:20

Behold, I have longed after thy
precepts: quicken me in thy righteousness.   —Psa. 119:40

I have longed for thy salvation,
O Lord.   —Psa. 119:174

I stretch forth my hands unto
thee: my soul thirsteth after thee, as
a thirsty land.   —Psa. 143:6

Thou openest thine hand, and
satisfieth the desire of every living
thing.   —Psa. 145:16

If thou criest after knowledge,
and liftest up thy voice for understanding; If thou seekest her as
silver, and searchest for her as for
hid treasures; Then shalt thou understand the fear of the Lord, and
find the knowledge of God.
          —Prov. 2:3–5

Hope deferred maketh the heart
sick: but when the desire cometh,
it is a tree of life. —Prov. 13:12

The desire accomplished is sweet
to the soul.   —Prov. 13:19

Better is the sight of the eyes
than the wandering of the desire.
          —Eccl. 6:9

The desire of our soul is to thy
name, and to the remembrance of
thee.   —Isa. 26:8

With my soul have I desired thee
in the night; yea, with my spirit

within me will I seek thee early.
          —Isa. 26:9

Ho, every one that thirsteth,
come ye to the waters, and he that
hath no money; come ye, buy, and
eat; yea, come, buy wine and milk
without money and without price.
          —Isa. 55:1

Blessed are they which do hunger
and thirst after righteousness: for
they shall be filled. —Matt. 5:6

Desire spiritual gifts.
          —1 Cor. 14:1

DESPAIR

Fear not, neither be discouraged.
          —Deut. 1:21

My soul is weary of my life; I
will leave my complaint upon myself; I will speak in the bitterness
of my soul.   —Job 10:1

My God, my God, why hast
thou forsaken me? —Psa. 22:1

I said in my haste, I am cut off
from before thine eyes: nevertheless
thou heardest the voice of my supplications when I cried unto thee.
          —Psa. 31:22

Why art thou cast down, O my
soul? and why are thou disquieted
within me?   —Psa. 42:5

Will the Lord cast off for ever?
and will he be favourable no more?
          —Psa. 77:7

Hope deferred maketh the heart
sick: but when the desire cometh, it
is a tree of life.   —Prov. 13:12

A merry heart doeth good like a
medicine: but a broken spirit drieth
the bones.   —Prov. 17:22

The harvest is past, the summer is
ended, and we are not saved.
          —Jer. 8:20

When my soul fainted within me I remembered the Lord.

—JONAH 2:7

O Lord, how long shall I cry, and thou wilt not hear!   —HAB. 1:2

Men ought always to pray, and not to faint.   —LUKE 18:1

We are perplexed, but not in despair.   —2 COR. 4:8

Despondency, see DESPAIR, SADNESS, COMFORT

Determination, see RESOLUTION, CONSTANCY, INDECISION

Devotion, see CONSTANCY, LOVE, PIETY, WORSHIP, ZEAL

Difficulty, see TROUBLE

Diligence, see INDUSTRY, CONSTANCY

Disappointment, see COMFORT

Disapproval, see CENSURE, JUDGMENT, REPROOF

Disbelief, see UNBELIEF

Discernment, see UNDERSTANDING

Discipline, see CHASTENING, INSTRUCTION

DISCONTENT; see also COMPLAINT, ENVY, CONTENTMENT

Give me neither poverty nor riches; feed me with food convenient for me: Lest I be full, and deny thee, and say, Who is the Lord?   —PROV. 30:8, 9

All things are full of labour; man cannot utter it: the eye is not satisfied with seeing, nor the ear filled with hearing.   —ECCL. 1:8

There is one alone, and there is not a second; yea, he hath neither child nor brother: yet is there no end of all his labour; neither is his eye satisfied with riches; neither saith he, For whom do I labour, and bereave my soul of good?

—ECCL. 4:8

He that loveth silver shall not be satisfied with silver; nor he that loveth abundance with increase: this is also vanity. When goods increase, they are increased that eat them: and what good is there to the owners thereof, saving the beholding of them with their eyes?

—ECCL. 5:10, 11

Ye have sown much, and bring in little; ye eat, but ye have not enough; ye drink, but ye are not filled with drink; ye clothe you, but there is none warm; and he that earneth wages earneth wages to put it into a bag with holes.

—HAG. 1:6

Let us not be desirous of vain glory, provoking one another, envying one another.   —GAL. 5:26

Ye lust, and have not; ye kill, and desire to have, and cannot obtain.

—JAS. 4:2

Discord, see CONTENTION, ANGER, ENMITY

Discouragement, see DESPAIR, COMFORT

Discretion, see PRUDENCE

Disdain, see SCORN, PRIDE, CONCEIT

Disgrace, see DISHONOUR

Dishonesty, see DECEIT, FALSEHOOD

DISHONOUR; see also IRREVERENCE

For thy sake I have borne reproach.   —PSA. 69:7

Thou hast known my reproach, and my shame, and my dishonour.

—PSA. 69:19

Remove from me reproach and contempt. —Psa. 119:22

He that is of a perverse heart shall be despised. —Prov. 12:8

When the wicked cometh, then cometh also contempt, and with ignominy reproach. —Prov. 18:3

He that saith unto the wicked, Thou art righteous; him shall the people curse, nations shall abhor him. —Prov. 24:24

Do not disgrace the throne of thy glory. —Jer. 14:21

Blessed are you, when men . . . shall reproach you, and cast out your name as evil. —Luke 6:22

They departed . . . rejoicing that they were counted worthy to suffer shame for his name. —Acts 5:41

Thou that makest thy boast of the law, through breaking the law dishonourest thou God.
—Rom. 2:23

Hath not the potter power over the clay, of the same lump to make one vessel unto honour, and another unto dishonour? —Rom. 9:21

Therefore we both labour and suffer reproach, because we trust in the living God. —1 Tim. 4:10

Dislike, see Hatred, Enmity

Displeasure, see Anger, Hatred Sadness, Sorrow, Despair

Dispute, see Contention

Dissatisfaction, see Discontent, Envy, Complaint

Dissolution, see Licentiousness

Distress, see Affliction, Sorrow, Suffering, Trouble

Donation, see Giving

Doubt, see Unbelief, Infidelity

Drunkenness, see Intoxication, Abstinence, Temperance

DUTY; see also Responsibility, Reverence

Give unto the Lord the glory due unto his name. —1 Chron. 16:29

Withhold not good from them to whom it is due, when it is in the power of thine hand to do it.
—Prov. 3:27

Fear God, and keep his commandments: for this is the whole duty of man. —Eccl. 12:13

What doth the Lord require of thee, but to do justly, and to love mercy, and to walk humbly with thy God. —Mic. 6:8

Wist ye not that I must be about my Father's business?
—Luke 2:49

I have a baptism to be baptized with; and how am I straitened till it be accomplished! —Luke 12:50

We have done that which was our duty to do. —Luke 17:10

Render therefore unto Caesar the things which be Caesar's, and unto God the things which be God's.
—Luke 20:25

I must work the works of him that sent me, while it is day.
—John 9:4

We ought to obey God rather than men. —Acts 5:29

Render therefore to all their dues: tribute to whom tribute is due; custom to whom custom; fear to whom fear; honour to whom honour. —Rom 13:7

Owe no man any thing, but to love one another. —Rom. 13:8

We then that are strong ought to bear the infirmities of the weak, and not to please ourselves.
—ROM. 15:1

He that saith he abideth in him ought himself also so to walk, even as he walked.   —1 JOHN 2:6

If God so loved us, we ought also to love one another. —1 JOHN 4:11

E

Earnestness, see SINCERITY, RESO-
LUTION, ZEAL

Education, see INSTRUCTION

Egotism, see CONCEIT, PRIDE,
BOASTING

Employment, see INDUSTRY, SERV-
ICE, WORKS

Encouragement, see COMFORT,
COURAGE

Endowment, see GIVING

Endurance, see CONSTANCY, FAITH-
FULNESS, PATIENCE, TOLERANCE,
SUFFERING, RESIGNATION

Enjoyment, see PLEASURE, CHEER-
FULNESS, JOY, REJOICING

ENMITY

Thou preparest a table before
me in the presence of mine enemies.
—PSA. 23:5

Rejoice not when thine enemy
falleth, and let not thine heart be
glad when he stumbleth.
—PROV. 24:17

If thine enemy be hungry, give
him bread to eat: and if he be
thirsty, give him water to drink.
—PROV. 25:21

Love your enemies, bless them
that curse you, do good to them that
hate you, and pray for them which
despitefully use you, and persecute
you. —MATT. 5:44

If ye forgive men their trespasses,
your heavenly Father will also forgive you. —MATT. 6:14

Unto him that smiteth thee on
the one cheek offer also the other.
—LUKE 6:29

As ye would that men should do
to you, do ye also to them likewise.
—LUKE 6:31

Be ye therefore merciful, as
your Father also is merciful.
—LUKE 6:36

If thy brother trespass against
thee, rebuke him; and if he repent,
forgive him. —LUKE 17:3

Bless them which persecute you:
bless, and curse not. —ROM. 12:14

If thine enemy hunger, feed him;
if he thirst, give him drink: for in
so doing thou shalt heap coals of
fire on his head. —ROM. 12:20

Enthusiasm, see ZEAL

ENVY

Wrath killeth the foolish man,
and envy slayeth the silly one.
—JOB 5:2

Fret not thyself because of evildoers, neither be thou envious
against the workers of iniquity.
—PSA. 37:1

Fret not thyself because of him
who prospereth in his way, because of the man who bringeth
wicked devices to pass.
—PSA. 37:7

I was envious at the foolish, when I saw the prosperity of the wicked.
—Psa. 73:3

Envy thou not the oppressor, and choose none of his ways.
—Prov. 3:31

Be not thou envious against evil men, neither desire to be with them.
—Prov. 24:1

Who is able to stand before envy?
—Prov. 27:4

I considered all travail, and every right work, that for this a man is envied of his neighbour.
—Eccl. 4:4

Jealousy is cruel as the grave: the coals thereof are coals of fire, which hath a most vehement flame.
—S. of S. 8:6

Charity envieth not.
—1 Cor. 13:4

Let us not be desirous of vain glory, provoking one another, envying one another.   —Gal. 5:26

Where envying and strife is, there is confusion and every evil work.
—Jas. 3:16

The spirit that dwelleth in us lusteth to envy.   —Jas. 4:5

Equity, see Justice

Error, see Sin, Evil

ETERNITY; see also Immortality

The eternal God is thy refuge, and underneath are the everlasting arms.   —Deut. 33:27

The Lord shall endure for ever.
—Psa. 9:7

The counsel of the Lord standeth for ever, the thoughts of his heart to all generations.   —Psa. 33:11

Blessed be the Lord God of Israel from everlasting, and to everlasting.
—Psa. 41:13

His name shall endure for ever: his name shall be continued as long as the sun.   —Psa. 72:17

Before the mountains were brought forth, or ever thou hadst formed the earth and the world, even from everlasting to everlasting, thou art God.
—Psa. 90:2

Thou, O Lord, shalt endure for ever; and thy remembrance unto all generations.   —Psa. 102:12

His righteousness endureth for ever.   —Psa. 111:3

That which hath been is now; and that which is to be hath already been; and God requireth that which is past.   —Eccl. 3:15

For thine is the kingdom, and the power, and the glory, for ever.
—Matt. 6:13

His righteousness remaineth for ever.   —2 Cor. 9:9

To whom be glory for ever and ever.   —Gal. 1:5

Evidence, see Proof

EVIL; see also Sin, Imperfection, Harm, Injustice, Malice, Retribution

If I regard iniquity in my heart, the Lord will not hear me.
—Psa. 66:18

I had rather be a doorkeeper in the house of my God, than to dwell in the tents of wickedness.
—Psa. 84:10

The fear of the Lord is to hate evil.   —Prov. 8:13

He that walketh uprightly walketh surely: but he that perverteth his ways shall be known.
—Prov. 10:9

It is a sport to a fool to do mischief: but a man of understanding hath wisdom. —Prov. 10:23

He that diligently seeketh good procureth favour: but he that seeketh mischief, it shall come unto him. —Prov. 11:27

A man shall not be established by wickedness: but the root of the righteous shall not be moved. —Prov. 12:3

The wicked is snared by the transgression of his lips: but the just shall come out of trouble. —Prov. 12:13

Righteousness keepeth him that is upright in the way: but wickedness overthroweth the sinner. —Prov. 13:6

Evil pursueth sinners: but to the righteous good shall be repaid. —Prov. 13:21

Do they not err that devise evil? but mercy and truth shall be to them that devise good. —Prov. 14:22

In the house of the righteous is much treasure: but in the revenues of the wicked is trouble. —Prov. 15:6

The way of the wicked is an abomination unto the Lord: but he loveth him that followeth after righteousness. —Prov. 15:9

He that soweth iniquity shall reap vanity. —Prov. 22:8

As he thinketh in his heart, so is he. —Prov. 23:7

As a dog returneth to his vomit, so a fool returneth to his folly. —Prov. 26:11

The wicked flee when no man pursueth. —Prov. 28:1

There is no peace, saith my God, to the wicked. —Isa. 57:21

If thine eye be evil, thy whole body shall be full of darkness. If therefore the light that is in thee be darkness, how great is that darkness! —Matt. 6:23

A good man out of the good treasure of the heart bringeth forth good things: and an evil man out of the evil treasure bringeth forth evil things. —Matt. 12:35

Not that which goeth into the mouth defileth a man; but that which cometh out of the mouth, this defileth a man. —Matt. 15:11

For that which I do I allow not: for what I would, that do I not: but what I hate, that do I . . . For the good that I would I do not, but the evil which I would not, that I do. —Rom. 7:15, 19

There is nothing unclean of itself: but to him that esteemeth any thing to be unclean, to him it is unclean. —Rom. 14:14

Let not then your good be evil spoken of. —Rom. 14:16

All things indeed are pure; but it is evil for that man who eateth with offence. —Rom. 14:20

A little leaven leaveneth the whole lump. —1 Cor. 5:6

Charity . . . thinketh no evil. —1 Cor. 13:4, 5

Abstain from all appearance of evil. —1 Thess. 5:22

Unto the pure all things are pure. —Tit. 1:15

Exaltation, see GLORY, PRAISE

EXAMPLE

Make no friendship with an angry man; and with a furious man thou shalt not go: Lest thou learn his ways, and get a snare to thy soul.
—PROV. 22:24, 25

Like people, like priest.
—HOS. 4:9

Let your light so shine before men, that they may see your good works, and glorify your Father which is in heaven. —MATT. 5:16

Be ye therefore perfect, even as your Father which is in heaven is perfect. —MATT. 5:48

Be ye therefore merciful, as your Father also is merciful.
—LUKE 6:36

I have given you an example, that ye should do as I have done to you.
—JOHN 13:15

A little leaven leaveneth the whole lump. —1 COR. 5:6

Take heed lest by any means this liberty of yours become a stumblingblock to them that are weak.
—1 COR. 8:9

If meat make my brother to offend, I will eat no flesh while the world standeth, lest I make my brother to offend. —1 COR. 8:13

Walk in love, as Christ also hath loved us. —EPH. 5:2

Let this mind be in you, which was also in Christ Jesus.
—PHIL. 2:5

Even as Christ forgave you, so also do ye. —COL. 3:13

Be thou an example of the believers, in word, in conversation, in charity, in spirit, in faith, in purity.
—1 TIM. 4:12

Those things, which ye have both learned, and received, and heard, and seen in me, do. —PHIL. 4:9

In all things shewing thyself a pattern of good works.—TIT. 2:7

Take, my brethren, the prophets, who have spoken in the name of the Lord, for an example of suffering affliction, and of patience.
—JAS. 5:10

For even hereunto were ye called: because Christ also suffered for us, leaving us an example, that ye should follow his steps.
—1 PET. 2:21

He that saith he abideth in him ought himself also so to walk, even as he walked. —1 JOHN 2:6

Exculpation, see JUSTIFICATION, RE-MISSION

EXPECTATION; see also HOPE

The expectation of the poor shall not perish. —PSA. 9:18

On thee do I wait all the day.
—PSA. 25:5

Those that wait upon the Lord, they shall inherit the earth.
—PSA. 37:9

Wait thou only upon God; for my expectation is from him.
—PSA. 62:5

Our eyes wait upon the Lord our God, until that he have mercy upon us. —PSA. 123:2

My soul waiteth for the Lord more than they that watch for the morning. —PSA. 130:6

The eyes of all wait upon thee.
—PSA. 145:15

Blessed are all they that wait for him. —ISA. 30:18

It is good that a man should hope and quietly wait for the salvation of the Lord. —LAM. 3:26

Blessed are those servants, whom the Lord when he cometh shall find watching. —LUKE 12:37

The earnest expectation of the creature waiteth for the manifestation of the sons of God.

—ROM. 8:19

If we hope for that we see not, then do we with patience wait for it. —ROM. 8:25

We through the Spirit wait for the hope of righteousness by faith. —GAL. 5:5

Exultation, see BOASTING, REJOICING

F

Fairness, see JUSTICE

FAITH

Offer the sacrifices of righteousness, and put your trust in the Lord. —PSA. 4:5

They that know thy name will put their trust in thee: for thou, Lord, hast not forsaken them that seek thee. —PSA. 9:10

He that trusteth in the Lord, mercy shall compass him about. —PSA. 32:10

O taste and see that the Lord is good: blessed is the man that trusteth in him. —PSA. 34:8

How excellent is thy lovingkindness, O God! therefore the children of men put their trust under the shadow of thy wings. —PSA. 36:7

Commit thy way unto the Lord; trust also in him; and he shall bring it to pass. —PSA. 37:5

Blessed is that man that maketh the Lord his trust. —PSA. 40:4

What time I am afraid, I will trust in thee. —PSA. 56:3

My soul trusteth in thee: yea, in the shadow of thy wings will I make my refuge. —PSA. 57:1

The righteous shall be glad in the Lord, and shall trust in him. —PSA. 64:10

It is better to trust in the Lord than to put confidence in man. —PSA. 118:8

They that trust in the Lord shall be as mount Zion, which cannot be removed, but abideth for ever. —PSA. 125:1

Mine eyes are unto thee, O God the Lord: in thee is my trust. —PSA. 141:8

Trust in the Lord with all thine heart; and lean not unto thine own understanding. —PROV. 3:5

In the fear of the Lord is strong confidence: and his children shall have a place of refuge. —PROV. 14:26

Whoso putteth his trust in the Lord shall be safe. —PROV. 29:25

He is a shield unto them that put their trust in him. —PROV. 30:5

The Lord is good, a strong hold in the day of trouble; and he knoweth them that trust in him. —NAH. 1:7

As thou hast believed, so be it done unto thee. —MATT. 8:13

If ye have faith as a grain of mustard seed . . . nothing shall be impossible unto you. —MATT. 17:20

All things, whatsoever ye shall ask in prayer, believing, ye shall receive. —MATT. 21:22

If thou canst believe, all things are possible to him that believeth.
—MARK 9:23

`Lord, I believe; help thou mine unbelief. —MARK 9:24

The just shall live by faith.
—ROM. 1:17; GAL. 3:11

Your faith should not stand in the wisdom of men, but in the power of God. —1 COR. 2:5

We walk by faith, not by sight.
—2 COR. 5:7

By grace are ye saved through faith; and that not of yourselves: it is the gift of God. —EPH. 2:8

The end of the commandment is charity out of a pure heart, and of a good conscience, and of faith unfeigned. —1 TIM. 1:5

We trust in the living God, who is the Saviour of all men, specially of those that believe.—1 TIM. 4:10

Fight the good fight of faith.
—1 TIM. 6:12

I have fought a good fight, I have finished my course, I have kept the faith. —2 TIM. 4:7

Faith is the substance of things hoped for, the evidence of things not seen. —HEB. 11:1

He that cometh to God must believe that he is, and that he is a rewarder of them that diligently seek him. —HEB. 11:6

The trying of your faith worketh patience. —JAS. 1:3

Let him ask in faith, nothing wavering. —JAS. 1:6

Shew me thy faith without thy works, and I will shew thee my faith by my works. —JAS. 2:18

Faith without works is dead.
—JAS. 2:20

If our heart condemn us not, then have we confidence toward God. —1 JOHN 3:21

FAITHFULNESS; see also CONSTANCY

The Lord preserveth the faithful.
—PSA. 31:23

A friend loveth at all times, and a brother is born for adversity.
—PROV. 17:17

A faithful man who can find?
—PROV. 20:6

Confidence in an unfaithful man in time of trouble is like a broken tooth, and a foot out of joint.
—PROV. 25:19

Faithful are the wounds of a friend. —PROV. 27:6

He that endureth to the end shall be saved. —MATT. 10:22

Thou hast been faithful over a few things, I will make thee ruler over many things. —MATT. 25:23

He that is faithful in that which is least is faithful also in much: and he that is unjust in the least is unjust also in much. —LUKE 16:10

It is required in stewards, that a man be found faithful.
—1 COR. 4:2

Watch ye, stand fast in the faith, quit you like men, be strong.
—1 COR. 16:13

Let us hold fast the profession of our faith without wavering; (for he is faithful that promised).
—HEB. 10:23

Be thou faithful unto death, and I will give thee a crown of life.
—REV. 2:10

Faithlessness, see DECEIT, INFI-
DELITY, UNBELIEF

FALSEHOOD; see also DECEIT,
FLATTERY, HYPOCRISY

Thou shalt not bear false witness
against thy neighbour.
—Ex. 20:16

Ye shall not steal, neither deal
falsely, neither lie one to another.
—LEV. 19:11

My lips shall not speak wickedness, nor my tongue utter deceit.
—JOB 27:4

Keep thy tongue from evil, and
thy lips from speaking guile.
—PSA. 34:13

Thou lovest all devouring words,
O thou deceitful tongue.
—PSA. 52:4

The mouth of them that speak
lies shall be stopped. —PSA. 63:11

He that worketh deceit shall not
dwell within my house: he that
telleth lies shall not tarry in my
sight.   —PSA. 101:7

I said in my haste, All men are
liars.   —PSA. 116:11

Deliver my soul, O Lord, from
lying lips, and from a deceitful
tongue.   —PSA. 120:2

A naughty person, a wicked man,
walketh with a froward mouth. He
winketh with his eyes, he speaketh
with his feet, he teacheth with his
fingers.   —PROV. 6:12, 13

An hypocrite with his mouth
destroyeth his neighbour.
—PROV. 11:9

He that speaketh truth sheweth
forth righteousness: but a false witness deceit.   —PROV. 12:17

A lying tongue is but for a moment.   —PROV. 12:19

Lying lips are abomination to the
Lord.   —PROV. 12:22

A righteous man hateth lying:
but a wicked man is loathsome, and
cometh to shame.   —PROV. 13:5

A true witness delivereth souls:
but a deceitful witness speaketh lies.
—PROV. 14:25

A wicked doer giveth heed to
false lips: and a liar giveth ear to
a naughty tongue.   —PROV. 17:4

Excellent speech becometh not a
fool: much less do lying lips a
prince.   —PROV. 17:7

A false witness shall not be unpunished, and he that speaketh lies
shall not escape.   —PROV. 19:5

A poor man is better than a liar.
—PROV. 19:22

The getting of treasures by a
lying tongue is a vanity tossed to
and fro of them that seek death.
—PROV. 21:6

Be not a witness against thy
neighbour without cause; and deceive not with thy lips.
—PROV. 24:28

A lying tongue hateth those that
are afflicted by it. —PROV. 26:28

Family, see MARRIAGE, PARENTS,
CHILDREN

Fault, see IMPERFECTION, SIN,
EVIL

Faultfinding, see COMPLAINT

Fear, see ANXIETY, COURAGE

Fear of God, see REVERENCE

Feebleness, see INFIRMITY

Fellowship, see BROTHERHOOD,
COMPANIONS, EVIL, FRIENDSHIP

Fervor, see ZEAL

Fickleness, see INSTABILITY, INDE-CISION

Fidelity, see FAITHFULNESS, CON-STANCY

Fighting, see CONTENTION, WAR

FLATTERY, SYCOPHANCY

Men will praise thee, when thou doest well to thyself. —PSA. 49:18

The poor is hated even of his own neighbour: but the rich hath many friends.   —PROV. 14:20

Wealth maketh many friends.
—PROV. 19:4

Many will intreat the favour of the prince: and every man is a friend to him that giveth gifts.
—PROV. 19:6

Meddle not with him that flatter-eth with his lips.   —PROV. 20:19

A lying tongue hateth those that are afflicted by it; and a flattering mouth worketh ruin.
—PROV. 26:28

As the fining pot for silver, and the furnace for gold; so is a man to his praise.   —PROV. 27:21

He that rebuketh a man after-wards shall find more favour than he that flattereth with the tongue.
—PROV. 28:23

A man that flattereth his neigh-bour spreadeth a net for his feet.
—PROV. 29:5

Woe unto you, when all men shall speak well of you! for so did their fathers to the false prophets.
—LUKE 6:26

Flesh, see BODY, LUST

Foe, see ENMITY

FOLLY; see also FOOL, IGNORANCE

Forsake the foolish, and live; and go in the way of understanding.
—PROV. 9:6

The wisdom of the prudent is to understand his way: but the folly of fools is deceit.   —PROV. 14:8

The simple inherit folly: but the prudent are crowned with knowl-edge.   —PROV. 14:18

He that is slow to wrath is of great understanding: but he that is hasty of spirit exalteth folly.
—PROV. 14:29

Folly is joy to him that is desti-tute of wisdom: but a man of un-derstanding walketh uprightly.
—PROV. 15:21

Understanding is a wellspring of life unto him that hath it but the instruction of fools is folly.
—PROV. 16:22

He that answereth a matter be-fore he heareth it, it is folly and shame unto him.   —PROV. 18:13

The foolishness of man pervert-eth his way: and his heart fretteth against the Lord.   —PROV. 19:3

Speak not in the ears of a fool: for he will despise the wisdom of thy words.   —PROV. 23:9

The thought of foolishness is sin: and the scorner is an abomination to men.   —PROV. 24:9

Wisdom excelleth folly, as far as light excelleth darkness.
—ECCL. 2:13

Dead flies cause the ointment of the apothecary to send forth a stinking savour: so doth a little folly him that is in reputation for wisdom and honour. —ECCL. 10:1

Give not that which is holy unto the dogs, neither cast ye your pearls before swine, lest they trample them under their feet, and turn again and rend you.   —MATT. 7:6

Every one that heareth these sayings of mine, and doeth them not, shall be likened unto a foolish man, which built his house upon the sand.
—MATT. 7:26

God hath chosen the foolish things of the world to confound the wise.   —1 COR. 1:27

The wisdom of this world is foolishness with God.   —COR. 3:19

FOOL; see also FOLLY

The foolish shall not stand in thy sight: thou hatest all workers of iniquity.   —PSA. 5:5

The fear of the Lord is the beginning of knowledge: but fools despise wisdom and instruction.
—PROV. 1:7

How long, ye simple ones, will ye love simplicity? and the scorners delight in their scorning, and fools hate knowledge?   —PROV. 1:22

Wise men lay up knowledge: but the mouth of the foolish is near destruction.   —PROV. 10:14

The lips of the righteous feed many: but fools die for want of wisdom.   —PROV. 10:21

It is as sport to a fool to do mischief: but a man of understanding hath wisdom.   —PROV. 10:23

He that troubleth his own house shall inherit the wind: and the fool shall be servant to the wise of heart.
—PROV. 11:29

The way of a fool is right in his own eyes: but he that hearkeneth unto counsel is wise. —PROV. 12:15

A prudent man concealeth knowledge: but the heart of fools proclaimeth foolishness. —PROV. 12:23

Every prudent man dealeth with knowledge: but a fool layeth open his folly.   —PROV. 13:16

Go from the presence of a foolish man, when thou perceiveth not in him the lips of knowledge.
—PROV. 14:7

Fools make a mock at sin: but among the righteous there is favour.
—PROV. 14:9

A wise man feareth, and departeth from evil: but the fool rageth, and is confident.   —PROV. 14:16

The simple inherit folly: but the prudent are crowned with knowledge.   —PROV. 14:18

The crown of the wise is their riches: but the foolishness of fools is folly.   —PROV. 14:24

Wisdom resteth in the heart of him that hath understanding: but that which is in the midst of fools is made known.   —PROV. 14:33

The tongue of the wise useth knowledge aright: but the mouth of fools poureth out foolishness.
—PROV. 15:2

The heart of him that hath understanding seeketh knowledge: but the mouth of fools feedeth on foolishness.   —PROV. 15:14

Let a bear robbed of her whelps meet a man, rather than a fool in his folly.   —PROV. 17:12

A foolish son is a grief to his father, and bitterness to her that bare him.   —PROV. 17:25

A fool hath no delight in understanding, but that his heart may discover itself.   —PROV. 18:2

A fool's mouth is his destruction, and his lips are the snare of his soul. —PROV. 18:7

There is treasure to be desired and oil in the dwelling of the wise; but the foolish man spendeth it up. —PROV. 21:20

A whip for the horse, a bridle for the ass, and a rod for the fool's back. —PROV. 26:3

Answer not a fool according to his folly, lest thou also be like unto him. —PROV. 26:4

Answer a fool according to his folly, lest he be wise in his own conceit. —PROV. 26:5

As he that bindeth a stone in a sling, so is he that giveth honour to a fool. —PROV. 26:8

The great God that formed all things both rewardeth the fool, and rewardeth transgressors. —PROV. 26:10

As a dog returneth to his vomit, so a fool returneth to his folly. —PROV. 26:11

If a wise man contendeth with a foolish man, whether he rage or laugh, there is no rest. —PROV. 29:9

A fool uttereth all his mind: but a wise man keepeth it in till afterwards. —PROV. 29:11

The wise man's eyes are in his head; but the fool walketh in darkness. —ECCL. 2:14

The fool foldeth his hands together, and eateth his own flesh. —ECCL. 4:5

A wise man's heart is at his right hand; but a fool's heart at his left. —ECCL. 10:2

When he that is a fool walketh by the way, his wisdom faileth him, and he saith to every one that he is a fool. —ECCL. 10:3

The words of a wise man's mouth are gracious; but the lips of a fool will swallow up himself. —ECCL. 10:12

Professing themselves to be wise, they became fools. —ROM. 1:22

If any man among you seemeth to be wise in this world, let him become a fool, that he may be wise. —1 COR. 3:18

Forbearance, see ABSTINENCE, TEMPERANCE, PATIENCE, TOLERANCE, RENUNCIATION

FORGIVENESS; see also MERCY, REMISSION

The discretion of a man deferreth his anger; and it is his glory to pass over a transgression. —PROV. 19:11

Rejoice not when thine enemy falleth, and let not thine heart be glad when he stumbleth. —PROV. 24:17

Say not, I will do so to him as he hath done to me: I will render to the man according to his work. —PROV. 24:29

If thine enemy be hungry, give him bread to eat; and if he be thirsty, give him water to drink. —PROV. 25:21

Resist not evil: but whosoever shall smite thee on thy right cheek, turn to him the other also. —MATT. 5:39

Love your enemies, bless them that curse you, do good to them that hate you, and pray for them which despitefully use you, and persecute you. —MATT. 5:44

Forgive us our debts, as we forgive our debtors.   —MATT. 6:12

If ye forgive men their trespasses, your heavenly Father will also forgive you.   MATT. 6:14

Judge not, that ye be not judged.   —MATT. 7:1

Why beholdest thou the mote that is in thy brother's eye, but considerest not the beam that is in thine own eye?   —MATT. 7:3

When ye stand praying, forgive, if ye have ought against any: that your Father also which is in heaven may forgive you your trespasses.
   —MARK 11:25

Judge not, and ye shall not be judged: condemn not, and ye shall not be condemned: forgive, and ye shall be forgiven.   —LUKE 6:37

If thy brother trespass against thee, rebuke him; and if he repent, forgive him.   —LUKE 17:3

Bless them which persecute you: bless, and curse not.
   —ROM. 12:14

Recompense to no man evil for evil.   —ROM. 12:17

Avenge not yourselves, but rather give place unto wrath: for it is written, Vengeance is mine; I will repay, saith the Lord.
   —ROM. 12:19

If a man be overtaken in a fault, ye which are spiritual, restore such an one in the spirit of meekness; considering thyself, lest thou also be tempted.   —GAL. 6:1

Be ye kind one to another, tenderhearted, forgiving one another, even as God for Christ's sake hath forgiven you.
   —EPH. 4:32

Put on . . . bowels of mercies, kindness, humbleness of mind, meekness, longsuffering; Forbearing one another, and forgiving one another, if any man have a quarrel against any: even as Christ forgave you, so also do ye. —COL. 3:12, 13

Fornication, see ADULTERY

Fortitude, see COURAGE, RESOLUTION

Frankness, see SINCERITY

Fraternity, see BROTHERHOOD

Freedom, see LIBERTY

FRIENDSHIP; see also BROTHERHOOD, COMPANIONS, EVIL, LOVE, HOSPITALITY

To him that is afflicted pity should be shewed from his friend.
   —JOB 6:14

He that covereth a transgression seeketh love; but he that repeateth a matter separateth very friends.
   —PROV. 17:9

A friend loveth at all times, and a brother is born for adversity.
   —PROV. 17:17

A man that hath friends must shew himself friendly: and there is a friend that sticketh closer than a brother.   —PROV. 18:24

Make no friendship with an angry man; and with a furious man thou shalt not go: Lest thou learn his ways, and get a snare to thy soul.   —PROV. 22:24, 25

Confidence in an unfaithful man in time of trouble is like a broken tooth, and a foot out of joint.
   —PROV. 25:19

Faithful are the wounds of a friend; but the kisses of an enemy are deceitful.   —PROV. 27:6

Ointment and perfume rejoice the heart: so doth the sweetness of a man's friend by hearty counsel.

—PROV. 27:9

Better is a neighbour that is near than a brother far off.

—PROV. 27:10

Iron sharpeneth iron; so a man sharpeneth the countenance of his friend.   —PROV. 27:17

As in water face answereth to face, so the heart of man to man.

—PROV. 27:19

Two are better than one; because they have a good reward for their labour. For if they fall, the one will lift up his fellow. —ECCL. 4:9, 10

If two be together, then they have heat: but how can one be warm alone?   —ECCL. 4:11

A threefold cord is not quickly broken.   —ECCL. 4:12

Can two walk together, except they be agreed?   —AMOS 3:3

Make to yourself friends.

—LUKE 16:9

Greater love hath no man than this, that a man lay down his life for his friends.   —JOHN 15:13

Frugality, see THRIFT

Futility, see DESPAIR, PESSIMISM

G

Generosity, see GIVING

Gentleness, see MEEKNESS, KINDNESS

Gift, see GIVING, TALENT

GIVING; see also BRIBERY

Blessed is he that considereth the poor: the Lord will deliver him in time of trouble.   —PSA. 41:1

A good man sheweth favour, and lendeth; he will guide his affairs with discretion.   —PSA. 112:5

Withhold not good from them to whom it is due, when it is in the power of thine hand to do it.
—PROV. 3:27

The liberal soul shall be made fat: and he that watereth shall be watered also himself.
—PROV. 11:25

He that hath mercy on the poor, happy is he.   —PROV. 14:21

A gift is as a precious stone in the eyes of him that hath it: whithersoever it turneth, it prospereth.
—PROV. 17:8

Every man is a friend to him that giveth gifts.   —PROV. 19:6

He that hath pity upon the poor lendeth unto the Lord; and that which he hath given will he pay him again.   —PROV. 19:17

He that hath a bountiful eye shall be blessed; for he giveth of his bread to the poor. —PROV. 22:9

If thine enemy be hungry, give him bread to eat; and if he be thirsty, give him water to drink.
—PROV. 25:21

He that giveth unto the poor shall not lack: but he that hideth his eyes shall have many a curse.
—PROV. 28:27

Cast thy bread upon the waters: for thou shalt find it after many days.   —ECCL. 11:1

The liberal deviseth liberal things; and by liberal things shall he stand.
—ISA. 32:8

If thou draw out thy soul to the hungry, and satisfy the afflicted soul; then shall thy light rise in obscurity, and thy darkness be as the noon day.   —ISA. 58:10

Give to him that asketh thee, and from him that would borrow of thee turn not thou away.
—MATT. 5:42

Take heed that ye do not your alms before men, to be seen of them . . . But when thou doest alms, let not thy left hand know what thy right hand doeth.
—MATT. 6:1, 3

Freely ye have received; freely give.   —MATT. 10:8

Inasmuch as ye have done it unto one of the least of these my brethren, ye have done it unto me.
—MATT. 25:40

Whosoever shall give you a cup of water to drink in my name . . . shall not lose his reward.

—MARK 9:41

He that hath two coats, let him impart to him that hath none; and he that hath meat, let him do likewise.   —LUKE 3:11

Give, and it shall be given unto you; good measure, pressed down, and shaken together, and running over.   —LUKE 6:38

Give alms of such things as ye have.   —LUKE 11:41

Sell that ye have, and give alms; provide yourselves bags which wax not old, a treasure in the heavens that faileth not, where no thief approacheth, neither moth corrupteth. For where your treasure is, there will your heart be also.

—LUKE 12:33, 34

It is more blessed to give than to receive.   —ACTS 20:35

He that giveth, let him do it with simplicity.   —ROM. 12:8

Though I bestow all my goods to feed the poor, and though I give my body to be burned, and have not charity, it profiteth me nothing.

—1 COR. 13:3

If there be first a willing mind, it is accepted according to that a man hath, and not according to that he hath not.   —2 COR. 8:12

God loveth a cheerful giver.

—2 COR. 9:7

We should remember the poor.

—GAL. 2:10

If any provide not for his own, and specially for those of his own house, he hath denied the faith, and is worse than an infidel.

—1 TIM. 5:8

Thy benefit should not be as it were of necessity, but willingly.

—PHILEM. 1:14

To do good and to communicate forget not: for with such sacrifices God is well pleased.

—HEB. 13:16

Whoso hath this world's good, and seeth his brother have need, and shutteth up his bowels of compassion from him, how dwelleth the love of God in him?

—1 JOHN 3:17

Gladness, see CHEERFULNESS, JOY, REJOICING

Gloom, see SADNESS, SORROW

GLORY; see also BOASTING, PRAISE, REJOICING, HEAVEN

All the earth shall be filled with the glory of the Lord.

—NUM. 14:21

Thine, O Lord, is the greatness, and the power, and the glory.

—1 CHRON. 29:11

The heavens declare the glory of God.   —PSA. 19:1

O magnify the Lord with me, and let us exalt his name together.

—PSA. 34:3

Let the Lord be magnified.

—PSA. 35:27

Give unto the Lord the glory due unto his name.   —PSA. 96:8

Exalt the Lord our God, and worship at his holy hill. —PSA. 99:9

For men to search their own glory is not glory. —PROV. 25:27

Holy, holy, holy, is the Lord of hosts: the whole earth is full of his glory.   —Isa. 6:3

Let not the wise man glory in his wisdom, neither let the mighty man glory in his might, let not the rich man glory in his riches: But let him that glorieth glory in this, that he understandeth and knoweth me.
—Jer. 9:23, 24

My soul doth magnify the Lord.
—Luke 1:46

Glory to God in the highest.
—Luke 2:14

Now is the Son of man glorified, and God is glorified in him.
—John 13:31

Of him, and through him, and to him, are all things: to whom be glory for ever.   —Rom. 11:36

No flesh should glory in his presence.   —1 Cor. 1:29

He that glorieth, let him glory in the Lord.   —1 Cor. 1:31

Glorify God in your body, and in your spirit, which are God's.
—1 Cor. 6:20

We all, with open face beholding as in a glass the glory of the Lord, are changed into the same image from glory to glory, even as by the Spirit of the Lord.
—2 Cor. 3:18

God forbid that I should glory, save in the cross of our Lord Jesus Christ.   —Gal. 6:14

Unto him be glory. —Eph. 3:21

Christ shall be magnified in my body, whether it be by life, or by death.   —Phil. 1:20

Pray for us, that the word of the Lord may have free course, and be glorified.   —2 Thess. 3:1

All flesh is as grass, and all the glory of man as the flower of grass.
—1 Pet. 1:24

The spirit of glory and of God resteth upon you.   —1 Pet. 4:14

Let us be glad and rejoice, and give honour to him.   —Rev. 19:7

GOD; see also Providence, Preservation, Protection, Creation, Eternity, Omnipotence, Omnipresence, Ominiscience, Impartiality

The Lord our God is one Lord.
—Deut. 6:4

The Lord your God is God of gods, and Lord of lords, a great God, a mighty, and a terrible, which regardeth not persons, nor taketh reward.   —Deut. 10:17

He is thy life, and the length of thy days.   —Deut. 30:20

He is the Rock, his work is perfect: for all his ways are judgment; a God of truth and without iniquity, just and right is he.—Deut. 32:4

The eternal God is thy refuge, and underneath are the everlasting arms.   —Deut. 33:27

The Lord is a God of knowledge, and by him actions are weighed.
—1 Sam. 2:3

The Lord seeth not as man seeth; for man looketh on the outward appearance, but the Lord looketh on the heart.   —1 Sam. 16:7

There is none like thee, neither is there any God beside thee.
—2 Sam. 7:22

Canst thou by searching find out God? canst thou find out the Almighty unto perfection? It is as high as heaven; what canst thou do? deeper than hell; what canst thou know? The measure thereof is longer than the earth, and broader than the sea. —JOB 11:7–9

In whose hand is the soul of every living thing, and the breath of all mankind. —JOB 12:10

Behold, God is great, and we know him not, neither can the number of his years be searched out. —JOB 36:26

As for God, his way is perfect: the word of the Lord is tried: he is a buckler to all those that trust in him. —PSA. 18:30

The heavens declare the glory of God; and the firmament sheweth his handywork. —PSA. 19:1

Salvation belongeth unto the Lord: thy blessing is upon thy people. —PSA. 3:8

The fool hath said in his heart, There is no God. —PSA. 14:1

The Lord is my shepherd; I shall not want. —PSA. 23:1

God is our refuge and strength, a very present help in trouble.
—PSA. 46:1

God is the judge: he putteth down one, and setteth up another.
—PSA. 75:7

Thou, O Lord, art a God full of compassion, and gracious, long-suffering, and plenteous in mercy and truth. —PSA. 86:15

Thou art my father, my God, and

the rock of my salvation.
—PSA. 89:26

He that dwelleth in the secret place of the most High shall abide under the shadow of the Almighty.
—PSA. 91:1

The Lord is good; his mercy is everlasting; and his truth endureth to all generations. —PSA. 100:5

Gracious is the Lord, and righteous; yea, our God is merciful.
—PSA. 116:5

The Lord is righteous in all his ways, and holy in all his works.
—PSA. 145:17

Great is our Lord, and of great power: his understanding is infinite.
—PSA. 147:5

As thou knowest not what is the way of the spirit, nor how the bones do grow in the womb of her that is with child: even so thou knowest not the works of God who maketh all. —ECCL. 11:5

Holy, holy, holy, is the Lord of hosts: the whole earth is full of his glory. —ISA. 6:3

The Lord is our judge, the Lord is our lawgiver, the Lord is our king; he will save us. —ISA. 33:22

To whom then will ye liken God? or what likeness will ye compare unto him? —ISA. 40:18

Hast thou not known? hast thou not heard, that the everlasting God, the Lord, the Creator of the ends of the earth, fainteth not, neither is weary? there is no searching of his understanding. —ISA. 40:28

I am the first, and I am the last; and beside me there is no God.
—ISA. 44:6

I am the Lord thy God which teacheth thee to profit, which leadeth thee by the way that thou shouldest go.   —Isa. 48:17

My thoughts are not your thoughts, neither are your ways my ways, saith the Lord. —Isa. 55:8

Thou, O Lord, art our father, our redeemer; thy name is from everlasting.   —Isa. 63:16

But now, O Lord, thou art our father; we are the clay, and thou our potter; and we all are the work of thy hand.   —Isa. 64:8

Let him that glorieth glory in this, that he understandeth and knoweth me, that I am the Lord which exercise lovingkindness, judgment, and righteousness, in the earth; for in these things I delight, saith the Lord.   —Jer. 9:24

The Lord is the true God, he is the living God, and an everlasting king.   —Jer. 10:10

The Lord our God is righteous in all his works which he doeth.
                            —Dan. 9:14

The Lord is good, a strong hold in the day of trouble; and he knoweth them that trust in him.
                            —Nah. 1:7

I am with you, saith the Lord.
                            —Hag. 1:13

Our Father which art in heaven, Hallowed be thy name.—Matt. 6:9

Thine is the kingdom, and the power, and the glory, for ever.
                            —Matt. 6:13

Holy is his name. —Luke 1:49

God is a Spirit: and they that worship him must worship him in spirit and in truth. —John 4:24

In him we live, and move, and have our being.   —Acts 17:28

God is no respecter of persons.
                            —Acts 20:34

Of him, and through him, and to him, are all things. —Rom. 11:36

There is but one God, the Father, of whom are all things.
                            —1 Cor. 8:6

One God and Father of all, who is above all, and through all, and in you all.   —Eph. 4:6

The King eternal, immortal, invisible, the only wise God.
                            —1 Tim. 1:17

Who only hath immortality, dwelling in the light which no man can approach unto; whom no man hath seen, nor can see: to whom be honour and power everlasting.
                            —1 Tim. 6:16

God is light, and in him is no darkness at all.   —1 John 1:5

God is love.   —1 John 4:8

Holy, holy, holy, Lord God Almighty, which was, and is, and is to come.   —Rev. 4:8

I am Alpha and Omega, the beginning and the end, the first and the last.   —Rev. 22:13

Godlessness, see Infidelity, Unbelief, Evil

Godliness, see Piety, Righteousness

GOODNESS; see also Righteousness, Integrity, Veracity, Perfection, Charity, Kindness, Justice, Help, Service

I will make all my goodness pass before thee.   —Ex. 33:19

Surely goodness and mercy shall follow me all the days of my life. —PSA. 23:6

The earth is full of the goodness of the Lord. —PSA. 33:5

The steps of a good man are ordered by the Lord. —PSA. 37:23

Depart from evil and do good. —PSA. 37:27

No good thing will he withhold from them that walk uprightly. —PSA. 84:1

Oh that men would praise the Lord for his goodness, and for his wonderful works to the children of men! —PSA. 107:8

He satisfieth the longing soul, and filleth the hungry soul with goodness. —PSA. 107:9

Withhold not good from them to whom it is due, when it is in the power of thine hand to do it. —PROV. 3:27

Mercy and truth shall be to them that devise good. —PROV. 14:22

A word spoken in due season, how good it is! —PROV. 15:23

Learn to do well. —ISA. 1:17

A good man out of the good treasure of his heart bringeth forth that which is good. —LUKE 6:45

Why callest thou me good? none is good, save one, that is, God. —LUKE 18:19

Abhor that which is evil; cleave to that which is good. —ROM. 12:9

Overcome evil with good. —ROM. 12:21

I would have you wise unto that which is good, and simple concerning evil. —ROM. 16:19

It is good to be zealously affected always in a good thing. —GAL. 4:18

As we have therefore opportunity, let us do good unto all men. —GAL. 6:10

Whatsoever things are true, whatsoever things are honest, whatsoever things are just, whatsoever things are pure, whatsoever things are lovely, whatsoever things are of good report; if there be any virtue, and if there be any praise, think on these things. —PHIL. 4:8

Ever follow that which is good. —1 THESS. 5:15

Prove all things; hold fast that which is good. —1 THESS. 5:21

Let us consider one another to provoke unto love and good works. —HEB. 10:24

To do good and to communicate forget not: for with such sacrifices God is well pleased. —HEB. 13:6

Gospel, see SCRIPTURE

GOSSIP; see also SLANDER

Thou shalt not go up and down as a talebearer among thy people. —LEV. 19:16

Tell it not in Gath, publish it not in the streets of Askelon. —2 SAM. 1:20

A talebearer revealeth secrets: but he that is of a faithful spirit concealeth the matter. —PROV. 11:13

He that repeateth a matter separateth very friends. —PROV. 17:9

The words of a talebearer are as wounds, and they go down into the innermost parts of the belly. —PROV. 18:8

He that goeth about as a talebearer revealeth secrets.
—Prov. 20:19

Where no wood is, there the fire
goeth out: so where there is no
talebearer, the strife ceaseth.
—Prov. 26:20

Refuse profane and old wives'
fables.   —1 Tim. 4:7

Let none of you suffer as . . . a
busybody in other men's matters.
—1 Pet. 4:15

Gratification, see Pleasure, Sensuality, Licentiousness, Worldliness, Rejoicing

Gratitude, see Thanksgiving

Gravity, see Sobriety

Greatness, see Pride, Humility

Greed, see Avarice

Grief, see Sorrow, Remorse

Grudge, see Anger, Hatred, Retaliation

Guile, see Deceit

Guilt, see Conscience, Sin, Remission, Retribution

H

HALFHEARTEDNESS

How weak is thine heart, saith the Lord God, seeing thou doest all these things. —EZEK. 16:30

Your goodness is as a morning cloud, and as the early dew it goeth away. —HOS. 6:4

No man can serve two masters. —MATT. 6:24

Because iniquity shall abound, the love of many shall wax cold. —MATT. 24:12

The spirit indeed is willing, but the flesh is weak. —MATT. 26:41

A double minded man is unstable in all his ways. —JAS. 1:8

Purify your hearts, ye double minded. —JAS. 4:8

I know thy works, that thou art neither cold nor hot: I would thou wert cold or hot. —REV. 3:15

Because thou art lukewarm, and neither cold nor hot, I will spue thee out of my mouth. —REV. 3:16

Happiness, see CHEERFULNESS, CONTENTMENT, JOY, PLEASURE, REJOICING

Hardness, see IMPENITENCE

Hardship, see AFFLICTION, SUFFERING, TROUBLE

HARM; see also INJUSTICE, MALICE

Yea, though I walk through the valley of the shadow of death, I will fear no evil. —PSA. 23:4

I will not fear what flesh can do unto me. —PSA. 56:4

The Lord is on my side; I will not fear: what can man do unto me? —PSA. 118:6

Devise not evil against thy neighbour. —PROV. 3:29

He that seeketh mischief, it shall come unto him. —PROV. 11:27

Whoso causeth the righteous to go astray in an evil way, he shall fall himself into his own pit. —PROV. 28:10

Be ye therefore wise as serpents, and harmless as doves. —MATT. 10:16

Fear not them which kill the body, but are not able to kill the soul. —MATT. 10:28

Do thyself no harm. —ACTS 16:28

Recompense to no man evil for evil. —ROM. 12:17

Love worketh no ill to his neighbour. —ROM. 13:10

Take heed lest by any means this liberty of yours become a stumblingblock to them that are weak. —1 COR. 8:9

Be blameless and harmless, the sons of God, without rebuke.

—PHIL. 2:15

The Lord is my helper, and I will not fear what man shall do unto me.

—HEB. 13:6

Who is he that will harm you, if ye be followers of that which is good?   —1 PET. 3:13

HARMONY; see also BROTHER-HOOD, PEACE

Let there be no strife, I pray thee, between me and thee . . . for we be brethren.   —GEN. 13:8

Righteousness and peace have kissed each other.   —PSA. 85:10

Behold, how good and how pleasant it is for brethren to dwell together in unity!   —PSA. 133:1

Better is a dinner of herbs where love is, than a stalled ox and hatred therewith.   —PROV. 15:17

Can two walk together, except they be agreed?   —AMOS 3:3

First be reconciled to thy brother, and then come and offer thy gift.

—MATT. 5:24

Agree with thine adversary quickly, whiles thou art in the way with him.   —MATT. 5:25

Every kingdom divided against itself is brought to desolation; and every city or house divided against itself shall not stand.

—MATT. 12:25

Have peace one with another.

—MARK 9:50

A new commandment I give unto you, That ye love one another; as I have loved you, that ye also love one another.   —JOHN 13:34

The multitude of them that believed were of one heart and of one soul.   —ACTS 4:32

Be of the same mind one toward another.   —ROM. 12:16

Be likeminded one toward another.   —ROM. 15:5

I beseech you . . . that ye all speak the same thing, and that there be no divisions among you; but that ye be perfectly joined together in the same mind and in the same judgment.   —1 COR. 1:10

Be of one mind, live in peace; and the God of love and peace shall be with you.   —2 COR. 13:11

Keep the unity of the Spirit in the bond of peace.   —EPH. 4:3

Stand fast in one spirit, with one mind striving together for the faith of the gospel.   —PHIL. 1:27

Fulfil ye my joy, that ye be likeminded, having the same love, being of one accord, of one mind.

—PHIL. 2:2

Let us walk by the same rule, let us mind the same thing.

—PHIL. 3:16

Be ye all of one mind, having compassion one of another, love as brethren.   —1 PET. 3:8

HARVEST

Thou crownest the year with thy goodness.   —PSA. 65:11

They that sow in tears shall reap in joy.   —PSA. 126:5

He that goeth forth and weepeth, bearing precious seed, shall doubtless come again with rejoicing, bringing his sheaves with him.

—PSA. 126:6

He that sleepeth in harvest is a son that causeth shame.
—Prov. 10:5

He that regardeth the clouds shall not reap. —Eccl. 11:4

The harvest is past, the summer is ended, and we are not saved.
—Jer. 8:20

They have sown the wind, and they shall reap the whirlwind.
—Hos. 8:7

Sow to yourselves in righteousness, reap in mercy. —Hos. 10:12

Ye shall know them by their fruits. Do men gather grapes of thorns, or figs of thistles?
—Matt. 7:16

Every good tree bringeth forth good fruit; but a corrupt tree bringeth forth evil fruit. —Matt. 7:17

The harvest truly is plenteous, but the labourers are few.
—Matt. 9:37

Pray ye therefore the Lord of the harvest, that he will send forth labourers into his harvest.
—Matt. 9:38

The harvest is the end of the world; and the reapers are the angels. —Matt. 13:39

Every branch that beareth fruit, he purgeth it, that it may bring forth more fruit. —John 15:2

One soweth, and another reapeth.
—John 4:37

He which soweth sparingly shall reap also sparingly; and he which soweth bountifully shall reap also bountifully. —2 Cor. 9:6

Whatsoever a man soweth, that shall he also reap. —Gal. 6:7

He that soweth to his flesh shall of the flesh reap corruption; but he that soweth to the Spirit shall of the Spirit reap life everlasting.
—Gal. 6:8

Let us not be weary in well doing: for in due season we shall reap, if we faint not. —Gal. 6:9

Thrust in thy sickle, and reap: for the time is come for thee to reap; for the harvest of the earth is ripe. —Rev. 14:5

HATRED; see also Anger

Thou shalt not hate thy brother in thine heart. —Lev. 19:17

Hatred stirreth up strifes: but love covereth all sins.
—Prov. 10:12

He that hideth hatred with lying lips, and he that uttereth a slander, is a fool. —Prov. 10:18

Better is a dinner of herbs where love is, than a stalled ox and hatred therewith. —Prov. 15:17

He that despiseth his neighbour sinneth. —Prov. 14:21

He that hateth dissembleth with his lips, and layeth up deceit within him. —Prov. 26:24

Whose hatred is covered by deceit, his wickedness shall be shewed before the whole congregation.
—Prov. 26:26

Love your enemies, bless them that curse you, do good to them that hate you, and pray for them which despitefully use you, and persecute you. —Matt. 5:44

If ye forgive not men their trespasses, neither will your Father forgive your trespasses. —Matt. 6:15

He that hateth me hateth my Father also.   —JOHN 15:23

The works of the flesh are manifest . . . hatred, variance, emulations, wrath.   —GAL. 5:19, 20

Let all bitterness, and wrath, and anger, and clamour, and evil speaking, be put away from you, with all malice.   —EPH. 4:31

He that saith he is in the light, and hateth his brother, is in darkness.   —1 JOHN 2:9

He that hateth his brother is in darkness, and walketh in darkness, and knoweth not whither he goeth, because that darkness hath blinded his eyes.   —1 JOHN 2:11

Whosoever doeth not righteousness is not of God, neither he that loveth not his brother.
          —1 JOHN 3:10

He that loveth not his brother abideth in death.   —1 JOHN 3:14

Whosoever hateth his brother is a murderer.   —1 JOHN 3:15

If a man say, I love God, and hateth his brother, he is a liar: for he that loveth not his brother whom he hath seen, how can he love God whom he hath not seen?
          —1 JOHN 4:20

Haughtiness, see CONCEIT, PRIDE, SCORN

HEALING

Who forgiveth all thine iniquities; who healeth all thy diseases.
          —PSA 103:3

He healeth the broken in heart, and bindeth up their wounds.
          —PSA. 147:3

They that be whole need not a physician, but they that are sick.
          —MATT. 9:12

Thy faith hath made thee whole.
          —MATT. 9:22

Physician, heal thyself.
          —LUKE 4:23

Jesus said unto him, Receive thy sight: thy faith hath saved thee.
          —LUKE 18:42

He hath faith to be healed.
          —ACTS 14:9

The prayer of faith shall save the sick, and the Lord shall raise him up.   —JAS. 5:15

Health, see HEALING, INFIRMITY

HEART; see also SPIRIT, SOUL

The Lord seeth not as man seeth; for man looketh on the outward appearance, but the Lord looketh on the heart.   —SAM. 16:7

I have given thee a wise and an understanding heart. —1 KIN. 3:12

Thou, even thou only, knowest the hearts of all the children of men.
          —1 KIN. 8:39

The Lord searcheth all hearts and understandeth all the imaginations of the thoughts.
          —1 CHRON. 28:9

Shall not God search this out? for he knoweth the secrets of the heart.   —PSA. 44:21

Create in me a clean heart, O God; and renew a right spirit within me.   —PSA. 51:10

Keep thy heart with all diligence; for out of it are the issues of life.
          —PROV. 4:23

A sound heart is the life of the flesh.   —PROV. 14:30

The preparations of the heart in man, and the answer of the tongue, is from the Lord.   —PROV. 16:1

Who can say, I have made my heart clean, I am pure from my sin?　—Prov. 20:9

Every way of a man is right in his own eyes; but the Lord pondereth the hearts.　—Prov. 21:2

The heart is deceitful above all things, and desperately wicked: who can know it?　—Jer. 17:9

I the Lord search the heart.　—Jer. 17:10

Make you a new heart and a new spirit: for why will ye die?　—Ezek. 18:31

Blessed are the pure in heart: for they shall see God.　—Matt. 5:8

Those things which proceed out of the mouth come forth from the heart; and they defile the man.　—Matt. 15:18

Out of the heart proceed evil thoughts.　—Matt. 15:19

Cleanse first that which is within the cup and platter, that the outside of them may be clean also.　—Matt. 23:26

With the heart man believeth unto righteousness. —Rom. 10:10

God . . . hath shined in our hearts.　—2 Cor. 4:6

Harden not your hearts.　—Heb. 3:8

HEAVEN

There the wicked cease from troubling; and there the weary be at rest.　—Job 3:17

The Lord is in his holy temple, the Lord's throne is in heaven.　—Psa. 11:4

In thy presence is fulness of joy; at thy right hand there are pleasures for evermore.　—Psa. 16:11

I will dwell in the house of the Lord for ever.　—Psa. 23:6

Thine eyes shall see the king in his beauty: they shall behold the land that is very far off. —Isa. 33:7

The habitation of thy holiness and of thy glory.　—Isa. 63:15

Blessed are the poor in spirit: for theirs is the kingdom of heaven.　—Matt. 5:3

Lay up for yourselves treasures in heaven, where neither moth nor rust doth corrupt, and where thieves do not break through nor steal.　—Matt. 6:20

In my Father's house are many mansions.　—John 14:2

We know that if our earthly house of this tabernacle were dissolved, we have a building of God, an house not made with hands, eternal in the heavens.—2 Cor. 5:1

When Christ, who is our life, shall appear, then shall ye also appear with him in glory.—Col. 3:4

Ye have in heaven a better and an enduring substance.　—Heb. 10:34

Here have we no continuing city, but we seek one to come.　—Heb. 13:14

An inheritance incorruptible, and undefiled, and that fadeth not away, reserved in heaven for you.　—1 Pet. 1:4

We, according to his promise, look for new heavens and a new earth, wherein dwelleth righteousness.　—2 Pet. 3:13

God shall wipe away all tears from their eyes; and there shall be no more death, neither sorrow, nor crying, neither shall there be any more pain: for the former things are passed away.—Rev. 21:4

HELP; see also Giving, Service

God is our refuge and strength, a very present help in trouble.
—Psa. 46:1

Give us help from trouble: for vain is the help of man.
—Psa. 60:11

Withhold not good from them to whom it is due, when it is in the power of thine hand to do it.
—Prov. 3:27

A word spoken in due season, how good it is!   —Prov. 15:23

Relieve the oppressed, judge the fatherless, plead for the widow.
—Isa. 1:17

Strengthen ye the weak hands, and confirm the feeble knees.
—Isa. 35:3

If thou draw out thy soul to the hungry, and satisfy the afflicted soul; then shall thy light rise in obscurity, and thy darkness be as the noon day.   —Isa. 58:10

Inasmuch as ye have done it unto one of the least of these my brethren, ye have done it unto me.
—Matt. 25:40

So labouring ye ought to support the weak.   —Acts 20:35

Rejoice with them that do rejoice, and weep with them that weep.   —Rom. 12:15

We then that are strong ought to bear the infirmities of the weak, and not to please ourselves.
—Rom. 15:1

We should remember the poor.
—Gal. 2:10

Bear ye one another's burdens, and so fulfil the law of Christ.
—Gal. 6:2

As we have therefore opportunity, let us do good unto all men.
—Gal. 6:10

Comfort yourselves together, and edify one another.—1 Thess. 5:11

Thy benefit should not be as it were of necessity, but willingly.
—Philem. 1:14

Lift up the hands which hang down, and the feeble knees.
—Heb. 12:12

HERESY

In vain they do worship me, teaching for doctrines the commandments of men. —Matt. 15:9

Ye worship ye know not what.
—John 4:22

Be no more children, tossed to and fro, and carried about with every wind of doctrine.—Eph. 4:14

Beware lest any man spoil you through philosophy and vain deceit, after the tradition of men, after the rudiments of the world, and not after Christ.   —Col. 2:8

Keep that which is committed to thy trust, avoiding profane and vain babblings, and oppositions of science falsely so called.—1 Tim. 6:20

Be not carried about with divers and strange doctrines. —Heb. 13:9

Whosoever transgresseth, and abideth not in the doctrine of Christ, hath not God.   —2 John 1:9

Holiness, see Righteousness

Honesty, see Veracity, Integrity, Sincerity, Justice, Deceit, Falsehood

Honor, see GLORY, INTEGRITY, VE-
RACITY

HOPE; see also ASPIRATION, DE-
SIRE, FAITH, EXPECTATION

My heart is glad, and my glory
rejoiceth: my flesh also shall rest
in hope. —PSA. 16:9

Be of good courage, and he shall
strengthen your heart, all ye that
hope in the Lord. —PSA. 31:24

The eye of the Lord is upon
them that fear him, upon them that
hope in his mercy. —PSA. 33:18

Let thy mercy, O Lord, be upon
us, according as we hope in thee.
—PSA. 33:22

In thee, O Lord, do I hope.
—PSA. 38:15

Why art thou cast down, O my
soul? and why art thou disquieted
within me? hope in God.
—PSA. 43:5

I will hope continually, and will
yet praise thee more and more.
—PSA. 71:14

My soul fainteth for thy salvation; but I hope in thy word.
—PSA. 119:81

Lord, I have hoped for thy salvation. —PSA. 119:166

Happy is he that hath the God of
Jacob for his help, whose hope is
in the Lord his God. —PSA. 146:5

The hope of the righteous shall
be gladness. —PROV. 10:28

Hope deferred maketh the heart
sick: but when the desire cometh,
it is a tree of life. —PROV. 13:12

The righteous hath hope in his
death. —PROV. 14:32

Blessed is the man that trusteth
in the Lord, and whose hope the
Lord is. —JER. 17:7

The Lord is my portion, saith my
soul; therefore will I hope in him.
—LAM. 3:24

It is good that a man should both
hope and quietly wait for the salvation of the Lord. —LAM. 3:26

Turn you to the strong hold, ye
prisoners of hope. —ZECH. 9:12

Who against hope believed in
hope. —ROM. 4:18

Tribulation worketh patience;
and patience, experience; and experience, hope. —ROM. 5:3,4

Hope that is seen is not hope: for
what a man seeth, why doth he
yet hope for? —ROM. 8:24

If we hope for that we see not,
then do we with patience wait for it.
—ROM. 8:25

The God of hope fill you with all
joy and peace in believing, that ye
may abound in hope.
—ROM. 15:13

Now abideth faith, hope, charity.
—1 COR. 13:13

We through the Spirit wait for
the hope of righteousness by faith.
—GAL. 5:5

Ye are called in one hope of
your calling. —EPH. 4:4

The hope which is laid up for you
in heaven. —COL. 1:5

Christ in you, the hope of glory.
—COL. 1:27

Hold fast the confidence and the
rejoicing of the hope firm unto the
end. —HEB. 3:6

Hope we have as an anchor of the soul, both sure and stedfast.
—HEB. 6:19

Faith is the substance of things hoped for, the evidence of things not seen. —HEB. 11:1

Hopelessness, see DESPAIR, PESSIMISM

HOSPITALITY

The stranger that dwelleth with you shall be unto you as one born among you, and thou shalt love him as thyself. —LEV. 19:34

Ye shall have one manner of law, as well for the stranger, as for one of your own country. —LEV. 24:22

I was an hungred, and ye gave me meat: I was thirsty, and ye gave me drink: I was a stranger, and ye took me in. —MATT. 25:35

When thou makest a feast, call the poor, the maimed, the lame, the blind: And thou shalt be blessed.
—LUKE 14:13, 14

Receive ye one another, as Christ also received us to the glory of God.
—ROM. 15:7

Be not forgetful to entertain strangers: for thereby some have entertained angels unawares.
—HEB. 13:2

Use hospitality one to another without grudging. —1 PET. 4:9

Humanity, see CHARITY, KINDNESS, JUSTICE, MERCY, HELP, SERVICE, GIVING, MAN

HUMILITY; see also MEEKNESS, PRIDE

Behold even to the moon, and it shineth not; yea, the stars are not pure in his sight. How much less man, that is a worm? and the son of man, which is a worm?
—JOB 25:5,6

When I consider thy heavens . . . What is man, that thou art mindful of him? and the son of man, that thou visitest him?
—PSA. 8:3,4

He forgetteth not the cry of the humble. —PSA. 9:12

Lord, thou hast heard the desire of the humble: thou wilt prepare their heart, thou wilt cause thine ear to hear. —PSA. 10:17

Though the Lord be high, yet hath he respect unto the lowly.
—PSA. 138:6

Surely he scorneth the scorners: but he giveth grace unto the lowly.
—PROV. 3:34

With the lowly is wisdom.
—PROV. 11:2

Before honour is humility.
—PROV. 15:33

Better it is to be of an humble spirit with the lowly, than to divide the spoil with the proud.
—PROV. 16:19

By humility and the fear of the Lord are riches, and honour, and life. —PROV. 22:4

Honour shall uphold the humble in spirit. —PROV. 29:23

I dwell in the high and holy place, with him also that is of a contrite and humble spirit, to revive the spirit of the humble, and to revive the heart of the contrite ones.
—ISA. 57:15

Seekest thou great things for thyself? seek them not. —JER. 45:5

What doth the Lord require of thee, but to . . . walk humbly with thy God? —Mic. 6:8

Blessed are the poor in spirit: for theirs is the kingdom of heaven.
—Matt. 5:3

Take my yoke upon you, and learn of me; for I am meek and lowly in heart: and ye shall find rest unto your souls.
—Matt. 11:29

Whosoever therefore shall humble himself as this little child, the same is greatest in the kingdom of heaven. —Matt. 18:4

Whosoever will be great among you, let him be your minister; And whosoever will be chief among you, let him be your servant.
—Matt. 20:26, 27

Whosoever shall exalt himself shall be abased; and he that shall humble himself shall be exalted.
—Matt. 23:12

He hath put down the mighty from their seats, and exalted them of low degree. —Luke 1:52

Thou hast hid these things from the wise and prudent, and hast revealed them unto babes.
—Luke 10:21

Mind not high things, but condescend to men of low estate. Be not wise in your own conceits.
—Rom. 12:16

If any man among you seemeth to be wise in this world, let him become a fool, that he may be wise.
—1 Cor. 3:18

Let him that thinketh he standeth take heed lest he fall.
—1 Cor. 10:12

Charity vaunteth not itself, is not puffed up. —1 Cor. 13:4

When I am weak, then am I strong. —2 Cor. 12:10

Let us not be desirous of vain glory. —Gal. 5:26

God forbid that I should glory, save in the cross of our Lord Jesus Christ. —Gal. 6:14

Walk worthy of the vocation wherewith ye were called, With all lowliness and meekness, with longsuffering, forbearing one another in love. —Eph. 4:1,2

Let nothing be done through strife or vainglory; but in lowliness of mind let each esteem other better than themselves. —Phil. 2:3

Look not every man on his own things, but every man also on the things of others. —Phil. 2:4

Put on . . . humbleness of mind, meekness. —Col. 3:12

God resisteth the proud, but giveth grace unto the humble.
—Jas. 4:6

Humble yourselves in the sight of the Lord, and he shall lift you up.
—Jas. 4:10

All flesh is grass, and all the glory of man as the flower of grass.
—1 Pet. 1:24

Hunger, see Desire

Hurt, see Harm

Husband, see Marriage

HYPOCRISY; see also Bigotry, Self-righteousness, Flattery

The hypocrite's hope shall perish.
—Job 8:13

An hypocrite shall not come before him. —Job 13:16

What is the hope of the hypocrite, though he hath gained, when God taketh away his soul?
—JOB 27:8

The words of his mouth were smoother than butter, but war was in his heart: his words were softer than oil, yet were they drawn swords. —PSA. 55:21

An hypocrite with his mouth destroyeth his neighbour.
—PROV. 11:9

The sacrifice of the wicked is abomination: how much more, when he bringeth it with a wicked mind? —PROV. 21:27

Be not righteous over much.
—ECCL. 7:16

Which say, Stand by thyself, come not near to me; for I am holier than thou. These are a smoke in my nose, a fire that burneth all the day. —ISA. 65:5

Take heed that ye do not your alms before men, to be seen of them: otherwise ye have no reward of your Father which is in heaven.
—MATT. 6:1

When thou doest thine alms, do not sound a trumpet before thee, as the hypocrites do in the synagogues and in the streets, that they may have glory of men. —MATT. 6:2

When thou prayest, thou shalt not be as the hypocrites are: for they love to pray standing in the synagogues and in the corners of the streets, that they may be seen of men. —MATT. 6:5

When ye fast, be not, as the hypocrites, of a sad countenance: for they disfigure their faces, that they may appear unto men to fast.
—MATT. 6:16

No man can serve two masters: for either he will hate the one, and love the other; or else he will hold to the one, and despise the other. Ye cannot serve God and mammon.
—MATT. 6:24

Thou hypocrite, first cast out the beam out of thine own eye; and then shalt thou see clearly to cast out the mote out of thy brother's eye. —MATT. 7:5

Beware of false prophets, which come to you in sheep's clothing, but inwardly they are ravening wolves. —MATT. 7:15

Not every one that saith unto me, Lord, Lord, shall enter into the kingdom of heaven; but he that doeth the will of my Father which is in heaven. —MATT. 7:21

This people draweth nigh unto me with their mouth, and honoureth me with their lips; but their heart is far from me. —MATT. 15:8

They say, and do not.
—MATT. 23:3

All their works they do for to be seen of men. —MATT. 23:5

Ye blind guides, which strain at a gnat, and swallow a camel.
—MATT. 23:24

Woe unto you, scribes and Pharisees, hypocrites! for ye make clean the outside of the cup and of the platter, but within they are full of extortion and excess.
—MATT. 23:25

Woe unto you, scribes and Pharisees, hypocrites! for ye are like unto whited sepulchres, which indeed appear beautiful outward, but are within full of dead men's bones, and of all uncleanness. —MATT. 23:27

Why call ye me, Lord, Lord, and do not the things which I say?
—LUKE 6:46

Ye are they which justify yourselves before men; but God knoweth your hearts. —LUKE 16:15

The Pharisee stood and prayed thus with himself, God, I thank thee, that I am not as other men are.
—LUKE 18:11

Thou art inexcusable, O man, whosoever thou art that judgest: for wherein thou judgest another, thou condemnest thyself; for thou that judgest doest the same things.
—ROM. 2:1

Circumcision is that of the heart, in the spirit, and not in the letter; whose praise is not of men, but of God. —ROM. 2:29

Though I speak with the tongues of men and of angels, and have not charity, I am become as sounding brass, or a tinkling cymbal.
— 1 COR. 13:1

They profess that they know God; but in works they deny him.
—TIT. 1:16

A double minded man is unstable in all his ways. —JAS. 1:8

Be ye doers of the word, and not hearers only, deceiving your own selves. —JAS. 1:22

If any man among you seem to be religious, and bridleth not his tongue, but deceiveth his own heart, this man's religion is vain.
—JAS. 1:26

What doth it profit, my brethren, though a man say he hath faith, and have not works? can faith save him?
—JAS. 2:14

If we say that we have fellowship with him, and walk in darkness, we lie, and do not the truth.
—1 JOHN 1:6

He that saith, I know him, and keepeth not his commandments, is a liar, and the truth is not in him.
—1 JOHN 2:4

He that saith he is in the light, and hateth his brother, is in darkness. —1 JOHN 2:9

If a man say, I love God, and hateth his brother, he is a liar.
—1 JOHN 4:20

I

IDLENESS; see also INDUSTRY

Go to the ant, thou sluggard; consider her ways, and be wise.

—PROV. 6:6

He becometh poor that dealeth with a slack hand: but the hand of the diligent maketh rich.

—PROV. 10:4

He that sleepeth in harvest is a son that causeth shame.

—PROV. 10:5

As vinegar to the teeth, and as smoke to the eyes, so is the sluggard to them that send him.

—PROV. 10:26

The hand of the diligent shall bear rule: but the slothful shall be under tribute.   —PROV. 12:24

The slothful man roasteth not that which he took in hunting: but the substance of a diligent man is precious.   —PROV. 12:27

The soul of the sluggard desireth, and hath nothing: but the soul of of diligent shall be made fat.

—PROV. 13:4

In all labour there is profit: but the talk of the lips tendeth only to penury.   —PROV. 14:23

The way of the slothful man is an hedge of thorns: but the way of the righteous is made plain.

—PROV. 15:19

He also that is slothful in his work is brother to him that is a great waster.   —PROV. 18:9

Slothfulness casteth into a deep sleep; and an idle soul shall suffer hunger.   —PROV. 19:15

A slothful man hideth his hand in his bosom, and will not so much as bring it to his mouth again.

—PROV. 19:24

The sluggard will not plow by reason of the cold; therefore shall he beg in harvest, and have nothing.   —PROV. 20:4

Love not sleep, lest thou come to poverty.   —PROV. 20:13

The desire of the slothful killeth him; for his hands refuse to labour.

—PROV. 21:25

Drowsiness shall clothe a man with rags.   —PROV. 23:21

As the door turneth upon his hinges, so doth the slothful upon his bed.   —PROV. 26:14

The sluggard is wiser in his own conceit than seven men that can render a reason.   —PROV. 26:16

By much slothfulness the building decayeth; and through idleness of the hands the house droppeth through.   —ECCL. 10:18

He that observeth the wind shall not sow; and he that regardeth the clouds shall not reap. —ECCL. 11:4

Not slothful in business; fervent in spirit; serving the Lord.

—ROM. 12:11

If any would not work, neither should he eat. —2 THESS. 3:10

Be not slothful, but followers of them who through faith and patience inherit the promises.

—HEB. 6:12

Ignominy, see DISHONOUR

IGNORANCE; see also FOLLY, IN-COMPREHENSION

We are but of yesterday, and know nothing, because our days upon earth are a shadow.—JOB 8:9

Fools despise wisdom and instruction. —PROV. 1:7

How long, ye simple ones, will ye love simplicity? and the scorners delight in their scorning, and fools hate knowledge? —PROV. 1:22

The way of the wicked is as darkness: they know not at what they stumble. —PROV. 4:19

O ye simple, understand wisdom: and ye fools, be ye of an understanding heart. —PROV. 8:5

Fools die for want of wisdom.

—PROV. 10:21

Poverty and shame shall be to him that refuseth instruction.

—PROV. 13:18

There is a way which seemeth right unto a man, but the end thereof are the ways of death.

—PROV. 14:12

The simple inherit folly: but the prudent are crowned with knowledge. —PROV. 14:18

Folly is joy to him that is destitute of wisdom: but a man of understanding walketh uprightly.

—PROV. 15:21

That the soul be without knowledge, it is not good. —PROV. 19:2

Who knoweth what is good for man in this life, all the days of his vain life which he spendeth as a shadow? for who can tell a man what shall be after him under the sun? —ECCL. 6:12

As thou knowest not what is the way of the spirit, nor how the bones do grow in the womb of her that is with child: even so thou knowest not the works of God who maketh all. —ECCL. 11:5

They are wise to do evil, but to do good they have no knowledge.

—JER. 4:22

My people are destroyed for lack of knowledge. —HOS. 4:6

Then said Jesus, Father, forgive them; for they know not what they do. —LUKE 23:34

It is not for you to know the times or the seasons, which the Father hath put in his own power.

—ACTS 1:7

Professing themselves to be wise, they became fools. —ROM. 1:22

Eye hath not seen, nor ear heard, neither have entered into the heart of man, the things which God hath prepared for them that love him.

—1 COR. 2:9

The wisdom of this world is foolishness with God. —1 COR. 3:19

If any man think that he knoweth anything, he knoweth nothing yet as he ought to know. —1 COR. 8:2

Now we see through a glass, darkly; but then face to face: now I know in part; but then shall I know even as also I am known.

—1 COR. 13:12

Ever learning, and never able to come to the knowledge of the truth. —2 TIM. 3:7

He that loveth not knoweth not God; for God is love.
—1 JOHN 4:8

If any of you lack wisdom, let him ask of God. —JAS. 1:5

With well doing ye may put to silence the ignorance of foolish men.
—1 PET. 2:15

Illness, see AFFLICTION, INFIRMITY, HEALING

Imitation, see EXAMPLE

Immorality, see EVIL, SIN, IMPER-FECTION

IMMORTALITY; see also DEATH, ETERNITY, HEAVEN

Now he is dead, wherefore should I fast? can I bring him back again? I shall go to him, but he shall not return to me. —2 SAM. 12:23

In thy presence is fulness of joy; at thy right hand there are pleasures for evermore. —PSA. 16:11

Your heart shall live for ever.
—PSA. 22:26

The Lord knoweth the days of the upright: and their inheritace shall be for ever. —PSA. 37:18

Depart from evil, and do good; and dwell for evermore.
—PSA. 37:27

God will redeem my soul from the power of the grave: for he shall receive me. —PSA. 49:15

My flesh and my heart faileth: but God is the strength of my heart, and my portion for ever.
—PSA. 73:26

The Lord shall preserve thy going out and thy coming in from this time forth, and even for evermore.
—PSA. 121:8

The wicked is driven away in his wickedness: but the righteous hath hope in his death. —PROV. 14:32

Then shall the dust return to the earth as it was: and the spirit shall return unto God who gave it.
—ECCL. 12:7

They that be wise shall shine as the brightness of the firmament; and they that turn many to righteousness as the stars for ever and ever.
—DAN. 12:3

Fear not them which kill the body, but are not able to kill the soul. —MATT. 10:28

He shall receive . . . in the world to come eternal life.
—MARK 10:30

Neither can they die any more: for they are equal unto the angels; and are the children of God.
—LUKE 20:36

For God so loved the world, that he gave his only begotten Son, that whosoever believeth in him should not perish, but have everlasting life.
—JOHN 3:16

This is the will of him that sent me, that every one which seeth the Son, and believeth on him, may have everlasting life. —JOHN 6:40

I am the living bread which came down from heaven; if any man eat of this bread, he shall live for ever.
—JOHN 6:51

I give unto them eternal life; and they shall never perish, neither shall any man pluck them out of my hand. —JOHN 10:28

I am the resurrection, and the life: he that believeth in me, though he were dead, yet shall he live: And whosoever liveth and believeth in me shall never die.

—JOHN 11:25, 26

To them who by patient continuance in well doing seek for glory and honour and immortality, eternal life.   —ROM. 2:7

Being made free from sin, and become servants to God, ye have your fruit unto holiness, and the end everlasting life.   —ROM. 6:22

The gift of God is eternal life through Jesus Christ our Lord.

—ROM. 6:23

The last enemy that shall be destroyed is death.   —1 COR. 15:26

This corruptible must put on incorruption, and this mortal must put on immortality. —1 COR. 15:53

Death is swallowed up in victory.

—1 COR. 15:54

O death, where is thy sting? O grave, where is thy victory?

—1 COR. 15:55

He that soweth to his flesh shall of the flesh reap corruption; but he that soweth to the Spirit shall of the Spirit reap life everlasting.

—GAL. 6:8

Godliness is profitable unto all things, having promise of the life that now is, and of that which is to come.   —1 TIM. 4:8

Fight the good fight of faith, lay hold on eternal life. —1 TIM. 6:12

Ye have in heaven a better and an enduring substance.

—HEB. 10:34

The world passeth away, and the lust thereof: but he that doeth the will of God abideth for ever.

—1 JOHN 2:17

This is the promise that he hath promised us, even eternal life.

—1 JOHN 2:25

Keep yourselves in the love of God, looking for the mercy of our Lord Jesus Christ unto eternal life.

—JUDE 1:21

IMPARTIALITY; see also JUSTICE

Thou shalt not respect the person of the poor, nor honour the person of the mighty: but in righteousness shalt thou judge thy neighbour.

—LEV. 19:5

Ye shall hear the small as well as the great.   —DEUT. 1:17

The Lord your God . . . regardeth not persons.   —DEUT. 10:17

There is no iniquity with the Lord our God, nor respect of persons, nor taking of gifts.

—2 CHRON. 19:7

Behold, God is mighty and despiseth not any: he is mighty in strength and wisdom.   —JOB 36:5

The rich and poor meet together: the Lord is the maker of them all.

—PROV. 22:2

The profit of the earth is for all.

—ECCL. 5:9

All things come alike to all: there is one event to the righteous, and to the wicked.   —ECCL. 9:2

He maketh his sun to rise on the evil and on the good, and sendeth rain on the just and on the unjust.

—MATT. 5:45

God is no respecter of persons.

—ACTS 10:34

There is no respect of persons with God. —Rom. 2:11

Whatsoever good thing any man doeth, the same shall he receive of the Lord, whether he be bond or free. —Eph. 6:8

He that doeth wrong shall receive for the wrong which he hath done: and there is no respect of persons. —Col. 3:25

The wisdom that is from above is . . . without partiality.—Jas. 3:17

The Father . . . without respect of persons judgeth according to every man's work. —Pet. 1:17

Impatience, see PATIENCE

IMPENITENCE; see also REJECTION

God speaketh once, yea twice, yet man perceiveth it not. —Job 33:14

Be ye not as the horse, or as the mule, which have no understanding. —Psa. 32:9

They know not, neither will they understand; they walk on in darkness. —Psa. 82:5

Harden not your heart. —Psa. 95:8

I have called, and ye refused; I have stretched out my hand, and no man regarded. —Prov. 1:24

They hated knowledge, and did not choose the fear of the Lord. —Prov. 1:29

Correction is grievous unto him that forsaketh the way: and he that hateth reproof shall die. —Prov. 15:10

He that refuseth instruction despiseth his own soul.—Prov. 15:32

A wicked man hardeneth his face. —Prov. 21:29

As a dog returneth to his vomit, so a fool returneth to his folly. —Prov. 26:11

He that covereth his sins shall not prosper. —Prov. 28:13

He that hardeneth his heart shall fall into mischief. —Prov. 28:14

He, that being often reproved hardeneth his neck, shall suddenly be destroyed, and that without remedy. —Prov. 29:1

Because sentence against an evil work is not executed speedily, therefore the heart of the sons of men is fully set in them to do evil. —Eccl. 8:11

When I called, ye did not answer; when I spake, ye did not hear. —Isa. 65:12

I spake unto you, rising up early and speaking, but ye heard not; and I called you, but ye answered not. —Jer. 7:13

They hearkened not, nor inclined their ear, but walked in the counsels and in the imagination of their evil heart, and went backward, and not forward. —Jer. 7:24

The harvest is past, the summer is ended, and we are not saved. —Jer. 8:20

If thou warn the wicked, and he turn not from his wickedness, nor from his wicked way, he shall die in his iniquity. —Ezek. 3:19

As he cried, and they would not hear; so they cried, and I would not hear, saith the Lord of hosts. —Zech. 7:13

This people's heart is waxed gross, and their ears are dull of hearing, and their eyes they have closed; lest at any time they should see with their eyes, and hear with their ears, and should understand with their heart, and should be converted, and I should heal them.
—MATT. 13:15

O Jerusalem, Jerusalem, thou that killest the prophets, and stonest them which are sent unto thee, how often would I have gathered thy children together, even as a hen gathereth her chickens under her wings, and ye would not!
—MATT. 23:37

Ye will not come to me, that ye might have life.   —JOHN 5:40

Despisest thou the riches of his goodness and forbearance and long-suffering; not knowing that the goodness of God leadeth thee to repentance?   —ROM. 2:4

IMPERFECTION; see also WANT

There is no man which sinneth not.   —2 CHRON. 6:36

Behold, I was shapen in iniquity; and in sin did my mother conceive me.   —PSA. 51:5

If I justify myself, mine own mouth shall condemn me: if I say, I am perfect, it shall also prove me perverse.   —JOB 9:20

There is none that doeth good, no, not one.   —PSA. 14:3

If thou, Lord, shouldest mark iniquities, O Lord, who shall stand?
—PSA. 130:3

Who can say, I have made my heart clean, I am pure from my sin?
—PROV. 20:9

There is not a just man upon earth, that doeth good, and sinneth not.   —ECCL. 7:20

All we like sheep have gone astray; we have turned every one to his own way.   —ISA. 53:6

All our righteousnesses are as filthy rags.   —ISA. 64:6

The heart is deceitful above all things, and desperately wicked: who can know it?   —JER. 17:9

Why beholdest thou the mote that is in thy brother's eye, but considerest not the beam that is in thine own eye?   —MATT. 7:3

He that is without sin among you, let him first cast a stone.
—JOHN 8:7

Thou art inexcusable, O man, whosoever thou art that judgest: for wherein thou judgest another, thou condemnest thyself; for thou that judgest doest the same things.
—ROM. 2:1

There is none righteous, no, not one.   —ROM. 3:10

All have sinned, and come short of the glory of God. —ROM. 3:23

Wherefore, as by one man sin entered into the world, and death by sin; and so death passed unto all men, for that all have sinned.
—ROM. 5:12

The scripture hath concluded all under sin.   —GAL. 3:22

IMPERMANENCE

There is but a step between me and death.   —1 SAM. 20:3

We must needs die, and are as water spilt on the ground, which cannot be gathered up again.
—2 SAM. 14:14

Our days on the earth are as a shadow, and there is none abiding.
—1 CHRON. 29:15

My days are swifter than a weaver's shuttle. —JOB 7:6

Remember that my life is wind.
—JOB 7:7

My days are swifter than a post: they flee away, they see no good. They are passed away as the swift ships: as the eagle that hasteth to the prey. —JOB 9:25, 26

Your remembrances are like unto ashes, your bodies to bodies of clay.
—JOB 13:12

Man that is born of a woman is of few days, and full of trouble. He cometh forth like a flower, and is cut down: he fleeth also as a shadow, and continueth not.
—JOB 14:1, 2

Behold, thou hast made my days as an handbreadth; and mine age is as nothing before thee.—PSA. 39:5

He remembered that they were but flesh; a wind that passeth away, and cometh not again.
—PSA. 78:39

Remember how short my time is.
—PSA. 89:47

As for man, his days are as grass: as a flower of the field, so he flourisheth. For the wind passeth over it, and it is gone; and the place thereof shall know it no more.
—PSA. 103:15, 16

Man is like to vanity: his days are as a shadow that passeth away.
—PSA. 144:4

One generation passeth away, and another generation cometh.
—ECCL. 1:4

The living know that they shall die. —ECCL. 9:5

All flesh is grass, and all the goodliness thereof is as the flower of the field: The grass withereth, the flower fadeth. —ISA. 40:6, 7

We all do fade as a leaf.
—ISA. 64:6

The fashion of this world passeth away. —1 COR. 7:31

Charity never faileth: but whether there be prophecies, they shall fail; whether there be tongues, they shall cease; whether there be knowledge, it shall vanish away.
—1 COR. 15:51

We look not at the things which are seen, but at the things which are not seen: for the things which are seen are temporal; but the things which are not seen are eternal.
—2 COR. 4:18

What is your life? It is even a vapour, that appeareth for a little time, and then vanisheth away.
—JAS. 4:14

IMPROVEMENT; see also IN-STRUCTION

The righteous also shall hold on his way, and he that hath clean hands shall be stronger and stronger. —JOB 17:9

Behold, I go forward. —JOB 23:8

Promotion cometh neither from the east, nor from the west, nor from the south. But God is the judge. —PSA. 75:6, 7

The Lord shall increase you more and more. —PSA. 115:14

They shall prosper that love thee.
—PSA. 122:6

A wise man will hear, and will increase learning. —PROV. 1:5

The path of the just is as the shining light, that shineth more and more unto the perfect day.

—Prov. 4:18

A man of knowledge increaseth strength.   —Prov. 24:5

Give instruction to a wise man, and he will be yet wiser: teach a just man, and he will increase in learning.   —Prov. 9:9

Better is the end of a thing than the beginning thereof. —Eccl. 7:8

Be ye therefore perfect, even as your Father which is in heaven is perfect.   —Matt. 5:48

The last shall be first.

—Matt. 20:16

The earth bringeth forth fruit of herself; first the blade, then the ear, after that the full corn in the ear.

—Mark 4:28

The kingdom of God . . . is like a grain of mustard seed, which, when it is sown in the earth, is less than all the seeds that be in the earth: But when it is sown, it groweth up, and becometh greater than all herbs.   —Mark 4:30–32

Friend, go up higher.

—Luke 14:10

Increase our faith.—Luke 17:5

He must increase, but I must decrease.   —John 3:30

I have planted, Apollos watered; but God gave the increase.

—1 Cor. 3:6

Now I know in part; but then shall I know even as also I am known.   —1 Cor. 13:12

Let all things be done unto edifying.   —1 Cor. 14:26

Though our outward man perish, yet the inward man is renewed day by day.   —2 Cor. 4:16

I pray, that your love may abound yet more and more in knowledge and in all judgment; That ye may approve things that are excellent.   —Phil. 1:9, 10

Walk worthy of the Lord unto all pleasing, being fruitful in every good work, and increasing in the knowledge of God.   —Col. 1:10

We beseech you, brethren, that you increase more and more.

—1 Thess. 4:10

Let us go on unto perfection.

—Heb. 6:1

As newborn babes, desire the sincere milk of the word, that ye may grow thereby.   —1 Pet. 2:2

Add to your faith virtue.

—2 Pet. 1:5

Grow in grace, and in the knowledge of our Lord and Saviour Jesus Christ.   —2 Pet. 3:18

Imprudence, see Folly, Prudence

Impurity, see Evil, Sin

INCOMPREHENSION; see also Ignorance

Canst thou by searching find out God?   —Job 11:7

God speaketh once, yea twice, yet man perceiveth it not.

—Job 33:14

Can any understand the spreadings of the clouds, or the noise of his tabernacle?   —Job 36:29

God thundereth marvellously with his voice; great things doeth he, which we cannot comprehend.

—Job 37:5

Dost thou know the balancings of the clouds, the wondrous works of him which is perfect in knowledge?   —JOB 37:16

Be ye not as the horse, or as the mule, which have no understanding.   —PSA. 32:9

They know not, neither will they understand; they walk on in darkness.   —PSA. 82:5

Eyes have they, but they see not.   —PSA. 115:5

The way of the wicked is as darkness: they know not at what they stumble.   —PROV. 4:19

Man's goings are of the Lord; how can a man then understand his own way?   —PROV. 20:24

Speak not in the ears of a fool: for he will despise the wisdom of thy words.   —PROV. 23:9

Evil men understand not judgment: but they that seek the Lord understand all things.—PROV. 28:5

I beheld all the work of God, that a man cannot find out the work that is done under the sun.   —ECCL. 8:17

Hear ye indeed, but understand not; and see ye indeed, but perceive not.   —ISA. 6:9

Hear, ye deaf; and look, ye blind, that ye may see.   —ISA. 42:18

Seeing many things, but thou observest not; opening the ears, but he heareth not.   —ISA. 42:20

O foolish people, and without understanding; which have eyes, and see not; which have ears, and hear not.   —JER. 5:21

None of the wicked shall understand: but the wise shall understand.   —DAN. 12:10

The people that doth not understand shall fall.   —HOS. 4:14

Give not that which is holy to dogs, neither cast ye your pearls before swine.   —MATT. 7:6

They seeing see not; and hearing they hear not, neither do they understand.   —MATT. 13:13

By hearing ye shall hear, and and shall not understand; and seeing ye shall see, and shall not perceive.   —MATT. 13:14

They be blind leaders of the blind. And if the blind lead the blind, both shall fall into the ditch.   —MATT. 15:14

Then said Jesus, Father, forgive them; for they know not what they do.   —LUKE 23:34

The light shineth in darkness; and the darkness comprehended it not.   —JOHN 1:5

Why do ye not understand my speech? even because ye cannot hear my word.   —JOHN 8:43

The preaching of the cross is to them that perish foolishness.   —1 COR. 1:18

The world by wisdom knew not God.   —1 COR. 1:21

The natural man receiveth not the things of the Spirit of God: for they are foolishness unto him: neither can he know them, because they are spiritually discerned.   —1 COR. 2:14

Now we see through a glass, darkly.   —1 COR. 13:12

Having the understanding darkened, being alienated from the life of God through the ignorance that is in them, because of the blindness of their heart.   —EPH. 4:18

Ever learning, and never able to come to the knowledge of the truth.
—2 Tim. 3:7

Inconstancy, see Instability, Indecision

Incredulity, see Unbelief

INDECISION; see also Instability

How long halt ye between two opinions? if the Lord be God, follow him: but if Baal, then follow him.   —1 Kin. 18:21

No man can serve two masters: for either he will hate the one, and love the other; or else he will hold to the one, and despise the other. Ye cannot serve God and mammon.
—Matt. 6:24

The spirit indeed is willing, but the flesh is weak.   —Matt. 26:41

Lord, I will follow thee; but . . .
—Luke 9:61

No man, having put his hand to the plough, and looking back, is fit for the kingdom of God.
—Luke 9:62

Remember Lot's wife.
—Luke 17:32

He that wavereth is like a wave of the sea driven with the wind and tossed.   —Jas. 1:6

A double minded man is unstable in all his ways.   —Jas. 1:8

Purify your hearts, ye double minded.   —Jas. 4:8

To him that knoweth to do good, and doeth it not, to him it is sin.
—Jas. 4:17

Indifference, see Halfhearted-ness

Indignation, see Anger

Indolence, see Idleness

Inducement, see Persuasion

Indulgence, see Pleasure, Licentiousness, Tolerance

INDUSTRY; see also Idleness

Go to the ant, thou sluggard; consider her ways, and be wise.
—Prov. 6:6

He becometh poor that dealeth with a slack hand: but the hand of the diligent maketh rich.
—Prov. 10:4

He that gathereth in summer is a wise son.   —Prov. 10:5

He that tilleth his land shall be satisfied with bread.—Prov. 12:11

The hand of the diligent shall bear rule: but the slothful shall be under tribute.   —Prov. 12:24

The slothful man roasteth not that which he took in hunting: but the substance of a diligent man is precious.   —Prov. 12:27

The soul of the sluggard desireth, and hath nothing: but the soul of the diligent shall be made fat.
—Prov. 13:4

He that gathereth by labour shall increase.   —Prov. 13:11

In all labour there is profit.
—Prov. 14:23

He that laboureth laboureth for himself; for his mouth craveth it of him.   —Prov. 16:26

The thoughts of the diligent tend only to plenteousness; but of every one that is hasty only to want.
—Prov. 21:5

Seest thou a man diligent in his business? he shall stand before kings; he shall not stand before mean men.   —Prov. 22:29

Be thou diligent to know the state of thy flocks, and look well to thy herds. —Prov. 27:23

He that tilleth his land shall have plenty of bread. —Prov. 28:19

The ants are a people not strong, yet they prepare their meat in the summer. —Prov. 30:25

The conies are but a feeble folk, yet make they their houses in the rocks. —Prov. 30:26

What profit hath a man of all his labour which he taketh under the sun? —Eccl. 1:3

My heart rejoiced in all my labour: and this was my portion of all my labour. —Eccl. 2:10

The sleep of a labouring man is sweet. —Eccl. 5:12

Whatsoever thy hand findeth to do, do it with thy might.
—Eccl. 9:10

In the morning sow thy seed, and in the evening withhold not thine hand: for thou knowest not whether shall prosper, either this or that, or whether they both shall be alike good. —Eccl. 11:6

The labourer is worthy of his hire. —Luke 10:7

Not slothful in business; fervent in spirit; serving the Lord.
—Rom. 12:11

INFIDELITY; see also Unbelief

Who is the Lord, that I should obey his voice? —Ex. 5:2

What is the almighty, that we should serve him? and what profit should we have, if we pray unto him? —Job 21:15

How doth God know?
—Job 22:13

The wicked, through the pride of his countenance, will not seek after God: God is not in all his thoughts.
—Psa. 10:4

The fool hath said in his heart, There is no God. —Psa. 14:1

Swords are in their lips: for who, say they, doth hear? —Psa. 59:7

They say, How doth God know? and is there knowledge in the most High? —Psa. 73:11

A scorner seeketh wisdom, and findeth it not. —Prov. 14:6

Fools make a mock at sin.
—Prov. 14:9

The scorner is an abomination to men. —Prov. 24: 9

Hear the word of the Lord, ye scornful men. —Isa. 28:14

Woe unto them that seek deep to hide their counsel from the Lord, and their works are in the dark, and they say, Who seeth us? and who knoweth us? —Isa. 29:15

Shall the work say of him that made it, He made me not? or shall the thing framed say of him that framed it, He had no understanding? —Isa. 29:16

Shall the clay say to him that fashioneth it, What makest thou? or thy work, He hath no hands?
—Isa. 45:9

Thou hast said, None seeth me. Thy wisdom and thy knowledge, it hath perverted thee; and thou hast said in thine heart, I am, and none else beside me. —Isa. 47:10

Lo, they have rejected the word of the Lord; and what wisdom is in them? —Jer. 8:9

What have we to do with thee, Jesus, thou Son of God?

—MATT. 8:29

Whosoever shall deny me before men, him will I also deny before my Father which is in heaven.

—MATT. 10:33

He that is not with me is against me; and he that gathereth not with me scattereth. —LUKE 11:23

He that denieth me before men shall be denied before the angels of God. —LUKE 12:9

I fear not God, nor regard men.

—LUKE 18:4

Ye worship ye know not what.

—JOHN 4:22

Be not faithless, but believing.

—JOHN 20:27

O man, who art thou that repliest against God? Shall the thing formed say to him that formed it, Why hast thou made me thus?—ROM. 9:20

What part hath he that believeth with an infidel? —2 COR. 6:15

Having no hope and without God in the world. —EPH. 2:12

Who is a liar but he that denieth that Jesus is the Christ?

—1 JOHN 2:22

Whosoever denieth the Son, the same hath not the Father.

—1 JOHN 2:23

Infinity, see ETERNITY, IMMORTALITY, OMNIPRESENCE

INFIRMITY; see also INSTABILITY, INDECISION

Let the weak say, I am strong.

—JOB 3:10

Thou hast strengthened the weak hands. —JOB 4:3

I had fainted, unless I had believed to see the goodness of the Lord in the land of the living.

—PSA. 27:13

My flesh and my heart faileth: but God is the strength of my heart, and my portion for ever.

—PSA. 73:26

He remembered that they were but flesh. —PSA. 78:39

He knoweth our frame; he remembereth that we are dust.

—PSA. 103:14

I was brought low, and he helped me. —PSA. 116:6

The Lord upholdeth all that fall, and raiseth up all those that be bowed down. —PSA. 145:14

He healeth the broken in heart, and bindeth up their wounds.

—PSA. 147:3

The spirit of a man will sustain his infirmity. —PROV. 18:14

If thou faint in the day of adversity, thy strength is small.

—PROV. 24:10

Strengthen ye the weak hands, and confirm the feeble knees.

—ISA. 35:3

He giveth power to the faint; and to them that have no might he increaseth strength. —ISA. 40:29

We all do fade as a leaf.

—ISA. 64:6

When my soul fainted within me I remembered the Lord.

—JON. 2:7

Himself took our infirmities and bare our sicknesses.—MATT. 8:17

The spirit indeed is willing, but the flesh is weak. —MATT. 26:41

They that are whole have no need of the physician, but they that are sick. —MARK 2:17

Men ought always to pray, and not to faint. —LUKE 18:1

To will is present with me; but how to perform that which is good I find not. —ROM. 7:18

The Spirit also helpeth our infirmities. —ROM. 8:26

We then that are strong ought to bear the infirmities of the weak. —ROM. 15:1

God hath chosen the weak things of the world to confound the things which are mighty. —1 COR. 1:27

Take heed lest by any means this liberty of yours become a stumblingblock to them that are weak. —1 COR. 8:9

Though our outward man perish, yet the inward man is renewed day by day. —2 COR. 4:16

My grace is sufficient for thee: for my strength is made perfect in weakness. —2 COR. 12:9

I take pleasure in infirmities . . . for Christ's sake: for when I am weak, then am I strong. —2 COR. 12:10

We also are weak in him, but we shall live with him by the power of God. —2 COR. 13:4

Support the weak, be patient toward all men. —1 THESS. 5:14

Influence, see EXAMPLE, COMPANIONS, EVIL, PERSUASION

Iniquity, see EVIL, SIN, IMPERFECTION, INJUSTICE

Injury, see HARM, INJUSTICE

INJUSTICE

Ye shall do no unrighteousness in judgment: thou shalt not respect the person of the poor, nor honour the person of the mighty: but in righteousness shalt thou judge thy neighbour. —LEV. 19:15

Cursed be he that perverteth the judgment of the stranger, fatherless, and widow. —DEUT. 27:19

How long will ye judge unjustly, and accept the persons of the wicked? —PSA. 82:2

When a wicked man dieth, his expectation shall perish: and the hope of unjust men perisheth. —PROV. 11:7

He that justifieth the wicked, and he that condemneth the just, even they both are abomination to the Lord. —PROV. 17:5

It is not good to accept the person of the wicked, to overthrow the righteous in judgment. —PROV. 18:5

He that is first in his own cause seemeth just; but his neighbour cometh and searcheth him. —PROV. 18:17

Rob not the poor, because he is poor. —PROV. 22:22

If thou hast nothing to pay, why should he take away thy bed from under thee? —PROV. 22:27

It is not good to have respect of persons in judgment.—PROV. 24:23

He that by usury and unjust gain increaseth his substance, he shall gather it for him that will pity the poor. —PROV. 28:8

To have respect of persons is not good: for for a piece of bread that man will transgress.—PROV. 28:21

An unjust man is an abomination to the just: and he that is upright in the way is abomination to the wicked.   —Prov. 29:27

If thou seest the oppression of the poor, and violent perverting of judgment and justice in a province, marvel not at the matter: for he that is higher than the highest regardeth; and there be higher than they.   —Eccl. 5:8

Oppression maketh a wise man mad; and a gift destroyeth the heart.   —Eccl. 7:7

Woe unto them that . . . turn aside the needy from judgment.   —Isa. 10:1, 2

Let favour be shewed to the wicked, yet will he not learn righteousness; in the land of uprightness will he deal unjustly, and will not behold the majesty of the Lord.   —Isa. 26:10

Truth is fallen in the street, and equity cannot enter.   —Isa. 59:14

To subvert a man in his cause, the Lord approveth not.   —Lam. 3:34

The unjust knoweth no shame.   —Zeph. 3:5

He that is unjust in the least is unjust also in much.—Luke 16:10

Innocence, see Righteousness

Insincerity, see Hypocrisy, Flattery, Halfheartedness, Sincerity

INSTABILITY; see also Indecision, Infirmity, Halfheartedness

Turn not to the right or the left: remove thy foot from evil.   —Prov. 4:26

Meddle not with them that are given to change.   —Prov. 24:21

As a bird that wandereth from her nest, so is a man that wandereth from his place.   —Prov. 27:8

Why gaddest thou about so much to change thy way?   —Jer. 2:36

Your goodness is as a morning cloud, and as the early dew it goeth away.   —Hos. 6:4

No man can serve two masters: for either he will hate the one, and love the other; or else he will hold to the one, and despise the other. Ye cannot serve God and mammon.   —Matt. 6:24

Every kingdom divided against itself is brought to desolation; and every city or house divided against itself shall not stand.—Matt. 12:25

No man having put his hand to the plough, and looking back, is fit for the kingdom of God.   —Luke 9:62

Remember Lot's wife.   —Luke 17:32

Having begun in the Spirit, are ye now made perfect by the flesh?   —Gal. 3:3

After that ye have known God, or rather are known of God, how turn ye again to the weak and beggarly elements, whereunto ye desire again to be in bondage?—Gal. 4:9

Be no more children, tossed to and fro, and carried about with every wind of doctrine, by the sleight of men, and cunning craftiness, whereby they lie in wait to deceive.   —Eph. 4:14

Let us hold fast the profession of our faith without wavering.   —Heb. 10:23

Be not carried about with divers and strange doctrines. For it is a good thing that the heart be established with grace.   —HEB. 13:9

He that wavereth is like a wave of the sea driven with the wind and tossed.   —JAS. 1:6

A double minded man is unstable in all his ways.   —JAS. 1:8

INSTRUCTION; see also COUNSEL

Come, ye children, hearken unto me: I will teach you the fear of the Lord.   —PSA. 34:11

A wise man will hear, and will increase learning; and a man of understanding shall attain unto wise counsels.   —PROV. 1:5

The fear of the Lord is the beginning of knowledge: but fools despise wisdom and instruction.
—PROV. 1:7

My son, hear the instruction of thy father, and forsake not the law of thy mother.   —PROV. 1:8

Incline thine ear unto wisdom, and apply thine heart to understanding.   —PROV. 2:2

If thou criest after knowledge, and liftest up thy voice for understanding; If thou seekest her as silver and searchest for her as for hid treasures; Then shalt thou understand the fear of the Lord, and find the knowledge of God.
PROV. 2:3–5

Hear, ye children, the instruction of a father, and attend to know understanding.   —PROV. 4:1

Get wisdom, get understanding: forget it not.   —PROV. 4:5

Wisdom is the principal thing; therefore get wisdom: and with all thy getting get understanding.
—PROV. 4:7

Take fast hold of instruction; let her not go: keep her; for she is thy life.   —PROV. 4:13

Give instruction to a wise man, and he will be yet wiser: teach a just man, and he will increase in learning.   —PROV. 9:9

Hear instruction, and be wise, and refuse it not.   —PROV. 8:33

Whoso loveth instruction loveth knowledge.   —PROV. 12:1

A wise son heareth his father's instruction: but a scorner heareth not rebuke.   —PROV. 13:1

A fool despiseth his father's instruction: but he that regardeth reproof is prudent.   —PROV. 15:5

He that refuseth instruction despiseth his own soul.—PROV. 15:32

The fear of the Lord is the instruction of wisdom.—PROV. 15:33

Understanding is a wellspring of life unto him that hath it: but the instruction of fools is folly.
—PROV. 16:22

The heart of the wise teacheth his mouth, and addeth learning to his lips.   —PROV. 16:23

Hear counsel, and receive instruction, that thou mayest be wise in thy latter end.   —PROV. 19:20

Cease, my son, to hear the instruction that causeth to err from the words of knowledge.
—PROV. 19:27

Train up a child in the way he should go: and when he is old, he will not depart from it.—PROV. 22:6

Bow down thine ear, and hear the words of the wise, and apply thine heart unto my knowledge. —Prov. 22:17

Apply thine heart unto instruction, and thine ears to the words of knowledge. —Prov. 23:12

Buy the truth, and sell it not; also wisdom, and instruction, and understanding. —Prov. 23:23

Whom shall he teach knowledge? and whom shall he make to understand doctrine? them that are weaned from the milk, and drawn from the breasts. —Isa. 9:9

Precept must be upon precept, precept upon precept; line upon line, line upon line; here a little, and there a little. —Isa. 28:10

The father to the children shall make known thy truth. —Isa. 38:19

Tell ye your children of it, and let your children tell their children, and their children another generation. —Joel 1:3

Feed my lambs. —John 21:15

Let him that is taught in the word communicate unto him that teacheth in all good things. —Gal. 6:6

Provoke not your children to wrath: but bring them up in the nurture and admonition of the Lord. —Eph. 6:4

Study to shew thyself approved unto God, a workman that needeth not to be ashamed, rightly dividing the word of truth. —2 Tim. 2:15

INTEGRITY; see also Sincerity, Veracity, Righteousness, Goodness, Justice, Faithfulness

That which is altogether just shalt thou follow. —Deut. 16:20

My lips shall not speak wickedness, nor my tongue utter deceit. —Job 27:4

Till I die I will not remove mine integrity from me. —Job 27:5

If I have walked with vanity, or if my foot hath hasted to deceit; Let me be weighed in an even balance, that God may know mine integrity. —Job 31:5, 6

Judge me, O Lord, according to my righteousness, and according to mine integrity that is in me. —Psa. 7:8

He that putteth not out his money to usury, nor taketh reward against the innocent. He that doeth these things shall never be moved. —Psa. 15:5

Let integrity and uprightness preserve me; for I wait on thee. —Psa. 25:21

Judge me, O Lord; for I have walked in mine integrity: I have trusted also in the Lord; therefore I shall not slide. —Psa. 26:1

Behold, thou desirest truth in the inward parts. —Psa. 51:6

No good thing will he withhold from them that walk uprightly. —Psa. 84:11

Let not mercy and truth forsake thee: bind them about thy neck; write them upon the table of thine heart. —Prov. 3:3

Let thine eyes look right on, and let thine eyelids look straight before thee. —Prov. 4:25

He that walketh uprightly walketh surely. —Prov. 10:9

The integrity of the upright shall guide them. —Prov. 11:3

A sound heart is the life of the flesh. —Prov. 14:30

A man of understanding walketh uprightly. —Prov. 15:21

Better is the poor that walketh in his integrity, than he that is perverse in his lips, and is a fool. —Prov. 19:1

The just man walketh in his integrity: his children are blessed after him. —Prov. 20:7

A faithful man shall abound with blessings. —Prov. 28:20

The way of the just is uprightness: thou, most upright, dost weigh the path of the just. —Isa. 26:7

He that walketh righteously, and speaketh uprightly . . . He shall dwell on high. —Isa. 33:15, 16

What doth the Lord require of thee, but to do justly, and to love mercy, and to walk humbly with thy God? —Mic. 6:8

As ye would that men should do to you, do ye also to them likewise. —Matt. 7:12

Herein do I exercise myself, to have always a conscience void of offence toward God, and toward men. —Acts 24:16

Provide things honest in the sight of all men. —Rom. 12:17

Let us walk honestly, as in the day. —Rom. 13:13

Whatsoever things are true, whatsoever things are honest, whatsoever things are just . . . think on these things. —Phil. 4:8

Whatsoever ye do, do it heartily, as to the Lord, and not unto men. —Col. 3:23

Walk honestly. —1 Thess. 4:12

We trust we have a good conscience, in all things willing to live honestly. —Heb. 13:18

Intelligence, see Understanding

Intemperance, see Intoxication, Licentiousness, Temperance

Intolerance, see Bigotry, Tolerance

INTOXICATION; see also Abstinence, Temperance

How long wilt thou be drunken? put away thy wine from thee. —1 Sam. 1:14

Wine is a mocker, strong drink is raging: and whosoever is deceived thereby is not wise. —Prov. 20:1

He that loveth wine . . . shall not be rich. —Prov. 21:17

Be not among winebibbers. —Prov. 23:20

The drunkard and the glutton shall come to poverty. —Prov. 23:21

Who hath woe? who hath sorrow? who hath contentions? who hath babbling? who hath wounds without cause? who hath redness of eyes? They that tarry long at the wine; they that go to seek mixed wine. —Prov. 23:29, 30

Look not thou upon the wine when it is red, when it giveth his colour in the cup, when it moveth itself aright. At the last it biteth like a serpent, and stingeth like an adder. —Prov. 23:31, 32

Give strong drink unto him that is ready to perish, and wine unto those that be of heavy hearts. Let him drink, and forget his poverty, and remember his misery no more. —Prov. 31:6, 7

Let us eat and drink; for to morrow we shall die.   —Isa. 22:13

Woe unto them that are mighty to drink wine, and men of strength to mingle strong drink. —Isa. 5:22

Whoredom and wine and new wine take away the heart.

—Hos. 4:11

Be not drunk with wine, wherein is excess.   —Eph. 5:18

They that be drunken are drunken in the night. But let us, who are of the day, be sober.

—1 Thess. 5:7

Irreligion, see Heresy, Infidelity, Unbelief, Irreverence

Irresolution, see Indecision

IRREVERENCE

Thou shalt not take the name of the Lord thy God in vain.

—Ex. 20:7

Ye shall not swear by my name falsely, neither shalt thou profane the name of thy God.—Lev. 19:12

They shall not profane the holy things.   —Lev. 22:15

Whosoever curseth his God shall bear his sin.   —Lev. 24:15

They spend their days in wealth, and in a moment go down to the grave. Therefore they say unto God, Depart from us; for we desire not the knowledge of thy ways.

—Job 21:13, 14

Is it fit to say to a king, Thou art wicked? and to princes, Ye are ungodly? How much less to him

that accepteth not the persons of princes, nor regardeth the rich more than the poor? for they all are the work of his hands.—Job 34:18, 19

Wherefore doth the wicked contemn God? he hath said in his heart, Thou wilt not require it.

—Psa. 10:13

The enemy hath reproached, O Lord, and . . . the foolish people have blasphemed thy name.

—Psa. 74:18

Remove far from me vanity and lies: give me neither poverty nor riches; feed me with food convenient for me: Lest I be full, and deny thee, and say, Who is the Lord? or lest I be poor, and steal, and take the name of my God in vain.

—Prov. 30:8, 9

Shall the work say of him that made it, He made me not? or shall the thing framed say of him that framed it, He had no understanding?   —Isa. 29:16

Shall the clay say to him that fashioneth it, What makest thou? or thy work, He hath no hands?

—Isa. 45:9

Put off all these . . . blasphemy, filthy communication out of your mouth.   —Col. 3:8

Out of the same mouth proceedeth blessing and cursing. My brethren, these things ought not so to be.

—Jas. 3:10

J

Jealousy, see ENVY

Jesus, see CHRIST

JOY; see also REJOICING, CHEER-FULNESS, CONTENTMENT, PLEAS-URE

Glory and honour are in his presence; strength and gladness are in his place.   —1 CHRON. 16:27

The joy of the Lord is your strength.   —NEH. 8:10

The triumphing of the wicked is short, and the joy of the hypocrite but a moment.   —JOB 20:5

Let them . . . that love thy name be joyful in thee.   —PSA. 5:11

In thy presence is fulness of joy; at thy right hand there are pleasures for evermore.   —PSA. 16:11

Weeping may endure for a night, but joy cometh in the morning.
   —PSA. 30:5

My soul shall be joyful in the Lord: it shall rejoice in his salvation.
   —PSA. 35:9

My soul shall be satisfied as with marrow and fatness; and my mouth shall praise thee with joyful lips.
   —PSA. 63:5

The righteous shall be glad in the Lord, and shall trust in him; and all the upright in heart shall glory.   —PSA. 64:10

Light is sown for the righteous, and gladness for the upright in heart.   —PSA. 97:11

Serve the Lord with gladness: come before his presence with sing-ing.   —PSA. 104:34

My meditation of him shall be sweet: I will be glad in the Lord.
   —PSA. 104:34

They that sow in tears shall reap in joy.   —PSA. 126:5

Happy is that people, whose God is the Lord.   —PSA. 144:15

Happy is he whose hope is in the Lord his God.   —PSA. 146:5

The hope of the righteous shall be gladness.   —PROV. 10:28

Whoso trusteth in the Lord, happy is he.   —PROV. 16:20

God giveth to a man that is good in his sight wisdom, and knowledge, and joy.   —ECCL. 2:26

With joy shall ye draw water out of the wells of salvation.
   —ISA. 12:3

My servants shall sing for joy of heart.   —ISA. 65:14

These things have I spoken unto you, that my joy might remain in you, and that your joy might be full.
   —JOHN 15:11

These things I speak in the world, that they might have my joy ful-filled in themselves.—JOHN 17:13

Thou hast made known to me the ways of life; thou shalt make me full of joy with thy countenance.
   —ACTS 2:28

The kingdom of God is not meat and drink; but righteousness, and peace, and joy in the Holy Ghost.
—ROM. 14:17

Now the God of hope fill you with all joy and peace in believing, that ye may abound in hope.
—ROM. 15:13

The fruit of the Spirit is love, joy, peace.   —GAL. 5:22

Is any merry? let him sing psalms.   —JAS. 5:13

These things write we unto you, that your joy may be full.
—1 JOHN 1:4

JUDGMENT; see also JUSTICE, IN-JUSTICE, PRUDENCE, RETRIBUTION

The judges . . . shall justify the righteous and condemn the wicked.
—DEUT. 25:1

If I justify myself, mine own mouth shall condemn me.
—JOB 9:20

Let us choose to us judgment: let us know among ourselves what is good.   —JOB 34:4

How long will ye judge unjustly, and accept the persons of the wicked?   —PSA. 82:2

Teach me good judgment.
—PSA. 119:66

He that justifieth the wicked, and he that condemneth the just, even they both are abomination to the Lord.   —PROV. 17:15

It is not good to have respect of persons in judgment.—PROV. 24:23

Many seek the ruler's favour; but every man's judgment cometh from the Lord.   —PROV. 29:26

Because sentence against an evil work is not executed speedily, therefore the heart of the sons of men is fully set in them to do evil.
—ECCL. 8:11

Woe unto them that . . . turn aside the needy from judgment.
—ISA. 10:1, 2

The Lord will help me; who is he that shall condemn me? —ISA. 50:9

Execute judgment in the morning.   —JER. 21:12

Let judgment run down as waters, and righteousness as a mighty stream.   —AMOS 5:24

Execute the judgment of truth and peace in your gates.
—ZECH. 8:16

Judge not, that ye be not judged.
—MATT. 7:1

With what judgment ye judge, ye shall be judged: and with what measure ye mete, it shall be measured to you again.   —MATT. 7:2

Why beholdest thou the mote that is in thy brother's eye, but considerest not the beam that is in thine own eye?   —MATT. 7:3

First cast out the beam out of thine own eye; and then shalt thou see clearly to cast out the mote out of thy brother's eye. —MATT. 7:5

Judge not according to the appearance, but judge righteous judgment.   —JOHN 7:24

Doth our law judge any man, before it hear him, and know what he doeth?   —JOHN 7:51

He that is without sin among you, let him first cast a stone.
—JOHN 8:7

Woman, where are those thine accusers? hath no man condemned thee? —JOHN 8:10

Wherein thou judgest another, thou condemnest thyself; for thou that judgest doest the same things. —ROM. 2:1

With me it is a very small thing that I should be judged of you, or of man's judgment: yea, I judge not mine own self. For I know nothing by myself; yet am I not hereby justified: but he that judgeth me is the Lord. —1 COR. 4:3, 4

Who maketh thee to differ from another? and what hast thou that thou didst not receive?—1 COR. 4:7

If we would judge ourselves, we should not be judged. —1 COR. 11:31

Speak evil of no man. —TIT. 3:2

Speak not evil one of another. —JAS. 4:11

If our heart condemn us, God is greater than our heart, and knoweth all things. —1 JOHN 3:20

JUSTICE; see also IMPARTIALITY, JUDGMENT, INJUSTICE

Ye shall do no unrighteousness in judgment: thou shalt not respect the person of the poor, nor honour the person of the mighty: but in righteousness shalt thou judge thy neighbour. —LEV. 19:15

Ye shall hear the small as well as the great. —DEUT. 1:17

That which is altogether just shalt thou follow. —DEUT. 16:20

He that ruleth over men must be just. —2 SAM. 23:3

Defend the poor and fatherless; do justice to the afflicted and needy. —PSA. 82:3

The Lord . . . blesseth the habitation of the just. —PROV. 3:33

The path of the just is as the shining light, that shineth more and more unto the perfect day. —PROV. 4:18

The memory of the just is blessed. —PROV. 10:7

The tongue of the just is as choice silver. —PROV. 10:20

The just man walketh in his integrity: his children are blessed after him. —PROV. 20:7

To do justice and judgment is more acceptable to the Lord than sacrifice. —PROV. 21:3

It is joy to the just to do judgment. —PROV. 21:15

A just man falleth seven times, and riseth up again. —PROV. 24:16

The way of the just is uprightness: thou, most upright, dost weigh the path of the just. —ISA. 26:7

Keep ye judgment, and do justice. —ISA. 56:1

If a man be just, and do that which is lawful and right . . . he shall surely live, saith the Lord God. —EZEK. 18:5, 9

What doth the Lord require of thee, but to do justly, and to love mercy, and to walk humbly with thy God? —MIC. 6:8

As ye would that men should do to you, do ye also to them likewise. —MATT. 7:12

The labourer is worthy of his hire. —LUKE 10:7

Judge not according to the appearance, but judge righteous judgment. —JOHN 7:24

Doth our law judge any man, before it hear him, and know what he doeth? —JOHN 7:51

Whatsoever things are true, whatsoever things are honest, whatsoever things are just . . . think on these things. —PHIL. 4:8

Masters, give unto your servants that which is just and equal.

—COL. 4:1

JUSTIFICATION

He is near that justifieth me.

—ISA. 50:8

By his knowledge shall my righteous servant justify many; for he shall bear their iniquities.

—ISA. 53:11

By him all that believe are justified from all things.—ACTS 13:39

Not the hearers of the law are just before God, but the doers of the law shall be justified. —ROM. 2:13

By the deeds of the law there shall no flesh be justified in his sight. —ROM. 3:20

All have sinned and come short of the glory of God; Being justified freely by his grace, through the redemption that is in Christ Jesus.

—ROM. 3:23, 24

A man is justified by faith without the deeds of the law.

—ROM. 3:28

To him that worketh not, but believeth on him that justifieth the ungodly, his faith is counted for righteousness. —ROM. 4:5

Believe on him that raised up Jesus our Lord from the dead; Who was delivered for our offences, and was raised again for our justification. —ROM. 4:24, 25

Being justified by faith, we have peace with God through our Lord Jesus Christ. —ROM. 5:1

Not as it was by one that sinned, so is the gift: for the judgment was by one to condemnation, but the free gift is of many offences unto justification. —ROM. 5:16

As by the offence of one judgment came upon all men to condemnation; even so by the righteousness of one the free gift came upon all men unto justification of life. —ROM. 5:18

Christ is the end of the law for righteousness to every one that believeth. —ROM. 10:4

A man is not justified by the works of the law, but by the faith of Jesus Christ. —GAL. 2:16

Being justified by his grace, we should be made heirs according to the hope of eternal life. —TIT. 3:7

K

KINDNESS; see also CHARITY, GIVING, GOODNESS, MERCY, HELP, SERVICE

According to the kindness that I have done unto thee, thou shalt do unto me.   —GEN. 21:23

The stranger that dwelleth with you shall be unto you as one born among you, and thou shalt love him as thyself.   —LEV. 19:34

Thou shalt not see thy brother's ox or his sheep go astray, and hide thyself from them: thou shalt in any case bring them again unto thy brother.   —DEUT. 22:1

Withhold not good from them to whom it is due, when it is in the power of thine hand to do it.
          —PROV. 3:27

Heaviness in the heart of man maketh it stoop: but a good word maketh it glad.   —PROV. 12:25

A word spoken in due season, how good it is!   —PROV. 15:23

Pleasant words are as an honeycomb, sweet to the soul, and health to the bones.   —PROV. 16:24

The desire of a man is his kindness.   —PROV. 19:22

The words of a wise man's mouth are gracious. —ECCL. 10:12

With everlasting kindness will I have mercy on thee. —ISA. 54:8

Inasmuch as ye have done it unto one of the least of these my brethren, ye have done it unto me.
          —MATT. 25:40

As ye would that men should do to you, do ye also to them likewise.
          —LUKE 6:31

Love ye your enemies, and do good, and lend, hoping for nothing again; and your reward shall be great, and ye shall be the children of the Highest: for he is kind unto the unthankful and to the evil.
          —LUKE 6:35

Be kindly affectioned one to another with brotherly love; in honour preferring one another.
          —ROM. 12:10

Let every one of us please his neighbour for his good to edification.   —ROM. 15:2

Charity suffereth long, and is kind.   —1 COR. 13:4

If a man be overtaken in a fault, ye which are spiritual, restore such an one in the spirit of meekness; considering thyself, lest thou also be tempted.   —GAL. 6:1

As we have therefore opportunity, let us do good unto all men.
          —GAL. 6:10

Put on . . . bowels of mercies, kindness, humbleness of mind, meekness, longsuffering.
          —COL. 3:12

Speak evil of no man. —Tit. 3:2

Let us consider one another to provoke unto love and good works.
—Heb. 10:24

Let brotherly love continue.
—Heb. 13:1

Be ye all of one mind, having compassion one of another, love as brethren, be pitiful, be courteous.
—1 Pet. 3:8

Add to . . . godliness brotherly kindness; and to brotherly kindness charity. —2 Pet. 1:5, 7

KNOWLEDGE; see also Wisdom, Understanding, Omniscience, Instruction, Ignorance

Acquaint now thyself with him, and be at peace. —Job 22:21

Dost thou know the balancings of the clouds, the wondrous works of him which is perfect in knowledge?
—Job 37:16

A wise man will hear, and will increase learning. —Prov. 1:5

The fear of the Lord is the beginning of knowledge. —Prov. 1:7

How long, ye simple ones, will ye love simplicity? and the scorners delight in their scorning, and fools hate knowledge? —Prov. 1:22

If thou criest after knowledge, and liftest up thy voice for understanding; If thou seekest her as silver and searchest for her as for hid treasures; Then shalt thou understand the fear of the Lord, and find the knowledge of God.
—Prov. 2:3–5

The Lord giveth wisdom: out of his mouth cometh knowledge and understanding. —Prov. 2:6

Wise men lay up knowledge.
—Prov. 10:14

A scorner seeketh wisdom, and findeth it not: but knowledge is easy unto him that understandeth.
—Prov. 14:6

The simple inherit folly: but the prudent are crowned with knowledge. —Prov. 14:18

The heart of him that hath understanding seeketh knowledge.
—Prov. 15:14

The heart of the wise teacheth his mouth, and addeth learning to his lips. —Prov. 16:23

The heart of the prudent getteth knowledge: and the ear of the wise seeketh knowledge. —Prov. 18:15

That the soul be without knowledge, it is not good. —Prov. 19:2

When the wise is instructed, he receiveth knowledge.—Prov. 21:11

Bow down thine ear, and hear the words of the wise, and apply thine heart unto knowledge.
—Prov. 22:17

Apply thine heart unto instruction, and thine ears to the words of knowledge. —Prov. 23:12

By knowledge shall the chambers be filled with all precious and pleasant riches. —Prov. 24:14

In much wisdom is much grief: and he that increaseth knowledge increaseth sorrow. —Eccl. 1:18

They are wise to do evil, but to do good they have no knowledge.
—Jer. 4:22

My people are destroyed for lack of knowledge: because thou hast rejected knowledge, I will also reject thee. —Hos. 4:6

Then shall we know, if we follow on to know the Lord. —Hos. 6:3

This is life eternal, that they might know thee the only true God, and Jesus Christ whom thou hast sent. —John 17:3

It is not for you to know the times or the seasons, which the Father hath put in his own power. —Acts 1:7

Much learning doth make thee mad. —Acts 26:24

Knowledge puffeth up, but charity edifieth. —1 Cor. 8:1

If any man think that he knoweth any thing, he knoweth nothing yet as he ought to know. —1 Cor. 8:2

Now we see through a glass, darkly; but then face to face: now I know in part; but then shall I know even as also I am known. —1 Cor. 13:12

I count all things but loss for the excellency of the knowledge of Christ Jesus my Lord. —Phil. 3:8

Be filled with the knowledge of his will in all wisdom and spiritual understanding. —Col. 1:9

Walk worthy of the Lord unto all pleasing, being fruitful in every good work, and increasing in the knowledge of God. —Col. 1:10

Add to faith virtue; and to virtue knowledge. —2 Pet. 1:5

Grow in grace, and in the knowledge of our Lord and Saviour Jesus Christ. —2 Pet. 3:18

He that loveth not knoweth not God; for God is love. —1 John 4:8

L

Labour, see INDUSTRY

Lack, see IMPERFECTION, WANT, POVERTY

Lamentation, see SORROW, COMPLAINT

Lasciviousness, see ADULTERY, LICENTIOUSNESS

LAW

The law of the Lord is perfect, converting the soul: the testimony of the Lord is sure, making wise the simple. —PSA. 19:7

The statues of the Lord are right, rejoicing the heart: the commandment of the Lord is pure, enlightening the eyes. —PSA. 19:8

Blessed are the undefiled in the way, who walk in the law of the Lord. —PSA. 119:1

Blessed are they that keep his testimonies, and that seek him with the whole heart. —PSA. 119:2

Thou hast commanded us to keep thy precepts diligently.—PSA. 119:4

Then shall I not be ashamed, when I have respect unto all thy commandments. —PSA. 119:6

They that forsake the law praise the wicked: but such as keep the law contend with them.
  —PROV. 28:4

He that keepeth the law, happy is he. —PROV. 29:18

Think not that I am come to destroy the law, or the prophets: I am not come to destroy, but to fulfil. —MATT. 5:17

It is easier for heaven and earth to pass, than one tittle of the law to fail. —LUKE 16:17

The law was given by Moses, but grace and truth came by Jesus Christ. —JOHN 1:17

By him all that believe are justified from all things, from which ye could not be justified by the law of Moses. —ACTS 13:39

When the Gentiles, which have not the law, do by nature the things contained in the law, these, having not the law, are a law unto themselves: Which shew the work of the law written in their hearts, their conscience also bearing witness, and their thoughts the mean while accusing or else excusing one another.
  —ROM. 2:14, 15

Not the hearers of the law are just before God, but the doers of the law shall be justified.
  —ROM. 2:13

By the deeds of the law there shall no flesh be justified in his sight. —ROM. 3:20

A man is justified by faith without the deeds of the law.
  —ROM. 3:28

Where no law is, there is no transgression. —ROM. 4:15

Ye are not under the law, but under grace. —ROM. 6:14

Ye also are become dead to the law by the body of Christ.
—ROM. 7:4

We should serve in newness of spirit, and not in the oldness of the letter. —ROM. 7:6

I had not known sin, but by the law. —ROM. 7:7

Christ is the end of the law for righteousness to every one that believeth. —ROM. 10:4

He that loveth another hath fulfilled the law. —ROM. 13:8

Love is the fulfilling of the law.
—ROM. 13:10

All things are lawful unto me, but all things are not expedient.
—1 COR. 6:12

A man is not justified by the works of the law, but by the faith of Jesus Christ. —GAL. 2:16

The just shall live by faith. And the law is not of faith.
—GAL. 3:11, 12

Christ hath redeemed us from the curse of the law, being made a curse for us. —GAL. 3:13

The law was our schoolmaster to bring us unto Christ. —GAL. 3:24

The end of the commandment is charity out of a pure heart, and of a good conscience, and of faith unfeigned. —1 TIM. 1:5

The law is good, if a man use it lawfully. —1 TIM. 1:8

The law is not made for a righteous man, but for the lawless and disobedient. —1 TIM. 1:9

The law having a shadow of good things to come, and not the very image of the things, can never with those sacrifices which they offered year by year continually make the comers thereunto perfect.
—HEB. 10:1

If ye fulfil the royal law according to the scripture, Thou shalt love thy neighbour as thyself, ye do well.
—JAS. 2:8

So speak ye, and so do, as they that shall be judged by the law of liberty. —JAS. 2:12

Sin is the transgression of the law. —1 JOHN 3:4

This is the love of God, that we keep his commandments.
—1 JOHN 5:3

Laziness, see IDLENESS

Learning, see INSTRUCTION, KNOWLEDGE, IGNORANCE

Lending, see BORROWING AND LENDING

Liberality, see GIVING

LIBERTY; see also LICENTIOUSNESS

Proclaim liberty throughout all the land unto all the inhabitants thereof. —LEV. 25:10

Thou hast loosed my bonds.
—PSA. 116:16

I will walk at liberty: for I seek thy precepts. —PSA. 119:45

Ye shall know the truth, and the truth shall make you free.
—JOHN 8:32

If the Son therefore shall make you free, ye shall be free indeed.
—JOHN 8:36

We are not under the law, but under grace. —ROM. 6:15

Now we are delivered from the law . . . that we should serve in newness of spirit. —Rom. 7:6

The creature itself also shall be delivered from the bondage of corruption into the glorious liberty of the children of God. —Rom. 8:21

All things are lawful unto me, but all things are not expedient.
—1 Cor. 6:12

He that is called in the Lord, being a servant, is the Lord's freeman: likewise also he that is called, being free, is Christ's servant.
—1 Cor. 7:22

Take heed lest by any means this liberty of yours become a stumblingblock to them that are weak.
—1 Cor. 8:9

Am I not an apostle? am I not free? —1 Cor. 9:1

Though I be free from all men, yet have I made myself servant unto all, that I might gain the more.
—1 Cor. 9:19

Stand fast therefore in the liberty wherewith Christ hath made us free.
—Gal. 5:1

Use not liberty for an occasion to the flesh. —Gal. 5:13

Whoso looketh into the perfect law of liberty, and continueth therein . . . this man shall be blessed in his deed. —Jas. 1:25

So speak ye, and so do, as they that shall be judged by the law of liberty. —Jas. 2:12

So is the will of God, that with well doing ye may put to silence the ignorance of foolish men: As free, and not using your liberty for a cloke of maliciousness, but as the servants of God.—1 Pet. 2:15, 16

LICENTIOUSNESS; see also Adultery, Lust

Stolen waters are sweet, and bread eaten in secret is pleasant.
—Prov. 9:17

A whore is a deep ditch; and a strange woman is a narrow pit.
—Prov. 23:27

He that keepeth company with harlots spendeth his substance.
—Prov. 29:3

Give not thy strength unto women, nor thy ways to that which destroyeth kings. —Prov. 31:3

Rejoice, O young man, in thy youth; and let thy heart cheer thee in the days of thy youth, and walk in the ways of thine heart, and in the sight of thine eyes: but know thou, that for all these things God will bring thee to judgment.
—Eccl. 11:9

Let us eat and drink; for to morrow we shall die. —Isa. 22:13

From within, out of the heart of men, proceed evil thoughts, adulteries, fornications, murders, Thefts, covetousness, wickedness, deceit, lasciviousness, an evil eye, blasphemy, pride, foolishness: All these evil things come from within, and defile the man.
—Mark 7:21–23

Sin, taking occasion by the commandment, wrought in me all manner of concupiscence.
—Rom. 7:8

Let us walk honestly, as in the day; not in rioting and drunkenness, not in chambering and wantonness.
—Rom. 13:13

Make no provision for the flesh, to fulfil the lusts thereof.
—ROM. 13:14

Neither fornicators, nor idolaters, nor adulterers, nor effeminate, nor abusers of themselves with mankind, Nor thieves, nor covetous, nor drunkards, nor revilers, nor extortioners, shall inherit the kingdom of God.   —1 COR. 6:9, 10

Use not liberty for an occasion to the flesh.   —GAL. 5:13

Walk not as other Gentiles walk, in the vanity of their mind . . . Who being past feeling have given themselves over unto lasciviousness, to work all uncleanness with greediness.   —EPH. 4:17, 19

No whoremonger, nor unclean person, nor covetous man, who is an idolater, hath any inheritance in the kingdom of Christ and of God.
—EPH. 5:5

Mortify therefore your members which are upon the earth; fornication, uncleanness, inordinate affection, evil concupiscence.—COL. 3:5

Whoremongers, and adulterers, God will judge.   —HEB. 13:4

LIFE; see also IMPERMANENCE, IMMORTALITY

The days of the years of my pilgrimage.   —GEN. 47:9

Truly, as the Lord liveth, and as thy soul liveth, there is but a step between me and death.
—1 SAM. 20:3

All that a man hath will he give for his life.   —JOB 2:4

Remember that my life is wind.
—JOB 7:6

Our days upon earth are a shadow.   —JOB 8:9

Man that is born of woman is of few days, and full of trouble.
—JOB 14:1

No man is sure of life.
—JOB 24:22

Thou wilt shew me the path of life.   —PSA. 16:11

None can keep alive his own soul.
—PSA. 22:29

What man is he that desireth life, and loveth many days, that he may see good?   —PSA. 34:12

Lord, make me to know mine end, and the measure of my days, what it is; that I may know how frail I am.   —PSA. 39:4

Behold, thou hast made my days as an handbreadth; and mine age is as nothing before thee. —PSA. 39:5

We spend our year as a tale that is told.   —PSA. 90:9

If a man beget an hundred children, and live many years, so that the days of his years be many, and his soul be not filled with good, and also that he have no burial; I say, that an untimely birth is better than he.   —ECCL. 6:3

Who knoweth what is good for man in this life, all the days of his vain life which he spendeth as a shadow? for who can tell a man what shall be after him under the sun?   —ECCL. 6:12

A living dog is better than a dead lion.   —ECCL. 9:4

Seek the Lord, and ye shall live.
—AMOS 5:6

Seek good, and not evil, that ye may live.   —AMOS 5:14

He that loveth his life shall lose it. —JOHN 12:25

He giveth to all life, and breath, and all things. —ACTS 17:25

In him we live, and move, and have our being. —ACTS 17:28

None of us liveth to himself, and no man dieth to himself.
—ROM. 14:7

He that will love life, and see good days, let him refrain his tongue from evil, and his lips that they speak no guile.—1 PET. 3:10

Whosoever will, let him take the water of life freely. —REV. 22:17

LIGHT

The Lord is my light and my salvation. —PSA. 27:1

Thy word is a lamp unto my feet, and a light unto my path.
—PSA. 119:105

The entrance of thy words giveth light; it giveth understanding unto the simple. —PSA. 119:130

The commandment is a lamp: and the law is light. —PROV. 6:23

The Lord shall be thine everlasting light. —ISA. 60:20

Ye are the light of the world.
—MATT. 5:14

The light of the body is the eye: therefore when thine eye is single, thy whole body also is full of light; but when thine eye is evil, thy body also is full of darkness.
—LUKE 11:34

In him was life; and the life was the light of men. —JOHN 1:4

The light shineth in darkness; and the darkness comprehended it not.
—JOHN 1:5

This is the condemnation, that light is come into the world, and men loved darkness rather than light, because their deeds were evil.
—JOHN 3:19

Every one that doeth evil hateth the light, neither cometh to the light, lest his deeds should be reproved. —JOHN 3:20

I am the light of the world: he that followeth me shall not walk in darkness, but shall have the light of life. —JOHN 8:12

Walk while ye have the light, lest darkness come upon you: for he that walketh in darkness knoweth not whither he goeth.
—JOHN 12:35

While ye have light, believe in the light, that ye may be the children of light. —JOHN 12:36

Ye were sometimes darkness, but now are ye light in the Lord: walk as children of light. —EPH. 5:8

Awake thou that sleepest, and arise from the dead, and Christ shall give thee light. —EPH. 5:14

Ye are all the children of light, and the children of the day: we are not of the night, nor of darkness.
—1 THESS. 5:5

God is light, and in him is no darkness at all. —1 JOHN 1:5

If we walk in the light, as he is in the light, we have fellowship one with another, and the blood of Jesus Christ his Son cleanseth us from all sin. —1 JOHN 1:7

Longing, see DESIRE

Long-suffering, see CONSTANCY, PATIENCE, TOLERANCE, MEEKNESS

LOVE; see also CHARITY, BROTHER-HOOD, FRIENDSHIP

Thou shalt love thy neighbour as thyself.   —LEV. 19:18

Thou shalt love the Lord thy God with all thine heart, and with all thy soul, and with all thy might.
—DEUT. 6:5

Hatred stirreth up strifes: but love covereth all sins.
—PROV. 10:12

Better is a dinner of herbs where love is, than a stalled ox and hatred therewith.   —PROV. 15:17

He that covereth a transgression seeketh love; but he that repeateth a matter separateth very friends.
—PROV. 17:9

A friend loveth at all times, and a brother is born for adversity.
—PROV. 17:17

Love is strong as death.
—S. OF S. 8:6

Many waters cannot quench love, neither can the floods drown it.
—S. OF S. 8:7

If ye love them which love you, what thank have ye? for sinners also love those that love them.
—LUKE 6:32

Love ye your enemies, and do good, and lend, hoping for nothing again; and your reward shall be great.   —LUKE 6:35

A new commandment I give unto you, That ye love one another; as I have loved you, that ye also love one another.   —JOHN 13:34

By this shall all men know that ye are my disciples, if ye have love one to another.   —JOHN 13:35

Greater love hath no man than this, that a man lay down his life for his friends.   —JOHN 15:13

We know that all things work together for good to them that love God.   —ROM. 8:28

Let love be without dissimulation.
—ROM. 12:9

Be kindly affectioned one to another with brotherly love; in honour preferring one another.
—ROM. 12:10

Owe no man any thing, but to love one another.   —ROM. 13:8

He that loveth another hath fulfilled the law.   —ROM. 13:8

Love is the fulfilling of the law.
—ROM. 13:10

By love serve one another.
—GAL. 5:13

Walk in love, as Christ also hath loved us.   —EPH. 5:2

I pray, that your love may abound yet more and more in knowledge and in all judgment.
—PHIL. 1:9

The Lord make you to increase and abound in love one toward another, and toward all men.
—1 THESS. 3:12

Ye yourselves are taught of God to love one another. —1 THESS. 4:9

God hath not given us the spirit of fear; but of power and love.
—2 TIM. 1:7

Let us consider one another to provoke unto love and to good works.   —HEB. 10:24

If ye fulfil the royal law according to the scripture, Thou shalt love thy neighbour as thyself, ye do well.
—JAS. 2:8

Love one another with a pure heart fervently. —1 PET. 1:22

Honour all men. Love the brotherhood. —1 PET. 2:17

Be ye all of one mind, having compassion one of another, love as brethren, be pitiful, be courteous. —1 PET. 3:8

Whoso keepeth his word, in him verily is the love of God perfected. —1 JOHN 2:5

He that loveth his brother abideth in the light, and there is none occasion of stumbling in him. —1 JOHN 2:10

He that loveth not his brother abideth in death. —1 JOHN 3:14

My little children, let us not love in word, neither in tongue; but in deed and in truth. —1 JOHN 3:18

Every one that loveth is born of God. —1 JOHN 4:7

If God so loved us, we ought also to love one another.—1 JOHN 4:11

If we love one another, God dwelleth in us, and his love is perfected in us. —1 JOHN 4:12

God is love. —1 JOHN 4:16

Perfect love casteth out fear. —1 JOHN 4:18

If a man say, I love God, and hateth his brother, he is a liar: for he that loveth not his brother whom he hath seen, how can he love God whom he hath not seen? —1 JOHN 4:20

This commandment have we from him, That he who loveth God love his brother also.—1 JOHN 4:21

Every one that loveth him that begat loveth him also that is begotten of him. —1 JOHN 5:1

By this we know that we love the children of God, when we love God, and keep his commandments. —1 JOHN 5:2

Keep yourselves in the love of God. —JUDE 1:21

Lowliness, see HUMILITY, MEEKNESS

Loyalty, see FAITHFULNESS

Lukewarmness, see HALFHEARTEDNESS

LUST; see also DESIRE, ADULTERY

Lust not after her beauty in thine heart; neither let her take thee with her eyelids. —PROV. 6:25

Whosoever looketh on a woman to lust after her hath committed adultery with her already in his heart. —MATT. 5:28

The cares of this world, and the deceitfulness of riches, and the lusts of other things entering in, choke the word, and it becometh unfruitful. —MARK 4:19

Ye are of your father the devil, and the lusts of your father ye will do. —JOHN 8:44

Make no provision for the flesh, to fulfil the lusts thereof. —ROM. 13:14

I keep under my body, and bring it into subjection: lest that by any means, when I have preached to others, I myself should be a castaway. —1 COR. 9:27

We should not lust after evil things. —1 COR. 10:6

The flesh lusteth against the Spirit, and the Spirit against the flesh. —GAL. 5:17

Flee . . . youthful lusts. —2 TIM. 2:22

Denying ungodliness and worldly lusts, we should live soberly, righteously, and godly, in this present world. —Tit. 2:12

Every man is tempted, when he is drawn away of his own lust, and enticed. —Jas. 1:14

When lust hath conceived, it bringeth forth sin: and sin, when it is finished, bringeth forth death. —Jas. 1:15

Ye lust, and have not: ye kill, and desire to have, and cannot obtain. —Jas. 4:2

Abstain from fleshly lusts, which war against the soul. —1 Pet. 2:11

All that is in the world, the lust of the flesh, and the lust of the eyes, and the pride of life, is not of the Father, but is of the world. —1 John 2:16

The world passeth away, and the lust thereof: but he that doeth the will of God abideth for ever. —1 John 2:17

Lying, see Falsehood

M

MALICE; see also ANGER, HATRED, HARM, PERSECUTION, OPPRESSION, RETALIATION, SLANDER, INJUSTICE

Thou shalt not avenge, nor bear any grudge against the children of thy people. —LEV. 19:18

Thou beholdest mischief and spite, to requite it with thy hand. —PSA. 10:14

Workers of iniquity, which speak peace to their neighbours, but mischief is in their hearts—PSA. 28:3

The dark places of the earth are full of the habitations of cruelty. —PSA. 74:20

They draw nigh that follow after mischief: they are far from thy law. —PSA. 119:150

Deliver me, O Lord, from the evil man: preserve me from the violent man; Which imagine mischiefs in their heart. —PSA. 140:1, 2

Devise not evil against thy neighbour. —PROV. 3:29

A naughty person, a wicked man, walketh with a froward mouth . . . Frowardness is in his heart, he deviseth mischief continually; he soweth discord. —PROV. 6:12, 14

Violence covereth the mouth of the wicked. —PROV. 10:6

It is a sport to a fool to do mischief: but a man of understanding hath wisdom. —PROV. 10:23

The merciful man doeth good to his own soul: but he that is cruel troubleth his own flesh. —PROV. 11:17

He that seeketh mischief, it shall come unto him. —PROV. 11:27

A righteous man regardeth the life of his beast: but the tender mercies of the wicked are cruel. —PROV. 12:10

Deceit is in the heart of them that imagine evil. —PROV. 12:20

Do they not err that devise evil? but mercy and truth shall be to them that devise good. —PROV. 14:22

A froward man soweth strife: and a whisperer separateth chief friends. —PROV. 16:28

A violent man enticeth his neighbour, and leadeth him into the way that is not good. He shutteth his eyes to devise froward things: moving his lips he bringeth evil to pass. —PROV. 16:29, 30

Whoso mocketh the poor reproacheth his Maker: and he that is glad at calamities shall not be unpunished. —PROV. 17:5

Say not thou, I will recompense evil; but wait on the Lord, and he shall save thee. —PROV. 20:22

The soul of the wicked desireth evil: his neighbour findeth no favour in his eyes. —Prov. 21:10

He that deviseth to do evil shall be called a mischievous person.
—Prov. 24:8

Rejoice not when thine enemy falleth, and let not thine heart be glad when he stumbleth.
—Prov. 24:17

Whoso diggeth a pit shall fall therein: and he that rolleth a stone, it will return upon him.
—Prov. 26:27

Whoso causeth the righteous to go astray in an evil way, he shall fall himself into his own pit.
—Prov. 28:10

Let none of you imagine evil in your hearts against his neighbour.
—Zech. 8:17

All they that take the sword shall perish with the sword.
—Matt. 26:52

Let all bitterness, and wrath, and anger, and clamour, and evil speaking, be put away from you, with all malice. —Eph. 4:31

Put off all these; anger, wrath, malice . . . out of your mouth.
—Col. 3:8

He shall have judgment without mercy, that hath shewed no mercy.
—Jas. 2:13

Speak not evil one of another.
—Jas. 4:11

MAN

God created man in his own image. —Gen. 1:27

The Lord formed man of the dust of the ground. —Gen. 2:7

Ye shall be as gods, knowing good and evil. —Gen. 3:5

Them that dwell in houses of clay, whose foundation is the dust.
—Job 4:19

Man is born unto trouble, as the sparks fly upward. —Job 5:7

Man that is born of woman is of few days, and full of trouble. He cometh forth like a flower, and is cut down: he fleeth also as a shadow, and continueth not.
—Job 14:1, 2

Thou madest him to have dominion over the works of thy hands; thou hast put all things under his feet. —Psa. 8:6

He remembered that they were but flesh. —Psa. 78:39

He knoweth our frame; he remembereth that we are dust.
—Psa. 103:14

As for man, his days are as grass: as a flower of the field, so he flourisheth. —Psa. 103:15

I am fearfully and wonderfully made. —Psa. 139:14

Lord, what is man, that thou takest knowledge of him! or the son of man, that thou makest account of him! —Psa. 144:3

Man is like to vanity: his days are as a shadow that passeth away.
—Psa. 144:4

That which befalleth the sons of men befalleth beasts; even one thing befalleth them: as the one dieth, so dieth the other. —Eccl. 3:19

All are of the dust, and all turn to dust again. —Eccl. 3:20

God hath made man upright; but they have sought out many inventions. —Eccl. 7:29

O Lord, thou art our Father; we are the clay, and thou our potter; and we all are the works of thy hand. —ISA. 64:8

What man knoweth the things of a man, save the spirit of man which is in him? —1 COR. 2:11

A man . . . is the image and glory of God. —1 COR. 11:7

When I was a child, I spake as a child, I understood as a child, I thought as a child: but when I became a man, I put away childish things. —1 COR. 13:11

All flesh is as grass, and all the glory of man as the flower of grass. —1 PET. 1:24

MARRIAGE; see also CELIBACY

The Lord God said, It is not good that the man should be alone; I will make him an help meet for him. —GEN. 2:18

Therefore shall a man leave his father and his mother, and shall cleave unto his wife: and they shall be one flesh. —GEN. 2:23

Unto the woman he said . . . thy desire shall be to thy husband, and he shall rule over thee. —GEN. 3:16

The wife of thy bosom. —DEUT. 13:6

Let thy fountain be blessed: and rejoice with the wife of thy youth. —PROV. 5:18

A virtuous woman is a crown to her husband. —PROV. 12:4

Whoso findeth a wife findeth a good thing, and obtaineth favour of the Lord. —PROV. 18:22

Two are better than one. —ECCL. 4:9

Live joyfully with the wife whom thou lovest all the days of the life of thy vanity. —ECCL. 9:9

I will betroth thee unto me for ever; yea, I will betroth thee unto me in righteousness, and in judgment, and in lovingkindness, and in mercies. —HOS. 2:19

From the beginning of the creation God made them male and female. For this cause shall a man leave his father and mother, and cleave to his wife. —MARK 10:6, 7

They twain shall be one flesh: so then they are no more twain, but one flesh. —MARK 10:8

What therefore God hath joined together, let not man put asunder. —MARK 10:9

The woman which hath an husband is bound by the law to her husband so long as he liveth. —ROM. 7:2

Let every man have his own wife, and let every woman have her own husband. —1 COR. 7:2

Let the husband render unto the wife due benevolence: and likewise also the wife unto the husband. —1 COR. 7:3

The wife hath not power of her own body, but the husband: and likewise also the husband hath not power of his own body, but the wife. —1 COR. 7:4

Defraud ye not one the other, except it be with consent for a time. —1 COR. 7:5

If they cannot contain, let them marry: for it is better to marry than to burn. —1 COR. 7:9

He that is unmarried careth for the things that belong to the Lord, how he may please the Lord: But he that is married careth for the things that are of the world, how he may please his wife.

—1 COR. 7:32, 33

The head of the woman is the man. —1 COR. 11:3

The woman is the glory of the man. —1 COR. 11:7

The man is not of the woman; but the woman of the man. Neither was the man created for the woman; but the woman for the man.

—1 COR. 11:8, 9

Wives, submit yourselves unto your husbands, as unto the Lord.

—EPH. 5:22

The husband is the head of the wife, even as Christ is the head of the church. —EPH. 5:23

As the church is subject unto Christ, so let the wives be to their own husbands in every thing.

—EPH. 5:24

Husbands, love your wives, even as Christ also loved the church, and gave himself for it. —EPH. 5:25

He that loveth his wife loveth himself. —EPH. 5:28

They two shall be one flesh.

—EPH. 5:31

Wives, submit yourselves unto your own husbands, as it is fit in the Lord. Husbands, love your wives, and be not bitter against them.

—COL. 3:18, 19

Marriage is honourable in all.

—HEB. 13:4

Ye husbands, dwell with them according to knowledge, giving hon-

our unto the wife, as unto the weaker vessel. —1 PET. 3:7

Marvel, see WONDER

Materialism, see WORLDLINESS, WEALTH

MEDDLING

Why shouldest thou meddle to thy hurt? —2 KIN. 14:10

Forbear thee from meddling with God. —2 CHRON. 35:21

The heart knoweth his own bitterness; and a stranger doth not intermeddle with his joy.

—PROV. 14:10

Leave off contention, before it be meddled with. —PROV. 17:14

Through desire a man, having separated himself, seeketh and intermeddleth with all wisdom.

—PROV. 18:1

Every fool will be meddling.

—PROV. 20:3

Meddle not with him that flattereth with his lips. —PROV. 20:19

Meddle not with them that are given to change. —PROV. 24:21

He that passeth by, and meddleth with strife belonging not to him, is like one that taketh a dog by the ears. —PROV. 26:17

Let none of you suffer . . . as a busybody in other men's matters.

—1 PET. 4:15

MEDITATION

His delight is in the law of the Lord, and in his law doth he meditate day and night. —PSA. 1:2

Commune with your own heart upon your bed, and be still.

—PSA. 4:4

Let the words of my mouth, and the meditation of my heart, be acceptable in thy sight, O Lord.
—PSA. 19:14

My heart was hot within me, while I was musing the fire burned.
—PSA. 39:3

My mouth shall speak of wisdom; and the meditation of my heart shall be of understanding. —PSA. 49:3

I remember thee upon my bed, and meditate on thee in the night watches. —PSA. 63:6

I will meditate also of all thy work, and talk of thy doings.
—PSA. 77:12

My meditation of him shall be sweet: I will be glad in the Lord.
—PSA. 104:34

I will meditate in thy precepts, and have respect unto thy ways.
—PSA. 119:15

O how love I thy law! it is my meditation all the day.
—PSA. 119:97

I meditate on all thy works; I muse on the work of thy hands.
—PSA. 143:5

Whatsoever things are true, whatsoever things are honest, whatsoever things are just, whatsoever things are pure, whatsoever things are lovely, whatsoever things are of good report; if there be any virtue, and if there be any praise, think on these things. —PHIL. 4:8

Give attention to reading, to exhortation, to doctrine . . . Meditate upon these things; give thyself wholly to them.—1 TIM. 4:13, 15

MEEKNESS; see also HUMILITY, KINDNESS, PATIENCE, RESIGNATION

The meek shall eat and be satisfied. —PSA. 22:26

The meek will he guide in judgment: and the meek will he teach his way. —PSA. 25:9

The meek shall inherit the earth.
—PSA. 37:11

The Lord lifteth up the meek: he casteth the wicked down to the ground. —PSA. 147:6

He will beautify the meek with salvation. —PSA. 149:4

He that is slow to wrath is of great understanding.—PROV. 14:29

A soft answer turneth away wrath. —PROV. 15:1

He that is slow to anger appeaseth strife. —PROV. 15:18

He that is slow to anger is better than the mighty: and he that ruleth his spirit than he that taketh a city.
—PROV. 16:32

By long forbearing is a prince persuaded, and a soft tongue breaketh the bone. —PROV. 25:15

The patient in spirit is better than the proud in spirit. —ECCL. 7:8

Yielding pacifieth great offences.
—ECCL. 10:4

He putteth his mouth in the dust; if so be there may be hope. He giveth his cheek to him that smiteth him: he is filled full with reproach.
—LAM. 3:29, 30

Seek ye the Lord, all ye meek of the earth, which have wrought his judgment: seek righteousness, seek meekness. —ZEPH. 2:3

Blessed are the meek: for they shall inherit the earth.—MATT. 5:5

Whosoever shall smite thee on thy right cheek, turn to him the other also. —MATT. 5:39

Take my yoke upon you, and learn of me; for I am meek and lowly in heart: and ye shall find rest unto your souls.—MATT. 11:29

Bless them which persecute you: bless, and curse not.—ROM. 12:14

If it be possible, as much as lieth in you, live peaceably with all men. —ROM. 12:18

Charity suffereth long, and is kind; charity envieth not; charity vaunteth not itself, is not puffed up, Doth not behave itself unseemly, seeketh not her own, is not easily provoked, thinketh no evil; Beareth all things, believeth all things, hopeth all things, endureth all things. —1 COR. 13:4–7

The fruit of the Spirit is love, joy, peace, longsuffering, gentleness, goodness, faith, Meekness, temperance. —GAL. 5:22, 23

If a man be overtaken in a fault, ye which are spiritual, restore such an one in the spirit of meekness; considering thyself, lest thou also be tempted. —GAL. 6:1

Walk worthy of the vocation wherewith ye are called, With all lowliness and meekness, with longsuffering, forbearing one another in love. —EPH. 4:1, 2

Put on . . . bowels of mercies, kindness, humbleness of mind, meekness, longsuffering; Forbearing one another, and forgiving one another. —COL. 3:12, 13

Follow after righteousness, godliness, faith, love, patience, meekness. —1 TIM. 6:11

The servant of the Lord must not strive; but be gentle unto all men, apt to teach, patient, In meekness instructing those that oppose themselves. —2 TIM. 2:24, 25

Be no brawlers, but gentle, shewing all meekness unto all men. —TIT. 3:2

Be swift to hear, slow to speak, slow to wrath. —JAS. 1:19

Receive with meekness the engrafted word. —JAS. 1:21

Be ready always to give an answer to every man that asketh you a reason of the hope that is in you with meekness and fear. —1 PET. 3:15

MERCY; see also FORGIVENESS, REMISSION

With the merciful thou wilt shew thyself merciful. —2 SAM. 22:26

Surely goodness and mercy shall follow me all the days of my life. —PSA. 23:6

Thy mercy, O Lord, is in the heavens; and thy faithfulness reacheth unto the clouds. —PSA. 36:5

Mercy and truth are met together; righteousness and peace have kissed each other. —PSA. 85:10

I will sing of the mercies of the Lord for ever. —PSA. 89:1

Like as a father pitieth his children, so the Lord pitieth them that fear him. —PSA. 103:13

The mercy of the Lord is from everlasting to everlasting upon them that fear him. —PSA. 103:17

Let not mercy and truth forsake thee: bind them about thy neck; write them upon the table of thine heart. —PROV. 3:3

The merciful man doeth good to his own soul: he that is cruel troubleth his own flesh.

—Prov. 11:17

A righteous man regardeth the life of his beast: but the tender mercies of the wicked are cruel.

—Prov. 12:10

He that hath mercy on the poor, happy is he. —Prov. 14:21

Mercy and truth shall be to them that devise good. —Prov. 14:22

He that oppresseth the poor reproacheth his Maker: but he that honoureth him hath mercy on the poor. —Prov. 14:31

By mercy and truth iniquity is purged. —Prov. 16:6

He that followeth after righteousness and mercy findeth life, righteousness, and honour.

—Prov. 21:21

He that covereth his sins shall not prosper: but whoso confesseth and forsaketh them shall have mercy.

—Prov. 28:13

Keep mercy and judgment, and wait on thy God continually.

—Hos. 12:6

What doth the Lord require of thee, but to do justly, and to love mercy, and to walk humbly with thy God? —Mic. 6:8

Execute true judgment, and shew mercy and compassions every man to his brother. —Zech. 7:9

Blessed are the merciful: for they shall obtain mercy. —Matt. 5:7

Be ye therefore merciful, as your Father also is merciful.

—Luke 6:36

Put on . . . bowels of mercies.

—Col. 3:12

He shall have judgment without mercy, that hath shewed no mercy.

—Jas. 2:13

Merriment, see Cheerfulness, Rejoicing

MINISTRY; see also Calling, Ordination, Service

Let thy priests, O Lord God, be clothed with salvation, and let thy saints rejoice in goodness.

—2 Chron. 6:41

Let thy priests be clothed with righteousness. —Psa. 132:9

The fruit of the righteous is a tree of life; and he that winneth souls is wise. —Prov. 11:30

Follow me, and I will make you fishers of men. —Matt. 4:18

Ye are the light of the world.

—Matt. 5:14

Behold, I send you forth as sheep in the midst of wolves: be ye therefore wise as serpents, and harmless as doves. —Matt. 10:16

Can the blind lead the blind? shall they not both fall into the ditch? —Luke 6:39

The harvest is great, but the labourers are few: pray ye therefore the Lord of the harvest, that he should send forth labourers into his harvest. —Luke 10:1

He that reapeth receiveth wages, and gathereth fruit unto life eternal: that both he that soweth and he that reapeth may rejoice together.

—John 4:36

Go, stand and speak in the temple to the people all the words of this life. —Acts 5:20

How then shall they call on him in whom they have not believed? and how shall they believe in him of whom they have not heard? and how shall they hear without a preacher? —Rom. 10:14

How beautiful are the feet of them that preach the gospel of peace, and bring glad tidings of good things! —Rom. 10:15

We are ambassadors for Christ. —2 Cor. 5:20

He gave some, apostles; and some, prophets; and some, evange-lists; and some, pastors and teach-ers. —Eph. 4:11

Take heed to the ministry which thou hast received in the Lord, that thou fulfil it. —Col. 4:17

If a man desire the office of a bishop, he desireth a good work. A bishop then must be blameless, the husband of one wife, vigilant, sober, of good behaviour, given to hospi-tality, apt to teach; Not given to wine, no striker, not greedy of filthy lucre; but patient, not a brawler, not covetous; One that ruleth well his own house, having his children in subjection with gravity; (For if a man know not how to rule his own house, how shall he take care of the church of God?) Not a novice, lest being lifted up with pride he fall into the condemnation of the devil. Moreover he must have a good report of them which are with-out; lest he fall into reproach and the snare of the devil. —1 Tim. 3:1–7

Be thou an example of the be-lievers, in word, in conversation, in charity, in spirit, in faith, in purity. —1 Tim. 4:12

The husbandman that laboureth must be first partaker of the fruits. —2 Tim. 2:6

Study to shew thyself approved unto God, a workman that needeth not to be ashamed, rightly dividing the word of truth. —2 Tim. 2:15

The servant of the Lord must not strive; but be gentle unto all men, apt to teach, patient, In meekness instructing those that oppose them-selves. —2 Tim. 2:24, 25

Preach the word; be instant in season, out of season; reprove, re-buke, exhort with all longsuffering and doctrine. —2 Tim. 4:2

Watch thou in all things, endure afflictions, do the work of an evan-gelist, make full proof of thy min-istry. —2 Tim. 4:5

A bishop must be blameless, as the steward of God; not selfwilled, not soon angry, not given to wine, no striker, not given to filthy lucre; But a lover of hospitality, a lover of good men, sober, just, holy, temperate; Holding fast the faithful word as he hath been taught, that he may be able by sound doctrine both to exhort and to convince the gainsayers. —Tit. 1:7–9

As every man hath received the gift, even so minister the same one to another, as good stewards of the manifold grace of God. —1 Pet. 4:10

If any man minister, let him do it as of the ability which God giveth. —1 Pet. 4:11

Feed the flock of God which is among you, taking the oversight thereof, not by constraint, but willingly; not for filthy lucre, but of a ready mind; Neither as being lords over God's heritage, but being ensamples to the flock.

—1 PET. 5:2, 3

Miracle, see WONDER

Misanthropy, see ANGER, HATRED, MALICE, INJUSTICE, HARM, PERSECUTION, RETALIATION, SLANDER

Mischief, see MALICE

Misery, see AFFLICTION, SADNESS, SORROW

Misfortune, see AFFLICTION, TROUBLE

Mockery, see SCORN

Moderation, see TEMPERANCE

Modesty, see CHASTITY, HUMILITY, MEEKNESS

Money, see WEALTH

Morality, see GOODNESS, RIGHTEOUSNESS, INTEGRITY, VERACITY, EVIL, SIN

Mortality, see DEATH, IMPERMANENCE

Mourning, see SORROW

Murmuring, see COMPLAINT

N

NATURE

In the beginning God created the heaven and the earth. —GEN. 1:1

All the earth shall be filled with the glory of the Lord.

—NUM. 14:21

Blessed of the Lord be his land . . . for the precious things of the earth and fulness thereof.

—DEUT. 33:13, 16

Let the fields rejoice, and all that is therein. —1 CHRON. 16:32

Speak to the earth, and it shall teach thee. —JOB 12:8

Is not God in the height of heaven? and behold the height of the stars how high they are!

—JOB 22:12

The morning stars sang together, and all the sons of God shouted for joy. —JOB 38:7

Canst thou bind the sweet influences of Pleiades, or loose the bands of Orion? —JOB 38:31

The firmament sheweth his handywork. —PSA. 19:1

The earth is the Lord's, and the fulness thereof. —PSA. 24:1

The earth is full of thy riches.

—PSA. 104:24

Praise ye him, sun and moon: praise him, all ye stars of light.

—PSA. 148:3

He hath made every thing beautiful in his time. —ECCL. 3:11

The flowers appear on the earth; the time of the singing of birds is come. —S. OF S. 2:12

The desert shall rejoice, and blossom as the rose. —ISA. 35:1

All flesh is grass, and all the goodliness thereof is as the flower of the field. —ISA. 40:6

Break forth into singing, ye mountains, O forest, and every tree therein. —ISA. 44:23

Do not I fill heaven and earth? saith the Lord. —JER. 23:24

Consider the lilies of the field.

—MATT. 6:28

Doth not even nature itself teach you. —1 COR. 11:14

That was not first which is spiritual, but that which is natural; and afterward that which is spiritual.

—1 COR. 15:46

Need, see POVERTY, WANT

O

Oath, see IRREVERENCE, VOW

Obduracy, see IMPENITENCE

OBEDIENCE

All that the Lord hath said will we do, and be obedient. —Ex. 24:7

To obey is better than sacrifice, and to hearken than the fat of rams.
—1 SAM. 15:22

The mercy of the Lord is from everlasting to everlasting upon them that fear him . . . and to those that remember his commandments to do them. —PSA. 103:17, 18

The fear of the Lord is the beginning of wisdom: a good understanding have all they that do his commandments. —PSA. 111:10

Blessed is the man that feareth the Lord, that delighteth greatly in his commandments. —PSA. 112:1

Blessed are they that keep his testimonies, and that seek him with the whole heart. —PSA. 119:2

Thou has commanded us to keep thy precepts diligently.
—PSA. 119:4

I have refrained my feet from every evil way, that I might keep thy word. —PSA. 119:101

Thy testimonies are wonderful: therefore doth my soul keep them.
—PSA. 119:129

Teach me to do thy will.
—PSA. 143:10

Whoso hearkeneth unto me shall dwell safely, and shall be quiet from fear of evil. —PROV. 1:33

He that keepeth the commandment keepeth his own soul.
—PROV. 28:7

Fear God, and keep his commandments: for this is the whole duty of man. —ECCL. 12:13

If ye be willing and obedient, ye shall eat the good of the land.
—ISA. 1:19

Obey my voice, and I will be your God, and ye shall be my people.
—JER. 7:27

Why call ye me, Lord, Lord, and do not the things which I say?
—LUKE 6:46

Thy will be done, as in heaven, so in earth. —LUKE 11:2

If a man keep my saying, he shall never see death. —JOHN 8:51

My sheep hear my voice, and I know them, and they follow me.
—JOHN 10:27

If ye love me, keep my commandments. —JOHN 14:15

If ye keep my commandments, ye shall abide in my love.
—JOHN 15:10

We ought to obey God rather than men. —ACTS 5:29

Being made perfect, he became the author of eternal salvation unto all them that obey him.
—HEB. 5:9

He that saith, I know him, and keepeth not his commandments, is a liar, and the truth is not in him.
—1 JOHN 2:4

He that keepeth his commandments dwelleth in him, and he in him. —1 JOHN 3:24

By this we know that we love the children of God, when we love God, and keep his commandments.
—1 JOHN 5:2

This is the love of God, that we keep his commandments.
—1 JOHN 5:3

Ye have purified your souls in obeying the truth. —1 PET. 1:22

Obligation, see DUTY

Occupation, see CALLING, INDUSTRY, WORKS

Offence, see SIN, ANGER

Oldness, see AGE

OMNIPOTENCE

Is any thing too hard for the Lord? —GEN. 18:14

I know that thou canst do every thing. —JOB 42:2

In the Lord Jehovah is everlasting strength. —ISA. 26:4

With God all things are possible.
—MATT. 19:26

With God nothing shall be impossible. —LUKE 1:37

The Lord God omnipotent reigneth. —REV. 19:6

OMNIPRESENCE

Will God indeed dwell on the earth? behold, the heaven and the heaven of heavens cannot contain thee. —1 KIN. 8:27

Whither shall I go from thy spirit? or whither shall I flee from thy presence? —PSA. 139:7

The eyes of the Lord are in every place, beholding the evil and the good. —PROV. 15:3

Can any hide himself in secret places that I shall not see him? saith the Lord. Do I not fill heaven and earth? saith the Lord. —JER. 23:24

They should seek the Lord, if haply they might feel after him, and find him, though he be not far from every one of us. —ACTS 17:27

In him we live, and move, and have our being. —ACTS 17:28

Him that filleth all in all.
—EPH. 1:23

OMNISCIENCE

The Lord is a God of knowledge, and by him actions are weighed.
—1 SAM. 2:3

Thou, even thou only, knowest the hearts of all the children of men. —1 KIN. 8:39

I know thy abode, and thy going out, and thy coming in.
—2 KIN. 19:27

The Lord searcheth all hearts, and understandeth all the imaginations of the thoughts.
—1 CHRON. 28:9

The eyes of the Lord run to and fro throughout the whole earth.
—2 CHRON. 16:9

His eye seeth every precious thing. —JOB 28:10

He looketh to the ends of the earth, and seeth under the whole heaven. —JOB 28:24

He that is perfect of knowledge is with thee. —JOB 36:4

Dost thou know . . . the wondrous works of him which is perfect in knowledge? —JOB 37:16

He knoweth the secrets of the heart. —PSA. 44:21

Thou knowest my downsitting and mine uprising, thou understandest my thought afar off.
—PSA. 139:2

He telleth the number of the stars; he calleth them all by their names. —PSA. 147:4

Great is our Lord, and of great power: his understanding is infinite.
—PSA. 147:5

There is no searching of his understanding. —ISA. 40:28

The very hairs of your head are all numbered. —MATT. 10:29

Known unto God are all his works from the beginning of the world. —ACTS 15:18

God . . . knoweth all things.
—1 JOHN 3:20

OPPORTUNITY

The Lord called yet again, Samuel. —1 SAM. 3:6

God speaketh once, yea twice, yet man perceiveth it not.
—JOB 33:14

I have called, and ye refused; I have stretched out my hand, and no man regarded. —PROV. 1:24

To every thing there is a season, and a time to every purpose under the heaven. —ECCL. 3:1

The harvest is past, the summer is ended, and we are not saved.
—JER. 8:20

O Jerusalem, Jerusalem, thou that killest the prophets, and stonest them which are sent unto thee, how often would I have gathered thy children together, even as a hen gathereth her chickens under her wings, and ye would not!
—MATT. 23:37

Come: for all things are now ready. —LUKE 14:17

My time is not yet come: but your time is always ready.
—JOHN 7:6

I must work the works of him that sent me, while it is day: the night cometh, when no man can work. —JOHN 9:4

Now it is high time to awake out of sleep: for now is our salvation nearer than when we believed.
—ROM. 13:11

The time is short. —1 COR. 7:29

Behold, now is the accepted time; behold, now is the day of salvation.
—2 COR. 6:2

As we have therefore opportunity, let us do good unto all men.
—GAL. 6:10

OPPRESSION

Thou shalt neither vex a stranger, nor oppress him: for ye were strangers in the land of Egypt.
—EX. 22:21

Ye shall not oppress one another.
—LEV. 25:14

Thou shalt not oppress an hired servant that is poor and needy.
—DEUT. 24:14

The Lord heard our voice, and looked on our affliction, and our labour, and our oppression.
—DEUT. 26:7

Is it good unto thee that thou shouldst oppress?   —JOB 10:3

He delivereth the poor in his affliction, and openeth their ears in oppression.   —JOB 36:15

The Lord also will be a refuge for the oppressed, a refuge in times of trouble.   —PSA. 9:9

For the oppression of the poor, for the sighing of the needy, now will I arise, saith the Lord; I will set him in safety from him that puffeth at him.   —PSA. 12:5

Trust not in oppression.
—PSA. 62:10

He shall judge the poor of the people, he shall save the children of the needy, and shall break in pieces the oppressor.   —PSA. 72:4

O let not the oppressed return ashamed: let the poor and needy praise thy name.   —PSA. 74:21

Envy thou not the oppressor, and choose none of his ways.
—PROV. 3:31

He that oppresseth the poor reproacheth his Maker: but he that honoureth him hath mercy on the poor.   —PROV. 14:31

He that oppresseth the poor to increase his riches, and he that giveth to the rich, shall surely come to want.   —PROV. 22:16

Rob not the poor, because he is poor: neither oppress the afflicted in the gate.   —PROV. 22:22

A poor man that oppresseth the poor is like a sweeping rain which leaveth no food.   —PROV. 28:3

There is a generation, whose teeth are as swords, and their jaw teeth as knives, to devour the poor from off the earth, and the needy from among men.   —PROV. 30:14

I returned, and considered all the oppressions that are done under the sun: and behold the tears of such as were oppressed, and they had no comforter; and on the side of their oppressors there was power; but they had no comforter.
—ECCL. 4:1

If thou seest the oppression of the poor, and violent perverting of judgment and justice in a province, marvel not at the matter: for he that is higher than the highest regardeth; and there be higher than they.
—ECCL. 5:8

Surely oppression maketh a wise man mad.   —ECCL. 7:7

Seek judgment, relieve the oppressed, judge the fatherless, plead for the widow.   —ISA. 1:17

Is not this the fast that I have chosen? to loose the bands of wickedness, to undo the heavy burdens, and to let the oppressed go free.
—ISA. 58:6

Remove violence and spoil, and execute judgment and justice, take away your exactions from my people, saith the Lord God.
—EZEK. 45:9

Forasmuch therefore as your treading is upon the poor, and ye take from him burdens of wheat: ye have built houses of hewn stone, but ye shall not dwell in them; ye have planted pleasant vineyards, but ye shall not drink wine of them.
—AMOS 5:11

Optimism, see FAITH, HOPE, CHEER-FULNESS

ORDINATION; see also CALLING, MINISTRY

The Lord hath anointed me to preach good tidings.   —ISA. 61:1

I ordained thee a prophet unto the nations.   —JER. 1:5

Follow me, and I will make you fishers of men .   —MATT. 4:19

Ye have not chosen me, but I have chosen you, and ordained you, that ye should go and bring forth fruit, and that your fruit should remain.   —JOHN 15:16

The powers that be are ordained of God.   —ROM. 13:1

The Lord ordained that they which preach the gospel should live of the gospel.   —1 COR. 9:14

I am ordained a preacher, and an apostle . . . a teacher of the Gentiles in faith and verity.

— 1 TIM. 2:7

Every high priest taken from among men is ordained for men in things pertaining to God.

—HEB. 5:1

Origin, see CREATION

Ownership, see POSSESSION

P

Pacifism, see PEACE

Pain, see AFFLICTION, SADNESS, SORROW, SUFFERING

Paradise, see HEAVEN

Pardon, see FORGIVENESS, REMISSION

PARENTS; see also CHILDREN, INSTRUCTION

Honour thy father and thy mother. —EX. 10:12

I . . . am a jealous God, visiting the iniquity of the fathers upon the children unto the third and fourth generation. EX. 20:5

Like as a father pitieth his children, so the Lord pitieth them that fear him. —PSA. 103:13

My son, hear the instruction of thy father, and forsake not the law of thy mother. —PROV. 1:8

Whom the Lord loveth he correcteth; even as a father the son in whom he delighteth. —PROV. 3:12

A foolish son is the heaviness of his mother. —PROV. 10:1

A good man leaveth an inheritance to his children's children. —PROV. 13:22

He that spareth his rod hateth his son: but he that loveth him chasteneth him betimes.—PROV. 13:24

Children's children are the crown of old men; and the glory of children are their fathers.—PROV. 17:6

He that begetteth a fool doeth it to his sorrow: and the father of a fool hath no joy. —PROV. 17:21

He that wasteth his father, and chaseth away his mother, is a son that causeth shame, and bringeth reproach. —PROV. 19:26

Who curseth his father or his mother, his lamp shall be put out in obscure darkness. —PROV. 20:20

Hearken unto thy father that begat thee, and despise not thy mother when she is old. —PROV. 23:22

The father of the righteous shall greatly rejoice: and he that begetteth a wise child shall have joy of him. —PROV. 23:24

The father to the children shall make known thy truth.—ISA. 38:19

Can a woman forget her suckling child, that she should not have compassion on the son of her womb? —ISA. 49:15

As one whom his mother comforteth, so will I comfort you. —ISA. 66:13

The fathers have eaten a sour grape, and the children's teeth are set on edge. —JER. 31:29

He that loveth father or mother more than me is not worthy of me. —MATT. 10:37

Call no man your father upon the earth: for one is your Father, which is in heaven. —MATT. 23:9

If a son shall ask bread of any of you that is a father, will ye give him a stone? —LUKE 11:11

The children ought not to lay up for the parents, but the parents for the children. —2 COR. 12:14

Children, obey your parents in the Lord: for this is right.

—EPH. 6:1

· Fathers, provoke not your children to wrath: but bring them up in the nurture and admonition of the Lord. —EPH. 6:4

Fathers, provoke not your children to anger, lest they be discouraged. —COL. 3:21

If a man know not how to rule his own house, how shall he take care of the church of God?

—1 TIM. 3:5

If any provide not for his own, and specially for those of his own house, he hath denied the faith, and is worse than an infidel.

—1 TIM. 5:8

If ye endure chastening, God dealeth with you as with sons; for what son is he whom the father chasteneth not? —HEB. 12:7

PARSIMONY; see also AVARICE

There is that scattereth, and yet increaseth; and there is that withholdeth more than is meet, but it tendeth to poverty. —PROV. 11:24

He that withholdeth corn, the people shall curse him.

—PROV. 11:26

The poor useth intreaties; but the rich answereth roughly.

—PROV. 18:23

Who stoppeth his ears at the cry of the poor, he also shall cry himself, but shall not be heard.

—PROV. 21:13

He that giveth unto the poor shall not lack: but he that hideth his eyes shall have many a curse.

—PROV. 28:27

He that loveth silver shall not be satisfied with silver; nor he that loveth abundance with increase.

—ECCL. 5:10

There is a sore evil which I have seen under the sun, namely, riches kept for the owners thereof to their hurt. —ECCL. 5:13

He which soweth sparingly shall reap also sparingly. —2 COR. 9:6

If any provide not for his own, and specially for those of his own house, he hath denied the faith, and is worse than an infidel.

—1 TIM. 5:8

We brought nothing into this world, and it is certain we can carry nothing out. —1 TIM. 6:7

Your gold and silver is cankered; and the rust of them shall be a witness against you. —JAS. 5:3

Whoso hath this world's good, and seeth his brother have need, and shutteth up his bowels of compassion from him, how dwelleth the love of God in him? —1 JOHN 3:17

Partiality, see IMPARTIALITY, JUSTICE

PATIENCE; see also CONSTANCY, MEEKNESS, TOLERANCE, RESIGNATION

Rest in the Lord, and wait patiently for him. —PSA. 37:7

Those that wait upon the Lord, they shall inherit the earth.

—PSA. 37:9

I wait for the Lord, my soul doth wait, and in his word do I hope.

—PSA. 130:5

My son, despise not the chastening of the Lord; neither be weary of his correction.   —Prov. 3:11

He that is slow to wrath is of great understanding: but he that is hasty of spirit exalteth folly.
     —Prov. 14:29

He that is slow to anger appeaseth strife.   —Prov. 15:18

The spirit of a man will sustain his infirmity.   —Prov. 18:14

He that hasteth with his feet sinneth.   —Prov. 19:2

The thoughts of the diligent tend only to plenteousness; but of every one that is hasty only to want.
     —Prov. 21:5

By long forbearing is a prince persuaded, and a soft tongue breaketh the bone.   —Prov. 25:15

The patient in spirit is better than the proud in spirit.   —Eccl. 7:8

Be not hasty in thy spirit to be angry: for anger resteth in the bosom of fools.   —Eccl. 7:9

He that believeth shall not make haste.   —Isa. 28:6

It is good that a man should both hope and quietly wait for the salvation of the Lord.   —Lam. 3:26

He that shall endure unto the end, the same shall be saved.
     —Matt. 24:13

On the good ground are they, which in an honest and good heart, having heard the word, keep it, and bring forth fruit with patience.
     —Luke 8:15

In your patience possess ye your souls.   —Luke 21:19

By patient continuance in well doing seek for glory and honour and immortality.   —Rom. 2:7

Tribulation worketh patience; And patience, experience; and experience, hope.   —Rom. 5:3,4

If we hope for that we see not, then do we with patience wait for it.   —Rom. 8:25

Rejoicing in hope; patient in tribulation.   —Rom. 12:12

Now the God of patience and consolation grant you to be likeminded one toward another according to Christ Jesus.   —Rom. 15:5

Charity suffereth long, and is kind . . . is not easily provoked . . . Beareth all things, believeth all things, hopeth all things, endureth all things.   —1 Cor. 13:4, 5, 7

The fruit of the Spirit is love, joy, peace, longsuffering, gentleness, goodness, faith.—Gal. 5:22

Let us not be weary in well doing: for in due season we shall reap, if we faint not.   —Gal. 6:9

Walk worthy of the vocation wherewith ye are called, With all lowliness and meekness, with longsuffering, forbearing one another in love.   —Eph. 4:1, 2

Walk worthy of the Lord . . . unto all patience and longsuffering with joyfulness.   —Col. 1:10

Put on . . . bowels of mercies, kindness, humbleness of mind, meekness, longsuffering; Forbearing one another, and forgiving one another.   —Col. 3:12, 13

Be patient toward all men.
     —1 Thess. 5:14

The Lord direct your hearts into the love of God, and into the patient waiting for Christ.
     —2 Thess. 3:5

Follow after righteousness, godliness, faith, love, patience, meekness. —1 TIM. 6:11

The servant of the Lord must not strive; but be gentle unto all men, apt to teach, patient. —2 TIM. 2:24

Be not slothful, but followers of them who through faith and patience inherit the promises. —HEB. 6:12

Ye have need of patience, that, after ye have done the will of God, ye might receive the promise. —HEB. 10:36

Let us run with patience the race that is set before us. —HEB. 12:1

The trying of your faith worketh patience. —JAS. 1:3

Let patience have her perfect work, that ye may be perfect and entire, wanting nothing.—JAS. 1:4

Let every man be swift to hear, slow to speak, slow to wrath. —JAS. 1:19

Behold, the husbandman waiteth for the precious fruit of the earth, and hath long patience for it, until he receive the early and latter rain. —JAS. 5:7

Take, my brethren, the prophets, who have spoken in the name of the Lord, for an example of suffering affliction, and of patience. —JAS. 5:10

We count them happy which endure. —JAS. 5:11

Ye have heard of the patience of Job. —JAS. 5:11

What glory is it, if, when ye be buffeted for your faults, ye shall take it patiently? but if, when ye do

well, and suffer for it, ye take it patiently, this is acceptable with God. —1 PET. 2:20

Giving all diligence, add to your faith virtue; and to virtue knowledge; And to knowledge temperance; and to temperance patience; and to patience godliness. —2 PET. 1:5, 6

Pattern, see EXAMPLE

Payment, see RETRIBUTION, REWARD

PEACE; see also HARMONY

Let there be no strife, I pray thee, between me and thee . . . for we be brethren. —GEN. 13:8

Seek peace, and pursue it. —PSA. 34:14

The meek shall inherit the earth; and shall delight themselves in the abundance of peace. —PSA. 37:11

Righteousness and peace have kissed each other. —PSA. 85:10

I am for peace, but when I speak, they are for war. —PSA. 120:7

Behold, how good and how pleasant it is for brethren to dwell together in unity! —PSA. 133:1

To the counsellors of peace is joy. —PROV. 12:20

A soft answer turneth away wrath. —PROV. 15:1

Better is a dinner of herbs where love is, than a stalled ox and hatred therewith. —PROV. 15:17

He that is slow to anger appeaseth strife. —PROV. 15:18

When a man's ways please the Lord, he maketh even his enemies to be at peace with him. —PROV. 16:7

He that is slow to anger is better than the mighty; and he that ruleth his spirit than he that taketh a city.
—Prov. 16:32

Better is a dry morsel, and quietness therewith, than an house full of sacrifices with strife.
—Prov. 17:1

The beginning of strife is as when one letteth out water: therefore leave off contention, before it be meddled with. —Prov. 17:14

The discretion of a man deferreth his anger; and it is his glory to pass over a transgression. —Prov. 19:11

It is an honour for a man to cease from strife: but every fool will be meddling. —Prov. 20:3

Better is an handful with quietness, than both the hands full with travail and vexation of spirit.
—Eccl. 4:6

Yielding pacifieth great offences.
—Eccl. 10:4

They shall beat their swords into plowshares, and their spears into pruninghooks. —Isa. 2:4

Love the truth and peace.
—Zech. 8:19

Blessed are the peacemakers: for they shall be called the children of God. —Matt. 5:9

Agree with thine adversary quickly, whiles thou art in the way with him. —Matt. 5:25

Whosoever shall smite thee on thy right cheek, turn to him the other also. —Matt. 5:39

Have peace one with another.
—Mark 9:50

Guide our feet into the way of peace. —Luke 1:79

Glory to God in the highest, and on earth peace, good will toward men. —Luke 2:14

If it be possible, as much as lieth in you, live peaceably with all men.
—Rom. 12:18

Let us therefore follow after the things which make for peace.
—Rom. 14:19

God is not the author of confusion, but of peace.—1 Cor. 14:33

Be of one mind, live in peace; and the God of love and peace shall be with you. —2 Cor. 13:11

Keep the unity of the Spirit in the bond of peace. —Eph. 4:3

Be at peace among yourselves.
—1 Thess. 5:13

Lead a quiet and peaceable life in all godliness and honesty.
— 1 Tim. 2:2

Follow righteousness, faith, charity, peace, with them that call on the Lord out of a pure heart.
—2 Tim. 2:22

Follow peace with all men.
—Heb. 12:14

Let every man be swift to hear, slow to speak, slow to wrath.
—Jas. 1:19

The wisdom that is from above is first pure, then peaceable, gentle, and easy to be intreated.—Jas. 3:17

The fruit of righteousness is sown in peace of them that make peace. —Jas. 3:18

PEACE (SPIRITUAL)

Acquaint now thyself with him, and be at peace. —Job 22:21

I will both lay me down in peace, and sleep: for thou, Lord, only makest me dwell in safety.
—Psa. 4:8

Great peace have they which love thy law: and nothing shall offend them.   —PSA. 119:165

Thou wilt keep him in perfect peace, whose mind is stayed on thee.   —ISA. 26:3

The work of righteousness shall be peace; and the effect of righteousness quietness and assurance for ever.   —ISA. 32:17

O that thou hadst hearkened to my commandments! then had thy peace been as a river, and thy righteousness as the waves of the sea.   —ISA. 48:19

All thy children shall be taught of the Lord; and great shall be the peace of thy children. —ISA. 54:13

Peace, peace to him that is far off, and to him that is near, saith the Lord.   —ISA. 57:19

Peace I leave with you, my peace I give unto you: not as the world giveth, give I unto you. Let not your heart be troubled, neither let it be afraid.   —JOHN 14:27

Being justified by Faith, we have peace with God through our Lord Jesus Christ.   —ROM. 5:1

To be spiritually minded is life and peace.   —ROM. 8:6

The fruit of the Spirit is love, joy, peace.   —GAL. 5:22

The peace of God, which passeth all understanding, shall keep your hearts and minds through Christ Jesus.   —PHIL. 4:7

Let the peace of God rule in your heart.   —COL. 3:15

Now the Lord of peace himself give you peace always by all means.   —2 THESS. 3:16

Penalty, see RETRIBUTION

Penitence, see REMORSE, REPENTANCE, IMPENITENCE

Perception, see UNDERSTANDING

PERFECTION; see also IMPERFECTION

Be thou perfect.   —GEN. 17:1

Thou shalt be perfect with the Lord thy God.   —DEUT. 18:13

Let your heart therefore be perfect with the Lord our God, to walk in his statutes, and to keep his commandments.   —1 KIN. 8:61

Know thou the God of thy father, and serve him with a perfect heart and with a willing mind.   —1 CHRON. 28:9

It is God that girdeth me with strength, and maketh my way perfect.   —PSA. 18:32

I will behave myself wisely in a perfect way.   —PSA. 101:2

Blessed are the undefiled in the way, who walk in the law of the Lord.   —PSA. 119:1

The upright shall dwell in the land, and the perfect shall remain in it.   —PROV. 2:21

Be ye therefore perfect, even as your Father which is in heaven is perfect.   —MATT. 5:48

When that which is perfect is come, then that which is in part shall be done away. —1 COR. 13:10

Let us cleanse ourselves from all filthiness of the flesh and spirit, perfecting holiness in the fear of God.   —2 COR. 7:1

Be perfect, be of good comfort, be of one mind, live in peace; and the God of love and peace shall be with you.   —2 COR. 13:11

Till we all come in the unity of the faith, and of the knowledge of the Son of God, unto a perfect man, unto the measure of the stature of the fulness of Christ.   —Eph. 4:13

Be blameless and harmless, the sons of God, without rebuke, in the midst of a crooked and perverse nation, among whom ye shine as lights in the world.   —Phil. 2:15

Not as though I had already attained, either were already perfect: but I follow after, if that I may apprehend that for which also I am apprehended of Christ Jesus.
                    —Phil. 3:12

We preach, warning every man, and teaching every man in all wisdom; that we may present every man perfect in Christ Jesus.
                    —Col. 1:28

And above all these things put on charity, which is the bond of perfectness.   —Col. 3:14

Stand perfect and complete in all the will of God.   —Col. 4:12

Be perfect, thoroughly furnished unto all good works. —2 Tim. 3:17

Let us go on unto perfection.
                    —Heb. 6:1

By one offering he hath perfected for ever them that are sanctified.
                    —Heb. 10:14

Now the God of peace . . . Make you perfect in every good work to do his will, working in you that which is well pleasing in his sight.   —Heb. 13:20, 21

Let patience have her perfect work, that ye may be perfect and entire, wanting nothing.—Jas. 1:4

If any man offend not in word, the same is a perfect man, and able also to bridle the whole body.
                    —Jas. 3:2

Whoso keepeth his word, in him verily is the love of God perfected.
                    —1 John 2:5

Whosoever abideth in him sinneth not: whosoever sinneth hath not seen him, neither known him.
                    —1 John 3:6

Whosoever is born of God doth not commit sin.   —1 John 3:9

If we love one another, God dwelleth in us, and his love is perfected in us.   —1 John 4:12

Performance,   see   Accomplishment

PERSECUTION

The wicked bend their bow, they make ready their arrow upon the string, that they may privily shoot at the upright in heart.—Psa. 11:2

The wicked watcheth the righteous, and seeketh to slay him.
                    —Psa. 37:32

For thy sake are we killed all the day long; we are counted as sheep for the slaughter.   —Psa. 44:22

The bloodthirsty hate the upright.
                    —Prov. 29:10

He that is upright in the way is abomination to the wicked.
                    —Prov. 29:27

I, even I, am he that comforteth you: who art thou, that thou shouldest be afraid of a man that shall die, and of the son of man which shall be made as grass.
                    —Isa. 51:12

He that departeth from evil maketh himself a prey.—Isa. 59:15

They hate him that rebuketh in the gate, and they abhor him that speaketh uprightly.   —Amos 5:10

The wicked devoureth the man that is more righteous than he.
—Hab. 1:13

Blessed are they which are persecuted for righteousness' sake: for theirs is the kingdom of heaven. Blessed are ye, when men shall revile you, and persecute you, and shall say all manner of evil against you falsely, for my sake. Rejoice, and be exceeding glad: for great is your reward in heaven: for so persecuted they the prophets which were before you. —Matt. 5:10–12

Love your enemies, bless them that curse you, do good to them that hate you, and pray for them which despitefully use you, and persecute you.   —Matt. 5:44

I send you forth as sheep in the midst of wolves: be ye therefore wise as serpents, and harmless as doves.   —Matt. 10:16

Ye shall be hated of all men for my name's sake: but he that endureth to the end shall be saved.
—Matt. 10:22

Fear not them which kill the body, but are not able to kill the soul.   —Matt. 10:28

Then shall they deliver you up to be afflicted, and shall kill you: and ye shall be hated of all nations for my name's sake.   —Matt. 24:9

Whosoever will save his life shall lose it; but whosoever shall lose his life for my sake and the gospel's, the same shall save it. —Mark 8:35

If the world hate you, ye know that it hated me before it hated you.   —John 15:18

If ye were of the world, the world would love his own: but because ye are not of the world, but I have chosen you out of the world, therefore the world hateth you.
—John 15:19

Being reviled, we bless; being persecuted, we suffer it. —1 Cor. 4:12

Though I give my body to be burned, and have not charity, it profiteth me nothing.—1 Cor. 13:3

We are troubled on every side, yet not distressed; we are perplexed, but not in despair; Persecuted, but not forsaken; cast down, but not destroyed.   —2 Cor. 4:8, 9

I take pleasure in infirmities, in reproaches, in necessities, in persecutions, in distresses for Christ's sake: for when I am weak, then am I strong.   —2 Cor. 12:10

Unto you it is given in the behalf of Christ, not only to believe on him, but also to suffer for his sake.
—Phil. 1:29

If we suffer, we shall also reign with him: if we deny him, he also will deny us.   —2 Tim. 2:12

Take, my brethren, the prophets, who have spoken in the name of the Lord, for an example of suffering affliction, and of patience.
—Jas. 5:10

If ye suffer for righteousness' sake, happy are ye: and be not afraid of their terror, neither be troubled.   —1 Pet. 3:14

It is better, if the will of God be so, that ye suffer for well doing, than for evil doing. —1 Pet. 3:17

Rejoice, inasmuch as ye are partakers of Christ's sufferings; that, when his glory shall be revealed, ye may be glad also with exceeding joy. —1 PET. 4:13

If ye be reproached for the name of Christ, happy are ye; for the spirit of glory and of God resteth upon you. —1 PET. 4:14

If any man suffer as a Christian, let him not be ashamed; but let him glorify God on this behalf.
—1 PET. 4:16

Perseverance, see CONSTANCY, FAITHFULNESS, PATIENCE, RESOLUTION

PERSUASION

By long forbearing is a prince persuaded. —PROV. 25:15

If they hear not Moses and the prophets, neither will they be persuaded, though one rose from the dead. —LUKE 16:31

Almost thou persuadest me to be a Christian. —ACTS 26:28

Let every man be fully persuaded in his own mind. —ROM. 14:5

I . . . am persuaded that he is able to keep that which I have committed unto him against that day.
—2 TIM. 1:12

PESSIMISM; see also DESPAIR

My soul is weary of my life.
—JOB 10:1

Men see not the bright light which is in the clouds.—JOB 37:21

Clouds and darkness are round about him. —PSA. 97:2

All is vanity. —ECCL. 1:2

What profit hath a man of all his labour which he taketh under the sun? —ECCL. 1:3

I have seen all the works that are done under the sun: and, behold, all is vanity and vexation of spirit.
—ECCL. 1:14

In much wisdom is much grief; and he that increaseth knowledge increaseth sorrow. —ECCL. 1:18

I looked on all the works that my hands had wrought, and on the labour that I had laboured to do: and, behold, all was vanity and vexation of spirit, and there was no profit under the sun. —ECCL. 2:11

What hath man of all his labour, and of the vexation of his heart, wherein he hath laboured under the sun? —ECCL. 2:22

I perceive that there is nothing better, than that a man should rejoice in his own works: for that is his portion: for who shall bring him to see what shall be after him?
—ECCL. 3:22

For whom do I labour, and bereave my soul of good?—ECCL. 4:8

What profit hath he that hath laboured for the wind?
—ECCL. 5:16

It is better to go to the house of mourning, than to the house of feasting. —ECCL. 7:2

Sorrow is better than laughter.
—ECCL. 7:3

There is not a just man upon earth, that doeth good, and sinneth not. —ECCL. 7:20

The Lord hath forsaken the earth, and the Lord seeth not.
—EZEK. 9:9

Philanthropy, see CHARITY, GIVING, HELP, SERVICE

PIETY; see also RIGHTEOUSNESS

Know that the Lord hath set apart him that is godly for himself. —PSA. 4:3

Blessed is the man that feareth the Lord, that delighteth greatly in his commandments. —PSA. 112:1

Blessed are the undefiled in the way, who walk in the law of the Lord. —PSA. 119:1

The fruit of the Spirit is love, joy, peace, longsuffering, gentleness, goodness, faith, Meekness, temperance. —GAL. 5:22, 23

If we live in the Spirit, let us also walk in the Spirit. —GAL. 5:25

Lead a quiet and peaceable life in all godliness and honesty. —1 TIM. 2:2

Great is the mystery of godliness. —1 TIM. 3:16

Exercise thyself . . . unto godliness. —1 TIM. 4:7

Godliness is profitable unto all things, having promsie of the life that now is, and of that which is to come. —1 TIM. 4:8

Learn first to shew piety at home. —1 TIM. 5:4

Godliness with contentment is great gain. —1 TIM. 6:6

Follow after righteousness, godliness, faith, love, patience, meekness. —1 TIM. 6:11

Live soberly, righteously, and godly, in this present world. —TIT. 2:12

Let us have grace, whereby we may serve God acceptably with reverence and godly fear. —HEB. 12:28

If any man among you seem to be religious, and bridleth not his tongue, but deceiveth his own heart, this man's religion is vain. —JAS. 1:26

Blessed are they that keep his testimonies, and that seek him with the whole heart. —PSA. 119:2

Blessed is every one that feareth the Lord; that walketh in his ways. —PSA. 128:1

Forget not my law; but let thine heart keep my commandments. —PROV. 3:1

Fear God, and keep his commandments: for this is the whole duty of man. —ECCL. 12:13

What doth the Lord require of thee, but to do justly, and to love mercy, and to walk humbly with thy God? —MIC. 6:8

Blessed are they which do hunger and thirst after righteousness; for they shall be filled. —MATT. 5:6

Not every one that saith unto me Lord, Lord, shall enter into the kingdom of heaven; but he that doeth the will of my Father which is in heaven. —MATT. 7:21

To love him with all the heart, and with all the understanding, and with all the soul, and with all the strength, and to love his neighbour as himself, is more than all whole burnt offerings and sacrifices. —MARK 12:33

They that are after the flesh do mind the things of the flesh; but they that are after the Spirit the things of the Spirit. —ROM. 8:5

To be spiritually minded is life and peace. —ROM. 8:6

As many as are led by the Spirit of God, they are the sons of God.
—ROM. 8:14

Pure religion and undefiled before God the Father is this, To visit the fatherless and widows in their affliction, and to keep himself unspotted from the world.
—JAS. 1:27

What doth it profit, my brethren, though a man say he hath faith, and have not works? can faith save him?
—JAS. 2:14

Add to your faith virtue; and to virtue knowledge; And to knowledge temperance; and to temperance patience; and to patience godliness; And to godliness brotherly kindness; and to brotherly kindness charity.
—2 PET. 1:5-7

This is the love of God, that we keep his commandments.
—1 JOHN 5:3

Pity, see MERCY

PLEASURE; see also CONTENTMENT, CHEERFULNESS, JOY, REJOICING

In thy presence is fulness of joy; at thy right hand there are pleasures for evermore.
—PSA. 16:11

Let them praise his name in the dance.
—PSA. 149:3

Praise him with the timbrel and dance.
—PSA. 150:4

Stolen waters are sweet, and bread eaten in secret is pleasant.
—PROV. 9:17

He that is of a merry heart hath a continual feast.
—PROV. 15:15

He that loveth pleasure shall be a poor man: he that loveth wine and oil shall not be rich. —PROV. 21:17

I said in mine heart, Go to now, I will prove thee with mirth, therefore enjoy pleasure: and, behold, this also is vanity.
—ECCL. 2:1

A time to weep, and a time to laugh; a time to mourn, and a time to dance.
—ECCL. 3:4

Every man should eat and drink, and enjoy the good of all his labour, it is the gift of God. —ECCL. 3:13

The heart of fools is in the house of mirth.
—ECCL. 7:4

A man hath no better thing under the sun, than to eat, and to drink, and to be merry.
—ECCL. 8:15

A feast is made for laughter, and wine maketh merry. —ECCL. 10:19

Let us eat and drink; for to morrow we shall die.
—ISA. 22:13

That which fell among thorns are they, which, when they have heard, go forth, and are choked with cares and riches and pleasures of this life, and bring no fruit to perfection.
—LUKE 8:14

Take thine ease, eat, drink, and be merry.
—LUKE 12:19

It was meet that we should make merry, and be glad. —LUKE 15:32

The works of the flesh are manifest, which are these . . . drunkenness, revellings, and such like.
—GAL. 5:19, 21

She that liveth in pleasure is dead while she liveth.
—1 TIM. 5:6

Lovers of pleasures more than of God.
—2 TIM. 3:4

Is any merry? let him sing psalms.
—JAS. 5:13

Pledge, see Vow

PLENTY

In thy presence is fullness of joy.
—Psa. 16:11

The Lord . . . plentifully rewardeth the proud doer.
—Psa. 31:23

Thou, Lord, art . . . plenteous in mercy. —Psa. 86:5

With him is plenteous redemption. —Psa. 130:7

Honour the Lord with thy substance . . . So shall thy barns be filled with plenty. —Prov. 3: 9, 10

The thoughts of the diligent tend only to plenteousness. —Prov. 21:5

He that tilleth his land shall have plenty of bread. —Prov. 28:19

A faithful man shall abound with blessings. —Prov. 28:20

The earth shall be full of the knowledge of the Lord, as the waters cover the sea. —Isa. 11:9

Joy and gladness is taken from the plentiful field. —Jer. 48:33

Sufficient unto the day is the evil thereof. —Matt. 6:34

The harvest truly is plenteous, but the labourers are few.
—Matt. 9:37

Whosoever hath, to him it shall be given, and he shall have more abundance. —Matt. 13:12

Give and it shall be given unto you; good measure, pressed down, and shaken together, and running over. —Luke 6:38

I am come that they may have life, and that they might have it more abundantly. —John 10:10

God is able to make all grace abound toward you. —2 Cor. 9:8

My God shall supply all your need according to his riches in glory by Christ Jesus. —Phil. 4:19

POSSESSION; see also Avarice, Wealth

All things come of thee, and of thine own have we given thee.
—1 Chron. 29:14

The upright shall have good things in possession. —Prov. 28:10

When goods increase, they are increased that eat them; and what good is there to the owners thereof, saving the beholding of them with their eyes? —Eccl. 5:11

He that putteth his trust in me shall possess the land, and shall inherit my holy mountain.
—Isa. 57:13

The silver is mine, and the gold is mine, saith the Lord of hosts.
—Hag. 2:8

Where your treasure is, there will your heart be also. —Matt. 6:21

What is a man profited, if he shall gain the whole world, and lose his own soul? —Matt. 16:26

Whosoever hath, to him shall be given. —Luke 8:18

A man's life consisteth not in the abundance of the things which he possesseth. —Luke 12:15

Soul, thou hast much goods laid up for many years; take thine ease, eat, drink, and be merry.
—Luke 12:19

All things are yours; Whether . . . the world, or life, or death, or things present, or things to come; all are yours; And ye are Christ's; and Christ is God's.
—1 Cor. 3:21–23

Though I bestow all my goods to feed the poor, and though I give my body to be burned, and have not charity, it profiteth me nothing. —1 COR. 13:3

As poor, yet making many rich; as having nothing, yet possessing all things. —2 COR. 6:10

Set your affection on things above, not on things on the earth. —COL. 3:2

Ye have in heaven a better and an enduring substance. —HEB. 10:34

POVERTY

If thy brother be waxen poor, and fallen in decay with thee; then shalt thou relieve him. —LEV. 25:35

He delivereth the poor in his affliction, and openeth their ears in oppression. —JOB 36:6

The needy shall not always be forgotten: the expectation of the poor shall not perish for ever. —PSA. 9:18

A little that a righteous man hath is better than the riches of many wicked. —PSA. 37:16

Defend the poor and fatherless: do justice to the afflicted and needy. —PSA. 82:3

The rich man's wealth is his strong city: the destruction of the poor is their poverty.—PROV. 10:15

There is that maketh himself rich, yet hath nothing: there is that maketh himself poor, yet hath great riches. —PROV. 13:7

The ransom of a man's life are his riches: but the poor heareth not rebuke. —PROV. 13:8

The poor is hated even of his own neighbour: but the rich hath many friends. —PROV. 14:20

He that hath mercy on the poor, happy is he. —PROV. 14:21

He that oppresseth the poor reproacheth his Maker: but he that honoureth him hath mercy on the poor. —PROV. 14:31

Better is a little with the fear of the Lord, than great treasure and trouble therewith. —PROV. 15:16

Better is a little with righteousness than great revenues without right. —PROV. 16:18

The poor useth intreaties; but the rich answereth roughly. —PROV. 18:23

Better is the poor that walketh in his integrity, than he that is perverse in his lips, and is a fool. —PROV. 19:1

Wealth maketh many friends; but the poor is separated from his neighbour. —PROV. 19:4

He that hath pity upon the poor lendeth unto the Lord; and that which he hath given will he pay him again. —PROV. 19:17

A poor man is better than a liar. —PROV. 19:22

Love not sleep, lest thou come to poverty; open thine eyes, and thou shalt be satisfied with bread. —PROV. 20:13

Who stoppeth his ears at the cry of the poor, he also shall cry himself, but shall not be heard. —PROV. 21:13

The rich and poor meet together: the Lord is the maker of them all. —PROV. 22:2

The rich ruleth over the poor, and the borrower is servant to the lender.   —Prov. 22:7

Rob not the poor, because he is poor.   —Prov. 22:22

The drunkard and the glutton shall come to poverty: and drowsiness shall clothe a man with rags.
                    —Prov. 23:21

A poor man that oppresseth the poor is like a sweeping rain which leaveth no food.   —Prov. 28:3

Better is the poor that walketh in his uprightness, than he that is perverse in his ways, though he be rich.   —Prov. 28:6

The rich man is wise in his own conceit; but the poor that hath understanding searcheth him out.
                    —Prov. 28:11

He that tilleth his land shall have plenty of bread: but he that followeth after vain persons shall have poverty enough.
                    —Prov. 28:19

Give me neither poverty nor riches; feed me with food convenient for me: Or lest I be poor, and steal, and take the name of my God in vain.   —Prov. 30:8, 9

Better is an handful with quietness, than both the hands full with travail and vexation of spirit.
                    —Eccl. 4:6

Better is a poor and a wise child than an old and foolish king, who will no more be admonished.
                    —Eccl. 4:13

Wisdom is better than strength: nevertheless the poor man's wisdom is despised, and his words are not heard.   —Eccl. 9:16

We may buy the poor for silver, and the needy for a pair of shoes.
                    —Amos 8:4

Ye have the poor always with you; but me ye have not always.
                    —Matt. 26:11

We should remember the poor.
                    —Gal. 2:10

Power, see Strength, Ability, Omnipotence

PRAISE; see also Thanksgiving, Flattery

I will call on the Lord, who is worthy to be praised.—2 Sam. 22:4

Praise the Lord.
                    —1 Chron. 23:30

Magnify his work, which men behold.   —Job 36:24

I will praise the Lord according to his righteousness: and will sing praise to the name of the Lord most high.   —Psa. 7:17

I will declare thy name unto my brethren: in the midst of the congregation will I praise thee.
                    —Psa. 22:22

Sing unto the Lord, O ye saints of his, and give thanks at the remembrance of his holiness.
                    —Psa. 30:4

Praise the Lord with harp: sing unto him with the psaltery and an instrument of ten strings. Sing unto him a new song: play skilfully with a loud noise.   —Psa. 33:2, 3

I will bless the Lord at all times: his praise shall continually be in my mouth.   —Psa. 34:1

O magnify the Lord with me, and let us exalt his name together.
                    —Psa. 34:3

I will give thee thanks in the great congregation: I will praise thee among much people.—PSA. 35:18

My tongue shall speak of thy righteousness and of thy praise all the day long.			—PSA. 35:28

Sing praises to God, sing praises: sing praises unto our King, sing praises.			—PSA. 47:6

Great is the Lord, and greatly to be praised.			—PSA. 48:1

I will praise thee, O Lord, among the people: I will sing unto thee among the nations.			—PSA. 57:9

Because thy lovingkindness is better than life, my lips shall praise thee.			—PSA. 63:3

My soul shall be satisfied as with marrow and fatness; and my mouth shall praise thee with joyful lips.			—PSA. 63:5

O bless our God, ye people, and make the voice of his praise to be heard.			—PSA. 66:8

Let the people praise thee, O God; let all the people praise thee.			—PSA. 67:3

Sing unto God, ye kingdoms of the earth: O sing praises unto the Lord.			—PSA. 68:32

I will praise the name of God with a song, and will magnify him with thanksgiving.			—PSA. 69:30

Let the heaven and earth praise him, the seas, and every thing that moveth therein.			—PSA. 69:34

Let my mouth be filled with thy praise and with thy honour all the day.			—PSA. 71:8

Sing aloud unto God our strength: make a joyful noise unto the God of Jacob.			—PSA. 81:1

I will praise thee, O Lord my God, with all my heart: and I will glorify thy name for evermore.
			—PSA. 86:12

It is a good thing to give thanks unto the Lord, and to sing praises unto thy name, O most High.
			—PSA. 92:1

The Lord is great, and greatly to be praised.			—PSA. 96:4

Praise ye the Lord. O give thanks unto the Lord; for he is good: for his mercy endureth for ever.
			—PSA. 106:1

Oh that men would praise the Lord for his goodness, and for his wonderful works to the children of men!			—PSA. 107:8

O praise the Lord, all ye nations: praise him, all ye people.
			—PSA. 117:1

I will praise thee with uprightness of heart, when I shall have learned thy righteous judgments.
			—PSA. 119:7

I will extol thee, my God, O King; and I will bless thy name for ever and ever.			—PSA. 145:1

My mouth shall speak the praise of the Lord: and let all my flesh bless his holy name for ever and ever.			—PSA. 145:21

While I live will I praise the Lord: I will sing praises unto my God while I have any being.
			—PSA. 146:2

It is good to sing praises unto our God; for it is pleasant; and praise is comely.			—PSA. 147:1

Praise the Lord, call upon his name, declare his doings among all the people, make mention that his name is exalted.			—ISA. 12:4

I will declare thy name unto my brethren, in the midst of the church will I sing praise unto thee.
—HEB. 2:12

Let us offer the sacrifice of praise to God continually. —HEB. 13:15

PRAYER; see also WORSHIP, PRAISE, THANKSGIVING

If my people . . . shall humble themselves, and pray, and seek my face, and turn from their wicked ways; then will I hear from heaven, and will forgive their sin, and will heal their land. —2 CHRON. 7:14

Thou shalt make thy prayer unto him, and he shall hear thee.
—JOB 22:27

The eyes of the Lord are upon the righteous, and his ears are open unto their cry. —PSA. 34:15

As for me, I will call upon God; and the Lord shall save me.
—PSA. 55:16

Evening, and morning, and at noon, will I pray, and cry aloud: and he shall hear my voice.
—PSA. 55:17

Thou, Lord, art good, and ready to forgive; and plenteous in mercy unto all them that call upon thee.
—PSA. 86:5

Give ear, O Lord, unto my prayer; and attend to the voice of my supplications. —PSA. 86:6

In the day of my trouble I will call upon thee: for thou wilt answer me. —PSA. 86:7

He will regard the prayer of the destitute, and not despise their prayer. —PSA. 102:17

The Lord is nigh unto all them that call upon him, to all that call upon him in truth. —PSA. 145:18

The sacrifice of the wicked is an abomination to the Lord: but the prayer of the upright is his delight.
—PROV. 15:8

The Lord is far from the wicked: but he heareth the prayer of the righteous. —PROV. 15:29

Seek ye the Lord while he may be found, call ye upon him while he is near. —ISA. 55:6

Ye call upon me, and ye shall go and pray unto me, and I will hearken unto you. —JER. 29:12

Call unto me, and I will answer thee, and shew thee great and mighty things, which thou knowest not. —JER. 33:3

Let us lift up our heart with our hands unto God in the heavens.
—LAM. 3:41

Whosoever shall call on the name of the Lord shall be delivered.
—JOEL 2:32

When thou prayest, thou shalt not be as the hypocrites are: for they love to pray standing in the synagogues and in the corners of the streets, that they may be seen of men. —MATT. 6:5

When thou prayest, enter into thy closet, and when thou hast shut thy door, pray to thy Father which is in secret; and thy Father which seeth in secret shall reward thee openly. —MATT. 6:6

When ye pray, use not vain repetitions, as the heathen do: for they think that they shall be heard for their much speaking. —MATT. 6:7

Your Father knoweth what things ye have need of, before ye ask him.
—MATT. 6:8

Our Father which art in heaven, Hallowed be thy name. Thy kingdom come. Thy will be done in earth, as it is in heaven. Give us this day our daily bread. And forgive us our debts, as we forgive our debtors. And lead us not into temptation, but deliver us from evil: For thine is the kingdom, and the power, and the glory, for ever. —MATT. 6:9–13

Ask, and it shall be given you; seek, and ye shall find; knock, and it shall be opened unto you.
—MATT. 7:7

If two of you shall agree on earth as touching any thing that they shall ask, it shall be done for them of my Father which is in heaven.
—MATT. 18:19

All things, whatsoever ye shall ask in prayer, believing, ye shall receive. —MATT. 21:22

When ye stand praying, forgive, if ye have ought against any: that your Father also which is in heaven may forgive your your trespasses.
—MARK 11:25

Men ought always to pray, and not to faint. —LUKE 18:1

If any man be a worshipper of God, and doeth his will, him he heareth. —JOHN 9:31

If ye abide in me, and my words abide in you, ye shall ask what ye will, and it shall be done unto you.
—JOHN 15:7

Whatsoever ye shall ask the Father in my name, he will give it you. —JOHN 16:23

Ask, and ye shall receive, that your joy may be full.—JOHN 16:24

The same Lord over all is rich unto all that call upon him.
—ROM. 10:12

I will pray with the spirit, and I will pray with the understanding also. —1 COR. 14:15

In every thing by prayer and supplication with thanksgiving let your requests be made known unto God. —PHIL. 4:6

Continue in prayer, and watch in the same with thanksgiving.
—COL. 4:2

Pray without ceasing.
—1 THESS. 5:17

I exhort therefore, that, first of all, supplications, prayers, intercessions, and giving of thanks, be made for all men. —1 TIM. 2:1

Let us therefore come boldly unto the throne of grace, that we may obtain mercy, and find grace to help in time of need.—HEB. 4:16

Let us draw near with a true heart in full assurance of faith, having our hearts sprinkled from an evil conscience. —HEB. 10:22

He that cometh to God must believe that he is, and that he is a rewarder of them that diligently seek him. —HEB. 11:6

Ask in faith, nothing wavering.
—JAS. 1:6

Pray one for another.—JAS. 5:16

The effectual fervent prayer of a righteous man availeth much.
—JAS. 5:16

Whatsoever we ask, we receive of him, because we keep his commandments, and do those things that are pleasing in his sight. —1 JOHN 3:22

This is the confidence that we have in him, that, if we ask any thing according to his will, he heareth us. —1 JOHN 5:14

Preacher, see MINISTRY

Precept, see LAW, SCRIPTURE

Prejudice, see BIGOTRY, TOLERANCE

PREPARATION

Prepare your hearts unto the Lord, and serve him only.

—1 SAM. 7:3

Set thine house in order.

—2 KIN. 20:1

Go to the ant, thou sluggard; consider her ways, and be wise: Which having no guide, overseer, or ruler, Provideth her meat in summer, and gathereth her food in the harvest.

—PROV. 6:6–8

He that gathereth in summer is a wise son. —PROV. 10:5

The preparations of the heart in man, and the answer of the tongue, is from the Lord. —PROV. 16:1

Prepare thy work without, and make it fit for thyself in the field; and afterwards build thine house.

—PROV. 24:27

He that tilleth his land shall have plenty of bread. —PROV. 28:19

The ants are a people not strong, yet they prepare their meat in summer. —PROV. 30:25

He that regardeth the clouds shall not reap. —ECCL. 11:4

Prepare ye the way of the Lord, make straight in the desert a highway for our God. —ISA. 40:3

Prepare ye the way of the people. ، —ISA. 62:10

Prepare to meet thy God.

—AMOS 4:12

Be ye also ready: for in such an hour as ye think not the Son of man cometh. —MATT. 24:44

Provide yourselves bags which wax not old, a treasure in the heavens that faileth not, where no thief approacheth, neither moth corrupteth. —LUKE 12:33

Let your loins be girded about, and your lights burning.

—LUKE 12:35

Which of you, intending to build a tower, sitteth not down first, and counteth the cost, whether he have sufficient to finish it? —LUKE 14:28

What king, going to make war against another king, sitteth not down first, and consulteth whether he be able with ten thousand to meet him that cometh against him with twenty thousand?

—LUKE 14:31

If a man therefore purge himself . . . he shall be a vessel unto honour, sanctified, and meet for the master's use, and prepared unto every good work. —2 TIM. 2:21

Be ready to every good work.

—TIT. 3:1

PRESERVATION; see also SALVATION, PROTECTION

Thou, even thou, art Lord alone; thou hast made heaven, the heaven of heavens, with all their host, the earth, and all things that are therein, the seas, and all that is therein, and thou preservest them all.

—NEH. 9:6

Thou hast granted me life and favour, and thy visitation hath preserved my spirit. —JOB 10:12

Let integrity and uprightness preserve me; for I wait on thee.

—PSA. 25:21

The Lord preserveth the faithful, and plentifully rewardeth the proud doer. —Psa. 31:23

O Lord, thou preservest man and beast. —Psa. 36:6

The Lord loveth judgment, and forsaketh not his saints; they are preserved for ever. —Psa. 37:28

He shall give his angels charge over thee, to keep thee in all his ways. —Psa. 91:11

He preserveth the souls of his saints. —Psa. 97:10

The Lord preserveth the simple. —Psa. 116:6

He will not suffer thy foot to be moved: he that keepeth thee will not slumber. —Psa. 121:3

The Lord shall preserve thee from all evil: he shall preserve thy soul. —Psa. 121:7

The Lord shall preserve thy going out and thy coming in from this time forth, and even for evermore. —Psa. 121:8

They that rest in the Lord shall be as mount Zion, which cannot be removed, but abideth for ever. —Psa. 125:1

The Lord preserveth all them that love him. —Psa. 145:20

He keepeth the paths of judgment, and preserveth the way of his saints. —Prov. 2:8

The root of the righteous shall not be moved. —Prov. 12:3

The eyes of the Lord preserve knowledge, and he overthroweth the words of the transgressor. —Prov. 22:12

A just man falleth seven times, and riseth up again. —Prov. 24:16

Whosoever shall lose his life shall preserve it. —Luke 17:33

There shall not an hair of your head perish. —Luke 21:18

Pretense, see Hypocrisy, Deceit, Pride

PRIDE; see also Conceit, Boasting, Scorn, Humility, Meekness

Talk no more so exceeding proudly; let not arrogancy come out of your mouth: for the Lord is a God of knowledge, and by him actions are weighed. —1 Sam. 2:3

Let not him that girdeth on his harness boast himself as he that putteth it off. —1 Kin. 20:11

The Lord preserveth the faithful, and plentifully rewardeth the proud doer. —Psa. 31:23

My soul shall make her boast in the Lord. —Psa. 34:2

Him that hath an high look and a proud heart will not I suffer. —Psa. 101:5

Though the Lord be high, yet hath he respect unto the lowly: but the proud he knoweth afar off. —Psa. 138:6

Surely he scorneth the scorners; but he giveth grace unto the lowly. —Prov. 3:34

When pride cometh, then cometh shame: but with the lowly is wisdom. —Prov. 11:2

He that is void of wisdom despiseth his neighbour. —Prov. 11:12

Only by pride cometh contention. —Prov. 13:10

He that despiseth his neighbour sinneth. —Prov. 14:21

A fool despiseth his father's instruction. —Prov. 15:5

He that refuseth instruction despiseth his own soul. —Prov. 15:32

Every one that is proud in heart is an abomination to the Lord.
—Prov. 16:5

Pride goeth before destruction, and an haughty spirit before a fall.
—Prov. 16:18

Better it is to be of an humble spirit with the lowly, than to divide the spoil with the proud.
—Prov. 16:19

Before destruction the heart of man is haughty, and before honour is humility. —Prov. 18:12

An high look, and a proud heart . . . is sin. —Prov. 21:4

For men to search their own glory is not glory. —Prov. 25:27

He that is of a proud heart stirreth up strife. —Prov. 28:25

A man's pride shall bring him low: but honour shall uphold the humble in spirit. —Prov. 29:23

Shall the ax boast itself against him that heweth therewith? or shall the saw magnify itself against him that shaketh it? as if the rod should shake itself against them that lift it up, or as if the staff should lift up itself, as if it were no wood.
—Isa. 10:15

Let not the wise man glory in his wisdom, neither let the mighty man glory in his might, let not the rich man glory in his riches: But let him that glorieth glory in this, that he understandeth and knoweth me, that I am the Lord which exercise lovingkindness, judgment, and righteousness, in the earth: for in these things I delight, saith the Lord.
—Jer. 9:23, 24

Though thou exalt thyself as the eagle, and though thou set thy nest among the stars, thence will I bring thee down, saith the Lord.
—Obad. 1:4

Whosoever will be great among you, let him be your minister; And whosoever will be chief among you, let him be your servant.
—Matt. 20:26, 27

Whosoever shall exalt himself shall be abased; and he that shall humble himself shall be exalted.
—Matt. 23:12

If any man desire to be first, the same shall be last of all.
—Mark 9:35

He hath put down the mighty from their seats, and exalted them of low degree. —Luke 1:52

He that is greatest among you, let him be as the younger; and he that is chief, as he that doth serve.
—Luke 22:26

I say, through the grace given unto me, to every man that is among you, not to think of himself more highly than he ought to think; but to think soberly, according as God hath dealt to every man the measure of faith.
—Rom. 12:3

Mind not high things, but condescend to men of low estate. Be not wise in your own conceits.
—Rom. 12:16

Who maketh thee to differ from another? and what hast thou that thou didst not receive? now if thou didst receive it, why dost thou glory, as if thou hadst not received it?
—1 COR. 4:7

Knowledge puffeth up, but charity edifieth. —1 COR. 8:1

If any man think that he knoweth any thing, he knoweth nothing yet as he ought to know. —1 COR. 8:2

Let him that thinketh he standeth take heed lest he fall.
—1 COR. 10:12

Charity vaunteth not itself, is not puffed up. —1 COR. 13:4

If a man think himself to be something, when he is nothing, he deceiveth himself. —GAL. 6:3

Let us not be desirous of vain glory. —GAL. 5:26

God forbid that I should glory, save in the cross of our Lord Jesus Christ. —GAL. 6:14

Let nothing be done through strife or vainglory; but in lowliness of mind let each esteem other better than themselves. —PHIL. 2:3

God resisteth the proud, but giveth grace unto the humble.
—JAS. 4:6

Priest, see MINISTRY

Probity, see INTEGRITY, VERACITY, SINCERITY, RIGHTEOUSNESS, GOODNESS, JUSTICE, FAITHFULNESS

Profanity, see IRREVERENCE

Profession, see CALLING, MINISTRY

Promiscuity, see LICENTIOUSNESS

Promise, see VOW

PROOF

I have learned by experience that the Lord hath blessed me.
—GEN. 30:27

How long will this people provoke me? and how long will it be ere they believe me, for all the signs which I have shewed among them? —NUM. 14:11

Doth not the ear try words? and the mouth taste his meat?
—JOB 12:11

How great are his signs! and how mighty are his wonders!
—DAN. 4:3

By their fruits ye shall know them. —MATT. 7:20

If thou be the Son of God, come down from the cross.
—MATT. 27:40

Neither will they be persuaded, though one rose from the dead.
—LUKE 16:31

We speak that we do know, and testify that we have seen.
—JOHN 3:11

Ye are witnesses of these things.
—JOHN 4:44

Except ye see signs and wonders, ye will not believe. —JOHN 4:48

These men, when they had seen the miracle that Jesus did, said, This is of a truth that prophet that should come into the world.
—JOHN 6:14

If any man will do his will, he shall know of the doctrine, whether it be of God. —JOHN 7:17

One thing I know, that, whereas I was blind, now I see.—JOHN 9:25

Except I shall see in his hands the print of the nails, and put my finger into the print of the nails, and thrust my hand into his side, I will not believe. —JOHN 20:25

Because thou hast seen me, thou hast believed: blessed are they that have not seen, and yet have believed. —JOHN 20:29

Prove what is the good, and acceptable, and perfect, will of God. —ROM. 12:2

The Jews require a sign, and the Greeks seek after wisdom. —1 COR. 1:22

The things of the Spirit of God . . . are spiritually discerned. —1 COR. 2:14

We walk by faith, not by sight. —2 COR. 5:7

Shew ye . . . the proof of your love. —2 COR. 8:24

Let every man prove his own work. —GAL. 6:4

Walk as children of light . . . Proving what is acceptable unto the Lord. —EPH. 5:8, 10

Prove all things; hold fast that which is good. —1 THESS. 5:21

Make full proof of thy ministry. —2 TIM. 4:5

Your fathers tempted me, proved me, and saw my works. —HEB. 3:9

Faith is the substance of things hoped for, the evidence of things not seen. —HEB. 11:1

That which we have seen and heard declare we unto you. —1 JOHN 1:3

Hereby we know that he abideth in us, by the Spirit which he hath given us. —1 JOHN 3:24

Propitiation, see RECONCILIATION, REDEMPTION

PROTECTION; see also PRESERVATION

The eternal God is thy refuge. —DEUT. 33:27

With me thou shalt be in safeguard. —1 SAM. 22:23

He is my shield, and the horn of my salvation, my high tower, and my refuge. —2 SAM. 22:3

The eyes of the Lord run to and fro throughout the whole earth, to shew himself strong in behalf of them whose heart is perfect toward him. —2 CHRON. 16:9

Thou, O Lord, art a shield for me; my glory and the lifter of mine head. —PSA. 3:3

Thou, Lord, only makest me dwell in safety. —PSA. 4:8

Let all those that put their trust in thee rejoice: let them ever shout for joy, because thou defendest them. —PSA. 5:11

The Lord . . . will be a refuge for the oppressed, a refuge in time of trouble. —PSA. 9:9

Be thou my strong rock, for an house of defence to save me. —PSA. 31:2

Our soul waiteth for the Lord: he is our help and our shield. —PSA. 33:20

God is our refuge and strength, a very present help in trouble. —PSA. 46:1

Thou hast been a shelter for me, and a strong tower from the enemy. —PSA. 61:3

He is my defence; I shall not be greatly moved. —PSA. 62:2

He shall cover thee with his feathers, and under his wings shalt thou trust: his truth shall be thy shield and buckler. —PSA. 91:4

He shall give his angels charge over thee, to keep thee in all thy ways.   —PSA. 91:11

My God is the rock of my refuge.
—PSA. 94:22

The Lord is thy shade upon thy right hand.   —PSA. 121:5

As the mountains are round about Jerusalem, so the Lord is round about his people.
—PSA. 125:2

He is a buckler to them that walk uprightly.   —PROV. 2:7

The name of the Lord is a strong tower.   —PROV. 18:10

The horse is prepared against the day of battle: but safety is of the Lord.   —PROV. 21:31

Whoso putteth his trust in the Lord shall be safe. —PROV. 29:25

He is a shield unto them that put their trust in him.   —PROV. 30:5

In the shadow of his hand hath he hid me, and made me a polished shaft; in his quiver hath he hid me.
—ISA. 49:2

He is on my right hand, that I should not be moved.—ACTS 2:25

The Lord is faithful, who shall stablish you, and keep you from evil.   —2 THESS. 3:3

The Lord is my helper, and I will not fear what man shall do unto me.
—HEB. 13:6

Who is he that will harm you, if ye be followers of that which is good?   —1 PET. 3:13

PROVIDENCE; see also GOD, PRESERVATION, PROTECTION

God will provide. —GEN. 22:8

Both riches and honour come of thee, and thou reignest over all; and in thine hand is power and might; and in thine hand it is to make great, and to give strength unto all.
—1 CHRON. 29:12

All things come of thee, and of thine own have we given thee.
—1 CHRON. 29:14

He increaseth the nations, and destroyeth them: he enlargeth the nations, and straiteneth them again.
—JOB 12:23

The Lord is my shepherd; I shall not want.   —PSA. 23:1

Oh how great is thy goodness, which thou hast laid up for them that fear thee.   —PSA. 31:19

O fear the Lord, ye his saints: for there is no want to them that fear him.   —PSA. 34:9

They that seek the Lord shall not want any good thing. —PSA. 34:10

Thou visitest the earth, and waterest it: thou greatly enrichest it with the river of God, which is full of water.   —PSA. 65:9

Thou, O God, hast prepared of thy goodness for the poor.
—PSA. 68:10

The Lord shall give that which is good; and our land shall yield her increase.   —PSA. 85:12

He watereth the hills from his chambers: the earth is satisfied with the fruit of thy works.
—PSA. 104:13

He satisfieth the longing soul, and filleth the hungry soul with goodness.   —PSA. 107:9

Oh that men would praise the Lord for his goodness, and for his wonderful works to the children of men! —Psa. 107:15

He hath given meat unto them that fear him: he will ever be mindful of his covenant.
—Psa. 111:5

The earth hath he given to the children of men. —Psa. 115:16

The eyes of all wait upon thee; and thou givest them their meat in due season. —Psa. 145:15

Thou openest thine hand, and satisfiest the desire of every living thing. —Psa. 145:16

He giveth to the beast his food, and to the young ravens which cry.
—Psa. 147:9

The lot is cast into thy lap; but the whole disposing thereof is of the Lord. —Prov. 16:33

The upright shall have good things in possession.—Prov. 28:10

I give waters in the wilderness, and rivers in the desert, to give drink to my people. —Isa. 43:20

He maketh his sun to rise on the evil and on the good, and sendeth rain on the just and on the unjust.
—Matt. 5:45

Behold the fowls of the air: for they sow not, neither do they reap, nor gather into barns; yet your heavenly Father feedeth them. Are ye not much better than they?
—Matt. 6:26

Take no thought of your life, what ye shall eat. —Luke 12:22

He . . . gave us rain from heaven, and fruitful seasons, filling our hearts with food and gladness.
—Acts 14:17

Eye hath not seen, nor ear heard, neither have entered into the heart of man, the things which God hath prepared for them that love him. —1 Cor. 2:9

God is able to make all grace abound toward you; that ye, always having all sufficiency in all things, may abound to every good work.
—2 Cor. 9:8

PRUDENCE; see also Wisdom, Counsel

Let us choose to us judgment: let us know among ourselves what is good. —Job 34:4

I will take heed to my ways, that I sin not with my tongue: I will keep my mouth with a bridle, while the wicked is before me.—Psa. 39:1

A good man . . . will guide his affairs with discretion.
—Psa. 112:5

When wisdom entereth into thine heart, and knowledge is pleasant unto thy soul; Discretion shall preserve thee, understanding shall keep thee. —Prov. 2:10, 11

Keep sound wisdom and discretion. —Prov. 3:21

My son, if thou be surety for thy friend, if thou hast stricken thy hand with a stranger, Thou are snared with the words of thy mouth, thou art taken with the words of thy mouth. —Prov. 6:1, 2

I wisdom dwell with prudence, and find out knowledge of witty inventions. —Prov. 8:12

A talebearer revealeth secrets: but he that is of a faithful spirit concealeth the matter.
—Prov. 11:13

A man shall be commended according to his wisdom.
—Prov. 12:8

A fool's wrath is presently known: but a prudent man covereth shame.   —Prov. 12:16

A prudent man concealeth knowledge: but the heart of fools proclaimeth foolishness.
—Prov. 12:23

He that keepeth his mouth keepeth his life: but he that openeth wide his lips shall have destruction.
—Prov. 13:3

Every prudent man dealeth with knowledge: but a fool layeth open his folly.   —Prov. 13:16

The wisdom of the prudent is to understand his way. —Prov. 14:8

The simple believeth every word: but the prudent man looketh well to his going.   —Prov. 14:15

A wise man feareth, and departeth from evil: but the fool rageth, and is confident.   —Prov. 14:16

The simple inherit folly: but the prudent are crowned with knowledge.   —Prov. 14:18

He that is slow to wrath is of great understanding: but he that is hasty of spirit exalteth folly.
—Prov. 14:29

He that regardeth reproof is prudent.   —Prov. 15:5

He that handleth a matter wisely shall find good.   —Prov. 16:20

The wise in heart shall be called prudent.   —Prov. 16:21

He that answereth a matter before he heareth it, it is folly and shame to him.   —Prov. 18:13

The heart of the prudent getteth knowledge; and the ear of the wise seeketh knowledge. —Prov. 18:15

He that hasteth with his feet sinneth.   —Prov. 19:2

The thoughts of the diligent tend only to plenteousness; but of every one that is hasty only to want.
—Prov. 21:5

There is treasure to be desired and oil in the dwelling of the wise; but a foolish man spendeth it up.
—Prov. 21:20

Whoso keepeth his mouth and his tongue keepeth his soul from troubles.   —Prov. 21:23

A prudent man foreseeth the evil, and hideth himself: but the simple pass on, and are punished.
—Prov. 22:3

Speak not in the ears of a fool: for he will despise the wisdom of thy words.   —Prov. 23:9

Prepare thy work without, and make it fit for thyself in the field; and afterwards build thine house.
—Prov. 24:27

Go not forth hastily to strive, lest you know not what to do in the end thereof.   —Prov. 25:8

Answer not a fool according to his folly, lest thou also be like unto him.   —Prov. 26:4

Answer a fool according to his folly, lest he be wise in his own conceit.   —Prov. 26:5

Scornful men bring a city into a snare: but wise men turn away wrath.   —Prov. 29:8

A fool uttereth all his mind: but a wise man keepeth it in till afterwards.   —Prov. 29:11

Be not righteous over much; neither make thyself over wise: why shouldest thou destroy thyself?
—Eccl. 7:16

Be not over much wicked, neither be thou foolish: why shouldest thou die before thy time? —Eccl. 7:17

Dead flies cause the ointment of the apothecary to send forth a stinking savour: so doth a little folly him that is in reputation for wisdom and honour.   —Eccl. 10:1

Who is wise, and he shall understand these things? prudent, and he shall know them? for the ways of the Lord are right, and the just shall walk in them: but the transgressors shall fall therein.   —Hos. 14:9

Agree with thine adversary quickly, whiles thou art in the way with him.   —Matt. 5:25

Give not that which is holy unto the dogs, neither cast ye your pearls before swine, lest they trample them under their feet, and turn again and rend you.   —Matt. 7:6

Which of you, intending to build a tower, sitteth not down first, and counteth the cost, whether he have sufficient to finish it?—Luke 14:28

What king, going to make war against another king, sitteth not down first, and consulteth whether he be able with ten thousand to meet him that cometh against him with twenty thousand?
—Luke 14:31

Let not then your good be evil spoken of.   —Rom. 14:16

All things are lawful unto me, but all things are not expedient.
—1 Cor. 6:12

Take heed lest by any means this liberty of yours become a stumblingblock to them that are weak.
—1 Cor. 8:9

If meat make my brother to offend, I will eat no flesh while the world standeth, lest I make my brother to offend.   — 1 Cor. 8:13

Let every man be swift to hear, slow to speak, slow to wrath.
—Jas. 1:19

Punishment, see Retribution, Chastening

Purging, see Purification

PURIFICATION; see also Remission, Regeneration

Sanctify yourselves therefore, and be ye holy: for I am the Lord your God.   —Lev. 20:7

Cleanse thou me from secret faults.   —Psa. 19:12

Wash me thoroughly from mine iniquity, and cleanse me from my sin.   —Psa. 51:2

Wash me, and I shall be whiter than snow.   —Psa. 51:7

As for our transgressions, thou shalt purge them away.
—Psa. 65:3

Wherewithal shall a young man cleanse his way? by taking heed thereto according to thy word.
—Psa. 119:9

Take away the dross from the silver, and there shall come forth a vessel for the finer. —Prov. 25:4

Wash you, make you clean; put away the evil of your doings from before mine eyes.   —Isa. 1:16

Though your sins be as scarlet, they shall be as white as snow; though they be red like crimson, they shall be as wool. —Isa. 1:19

I will turn my hand upon thee, and purely purge away thy dross, and take away all thy tin.
—Isa. 1:25

Thine iniquity is taken away, and thy sin purged. —Isa. 6:7

Wash thine heart from wickedness, that thou mayest be saved.
—Jer. 4:14

Many shall be purified, and made white, and tried. —Dan. 12:10

He shall . . . purge them as gold and silver, that they may be offered unto the Lord an offering in righteousness. —Mal. 3:3

Lord, if thou wilt, thou canst make me clean. —Matt. 8:2

Cleanse first that which is within the cup and platter, that the outside of them may be clean also.
—Matt. 23:26

Every branch that beareth fruit, he purgeth it, that it may bring forth more fruit. —John 15:2

What God hath cleansed, that call not thou common.
—Acts 10:15

Arise, and be baptized, and wash away thy sins, calling on the name of the Lord. —Acts 22:16

Purge out therefore the old leaven, that ye may be a new lump, as ye are unleavened.—1 Cor. 5:7

But ye are washed, but ye are sanctified, but ye are justified in the name of the Lord Jesus, and by the Spirit of our God. —1 Cor. 6:11

Put on the new man, which after God is created in righteousness and true holiness. —Eph. 4:24

Christ . . . loved the church, and gave himself for it; That he might sanctify and cleanse it with the washing of water by the word, That he might present it to himself a glorious church, not having spot, or wrinkle, or any such thing; but that it should be holy and without blemish. —Eph. 5:25–27

The Lord Jesus Christ . . . shall change our vile body, that it may be fashioned like unto his glorious body. —Phil. 3:20, 21

If a man therefore purge himself . . . he shall be a vessel unto honour, sanctified, and meet for the master's use. —2 Tim. 2:21

He saved us, by the washing of regeneration. —Tit. 3:5

If the blood of bulls and of goats . . . sanctifieth to the purifying of the flesh: How much more shall the blood of Christ.—Heb. 9:13, 14

Worshippers once purged should have no more conscience of sins.
—Heb. 10:2

Let us draw near with a true heart in full assurance of faith, having our hearts sprinkled from an evil conscience, and our bodies washed with pure water.
—Heb. 10:22

Cleanse your hands, ye sinners; and purify your hearts, ye double minded. —Jas. 4:8

Seeing ye have purified your souls in obeying the truth through the Spirit unto unfeigned love of the brethren, see that ye love one another with a pure heart fervently.
—1 Pet. 1:22

The blood of Jesus Christ his Son cleanseth us from all sin.

—1 JOHN 1:7

If we confess our sins, he is faithful and just to forgive us our sins, and to cleanse us from all unrighteousness. —1 JOHN 1:9

Every man that hath this hope in him purifieth himself, even as he is pure. —1 JOHN 3:3

Purity, see RIGHTEOUSNESS, PURIFICATION

Purpose, see RESOLUTION

Q

Quarreling, see CONTENTION

R

Rashness, see PRUDENCE

Readiness, see PREPARATION

Reaping, see HARVEST, RETRIBUTION, REWARD

Rebuke, see REPROOF

Recompense, see RETALIATION, RETRIBUTION, REWARD

RECONCILIATION; see also REDEMPTION

If when we were enemies, we were reconciled to God by the death of his Son; much more, being reconciled, we shall be saved by his life. —ROM. 5:10

All things are of God, who hath reconciled us to himself by Jesus Christ, and hath given to us the ministry of reconciliation.
  —2 COR. 5:18

God was in Christ, reconciling the world unto himself, not imputing their trespasses unto them; and hath committed unto us the word of reconciliation. —2 COR. 5:19

Be ye reconciled to God.
  —2 COR. 5:20

It pleased the Father . . . to reconcile all things unto himself.
  —COL. 1:19, 20

You, that were sometime alienated and enemies in your mind by wicked works, yet now hath he reconciled In the body of his flesh through death, to present you holy and unblameable and unreprovable in his sight. —COL. 1:21, 22

In all things it behoved him to be made like unto his brethren, that he might be a merciful and faithful high priest in things pertaining to God, to make reconciliation for the sins of the people. —HEB. 2:17

Rectitude, see INTEGRITY, RIGHTEOUSNESS

REDEMPTION; see also RECONCILIATION, SALVATION

He sent redemption unto his people: he hath commanded his covenant for ever. —PSA. 111:9

With the Lord there is mercy, and with him is plenteous redemption. —PSA. 130:7

Surely he hath borne our griefs, and carried our sorrows: yet we did esteem him stricken, smitten of God, and afflicted. But he was wounded for our transgressions, he was bruised for our iniquities: the chastisement of our peace was upon him; and with his stripes we are healed. —ISA. 53:4, 5

All we like sheep have gone astray; we have turned every one to his own way; and the Lord hath laid on him the iniquity of us all. —ISA. 53:6

The Son of man came not to be ministered unto, but to minister, and to give his life a ransom for many. —MATT. 20:28

This is my blood of the new testament, which is shed for many for the remission of sins. —MATT. 26:28

Behold the Lamb of God, which taketh away the sin of the world. —JOHN 1:29

I am the good shepherd: the good shepherd giveth his life for the sheep. —JOHN 10:10

Christ died for the ungodly. —ROM. 5:6

By the righteousness of one the free gift came upon all men unto justification of life. —ROM. 5:18

Of him are ye in Christ Jesus, who of God is made unto us wisdom, and righteousness, and sanctification, and redemption. —1 COR. 1:30

Ye are bought with a price. —1 COR. 6:20

Christ died for our sins. —1 COR. 15:3

He hath made him to be sin for us, who knew no sin; that we might be made the righteousness of God. —2 COR. 5:21

The life which I now live in the flesh I live by the faith of the Son of God, who loved me, and gave himself for me. —GAL. 2:20

God sent forth his Son, made of a woman, made under the law, To redeem them that were under the law, that we might receive the adoption of sons. —GAL. 4:4, 5

In whom we have redemption through his blood, the forgiveness of sins, according to the riches of his grace. —EPH. 1:7

Ye who sometime were far off are made nigh by the blood of Christ. —EPH. 2:7

Walk in love, as Christ also hath loved us, and hath given himself for us an offering and a sacrifice to God for a sweetsmelling savour. —EPH. 5:2

In whom we have redemption through his blood, even the forgiveness of sins. —COL. 1:14

God hath not appointed us to wrath, but to obtain salvation by our Lord Jesus Christ, Who died for us. —1 THESS. 5:9, 10

There is one God, and one mediator between God and men, the man Christ Jesus; Who gave himself a ransom for all. —1 TIM. 5, 6

Who gave himself for us, that he might redeem us from all iniquity, and purify unto himself a peculiar people, zealous of good works. —TIT. 2:14

Neither by the blood of goats and calves, but by his own blood he entered in once into the holy place, having obtained eternal redemption for us. —HEB. 9:12

For this cause he is the mediator of the new testament, that by means of death, for the redemption of the transgressions that were under the first testament, they which are called might receive the promise of eternal inheritance. —HEB. 9:15

Ye were not redeemed with corruptible things, as silver and gold, from your vain conversation received by tradition from your fathers; But with the precious blood of Christ, as of a lamb without blemish and without spot.

—1 PET. 1:18, 19

REFORMATION; see also RE-PENTANCE, CONVERSION, REGEN-ERATION

If ye will not be reformed by me . . . but will walk contrary unto me; Then will I walk contrary to you. —LEV. 26:23, 24

I thought on my ways, and turned my feet unto thy testimonies. —PSA. 119:59

Remove thy foot from evil.

—PROV. 4:27

Forsake the foolish, and live; and go in the way of understanding.

—PROV. 9:6

The fear of the Lord is a fountain of life, to depart from the snares of death. —PROV. 14:27

Put away the evil of your doings from before mine eyes; cease to do evil; Learn to do well.

—ISA. 1:16, 17

Let the wicked forsake his way, and the unrighteous man his thoughts. —ISA. 55:7

Turn, O backsliding children, saith the Lord. —JER. 3:14

Stand ye in the ways, and see, and ask for the old paths, where is the good way, and walk therein, and ye shall find rest for your souls.

—JER. 6:16

Amend your ways and your doings, and I will cause you to dwell in this place. —JER. 7:3

Can the Ethiopian change his skin or the leopard his spots? then may ye also do good, that are accustomed to do evil.

—JER. 13:23

Return ye now every one from his evil way, and make your ways and your doings good.—JER. 18:11

Turn ye again now every one from his evil way, and from the evil of your doings. —JER. 25:5

Amend your ways and your doings, and obey the voice of the Lord your God. —JER. 26:13

Let us search and try our ways, and turn again to the Lord.

—LAM. 3:40

If the wicked will turn from all his sins that he hath committed, and keep all my statutes, and do that which is lawful and right, he shall surely live, he shall not die.

—EZEK. 18:21

When the wicked man turneth away from his wickedness that he hath committed, and doeth that which is lawful and right, he shall save his soul alive. —EZEK. 18:27

Cast away from you all your transgressions, whereby ye have transgressed; and make you a new heart and a new spirit.

—Ezek. 18:31

Turn ye, turn ye from your evil ways.   —Ezek. 33:11

Let them turn every one from his evil way, and from the violence that is in their hands.   —Jon. 3:8

Refuge, see Protection

Refusal, see Rejection

REGENERATION; see also Con-version, Reformation, Purifica-tion

Create in me a clean heart, O God; and renew a right spirit within me.   —Psa. 51:10

Wash you, make you clean; put away the evil of your doings from before mine eyes; cease to do evil.

—Isa. 1:16

Heal me, O Lord, and I shall be healed; save me, and I shall be saved: for thou art my praise.

—Jer. 17:14

I will give them an heart to know me, that I am the Lord.—Jer. 24:7

Cast away from you all your transgressions, whereby ye have transgressed; and make you a new heart and a new spirit.

—Ezek. 18:31

A new heart also will I give you, and a new spirit will I put within you: and I will take away the stony heart out of your flesh, and I will give you an heart of flesh.

—Ezek. 36:26

I will put my spirit within you, and cause you to walk in my stat-utes, and ye shall keep my judg-ments, and do them. —Ezek. 36:27

I have caused thine iniquity to pass from thee, and will clothe thee with change of raiment.

—Zech. 3:4

No man putteth new wine into old bottles: else the new wine doth burst the bottles, and the wine is spilled, and the bottles will be marred: but new wine must be put in new bottles.   —Mark 2:22

As many as received him, to them gave he the power to become the sons of God, even to them that believe on his name: Which were born, not of blood, nor of the will of the flesh, nor of the will of man, but of God.—John 1:12, 13

Except a man be born again, he cannot see the Kingdom of God.

—John 3:3

Except a man be born of water and of the Spirit, he cannot enter into the kingdom of God.

—John 3:5

Marvel not that I said unto thee, Ye must be born again.—John 3:7

The wind bloweth where it list-eth, and thou hearest the sound thereof, but canst not tell whence it cometh, and whither it goeth: so is every one that is born of the Spirit.   —John 3:8

Whosoever drinketh of the water that I shall give him shall never thirst; but the water that I shall give him shall be in him a well of water springing up into everlasting life.

—John 4:14

I am the light of the world: he that followeth me shall not walk in darkness, but shall have the light of life.   —John 8:12

Ye shall know the truth, and the truth shall make you free.

—JOHN 8:32

I am come that they might have life, and that they might have it more abundantly. —JOHN 10:10

Like as Christ was raised up from the dead by the glory of the Father, even so we also should walk in newness of life. —ROM. 6:4

Our old man is crucified with him, that the body of sin might be destroyed, that henceforth we should not serve sin. —ROM. 6:6

Reckon ye also yourselves to be dead indeed unto sin, but alive unto God through Jesus Christ our Lord. —ROM. 6:11

Yield yourselves unto God, as those that are alive from the dead, and your members as instruments of righteousness unto God.

—ROM. 6:13

Sin shall not have dominion over you: for ye are not under the law, but under grace. —ROM. 6:14

Being made free from sin, and become servants to God, ye have your fruit unto holiness, and the end everlasting life. —ROM. 6:22

Now we are delivered from the law, that being dead wherein we were held; that we should serve in newness of spirit, and not in the oldness of the letter. —ROM. 7:6

They that are after the flesh do mind the things of the flesh; but they that are after the Spirit the things of the Spirit. —ROM 8:5

Ye are not in the flesh, but in the Spirit, if so be that the Spirit of God dwell in you. —ROM. 8:9

Be not conformed to this world: but be ye transformed by the renewing of your mind, that ye may prove what is that good, and acceptable, and perfect, will of God.

—ROM. 12:2

We have received, not the spirit of the world, but the spirit which is of God; that we might know the things that are freely given to us of God. —1 COR. 2:12

We all, with open face beholding as in a glass the glory of the Lord, are changed into the same image from glory to glory, even as by the Spirit of the Lord. —2 COR. 3:18

If any man be in Christ, he is a new creature: old things are passed away; behold, all things are become new. —2 COR. 5:17

I live; yet not I, but Christ liveth in me. —GAL. 2:20

In Christ Jesus neither circumcision availeth any thing, nor uncircumsion, but a new creature.

—GAL. 6:15

Put off concerning the former conversation the old man, which is corrupt according to the deceitful lusts; And be renewed in the spirit of your mind. —EPH. 4:22, 23

Put on the new man.—EPH. 4:24

Ye have put off the old man with his deeds; And have put on the new man, which is renewed in knowledge after the image of him that created him. —COL. 3:9, 10

According to his mercy he saved us, by the washing of regeneration, and renewing of the Holy Ghost.

—TIT. 3:5

Let us draw near with a true heart in full assurance of faith, having our hearts sprinkled from an evil conscience, and our bodies washed with pure water.

—HEB. 10:22

Seeing ye have purified your souls in obeying the truth through the Spirit unto unfeigned love of the brethren, see that ye love one another with a pure heart fervently: Being born again not of corruptible seed, but of incorruptible, by the word of God, which liveth and abideth forever. —1 PET. 1:22, 23

Every one that doeth righteousness is born of him. —1 JOHN 2:29

Whosoever is born of God doth not commit sin; for his seed remaineth in him: and he cannot sin, because he is born of God.

—1 JOHN 3:9

We know that we have passed from death unto life, because we love the brethren. —1 JOHN 3:14

Beloved, let us love one another: for love is of God; and every one that loveth is born of God, and knoweth God. —1 JOHN 4:7

Whosoever believeth that Jesus is the Christ is born of God.

—1 JOHN 5:1

Whatsoever is born of God overcometh the world: and this is the victory that overcometh the world, even our faith. —1 JOHN 5:4

Whosoever is born of God sinneth not; but he that is begotten of God keepeth himself, and that wicked one toucheth him not.

—1 JOHN 5:18

Regret, see REMORSE, REPENTANCE

REJECTION; see also IMPENITENCE, UNBELIEF

Ye have this day rejected your God. —1 SAM. 10:19

The fool hath said in his heart, There is no God. —PSA. 53:1

The stone which the builders refused is become the headstone of the corner. —PSA. 118:22

Hear instruction, and be wise, and refuse it not. —PROV. 8:33

He is despised and rejected of men; a man of sorrows and acquainted with grief. —ISA. 53:3

Lo, they have rejected the word of the Lord; and what wisdom is in them? —ISA. 8:9

Because thou hast rejected knowledge, I will also reject thee.

—HOS. 4:6

Every one that heareth these sayings of mine, and doeth them not, shall be likened unto a foolish man, which built his house upon the sand.

—MATT. 7:26

Whosoever shall deny me before men, him will I also deny before my Father which is in heaven.

—MATT. 10:33

A prophet is not without honour, but in his own country.—MARK 6:4

He that is not with me is against me; and he that gathereth not with me scattereth. —LUKE 11:23

He that denieth me before men shall be denied before the angels of God. —LUKE 12:9

O Jerusalem, Jerusalem, which killest the prophets, and stonest them that are sent unto thee; how often would I have gathered thy children together, as a hen doth gather her brood under her wings, and ye would not! —LUKE 13:34

He came unto his own, and his own received him not.—JOHN 1:11

We speak that we do know, and testify that we have seen; and ye receive not our witness. —JOHN 3:11

This is the condemnation, that light is come into the world, and men loved darkness rather than light, because their deeds were evil. —JOHN 3:19

Ye will not come to me, that ye might have life. —JOHN 5:40

I am come in my Father's name, and ye receive me not.—JOHN 5:43

He that rejecteth me, and receiveth not my words, hath one that judgeth him: the word that I have spoken, the same shall judge him in the last day. —JOHN 12:48

They will not receive thy testimony concerning me.—ACTS 22:18

The heart of this people is waxed gross, and their ears are dull of hearing, and their eyes have they closed; lest they should see with their eyes, and hear with their ears, and understand with their heart, and should be converted, and I should heal them. —ACTS 28:27

If we deny him, he also will deny us. —2 TIM. 2:12

Who is a liar but he that denieth that Jesus is the Christ? —1 JOHN 2:22

Whosoever denieth the Son, the same hath not the Father. —1 JOHN 2:23

REJOICING; see also JOY

Thou shalt rejoice before the Lord thy God in all that thou puttest thine hands unto. —DEUT. 12:18

My heart rejoiceth in the Lord, mine horn is exalted in the Lord. —1 SAM. 2:1

Let all those that put their trust in thee rejoice: let them ever shout for joy. —PSA. 5:11

I will be glad and rejoice in thee: I will sing praise to thy name, O thou most High. —PSA. 9:2

My heart shall rejoice in thy salvation. —PSA. 13:5

The statutes of the Lord are right, rejoicing the heart. —PSA. 19:8

We will rejoice in thy salvation, and in the name of our God we will set up our banners. —PSA. 20:5

The Lord is my strength and my shield; my heart trusted in him, and I am helped: therefore my heart greatly rejoiceth; and with my song will I praise him. —PSA. 28:7

Be glad in the Lord, and rejoice, ye righteous: and shout for joy, all ye that are upright in heart. —PSA. 32:11

Our heart shall rejoice in him, because we have trusted in his holy name. —PSA. 33:21

My soul shall be joyful in the Lord: it shall rejoice in his salvation. —PSA. 35:9

Let all those that seek thee rejoice and be glad in thee. —PSA. 40:16

Let the righteous be glad; let them rejoice before God: yea, let them exceedingly rejoice. —PSA. 68:3

My lips shall greatly rejoice when I sing unto thee; and my soul, which thou has redeemed. —PSA. 71:23

Rejoice in the Lord, ye righteous.
—Psa. 97:12

Make a joyful noise unto the Lord, all ye lands. —Psa. 100:1

Glory ye in his holy name: let the heart of them rejoice that seek the Lord. —Psa. 105:3

I rejoice at thy word, as one that findeth great spoil. —Psa. 119:162

He that goeth forth and weepeth, bearing precious seed, shall doubtless come again with rejoicing, bringing his sheaves with him.
—Psa. 126:6

The light of the righteous rejoiceth. —Prov. 13:9

The righteous doth sing and rejoice. —Prov. 29:6

Sing unto the Lord; for he hath done excellent things. —Isa. 12:5

This is the Lord; we have waited for him, we will be glad, and rejoice in his salvation. —Isa. 25:9

Sing, O ye heavens . . . shout, ye lower parts of the earth: break forth into singing, ye mountains, O forest, and every tree therein.
—Isa. 44:23

I will greatly rejoice in the Lord, my soul shall be joyful in my God; for he hath clothed me with the garments of salvation, he hath covered me with the robe of righteousness. —Isa. 61:10

Be glad and rejoice for ever in that which I create. —Isa. 65:18

My spirit hath rejoiced in God my Saviour. —Luke 1:47

Rejoice, because your names are written in heaven. —Luke 10:20

Rejoice in the Lord alway: and again I say, Rejoice. —Phil. 4:4

Rejoice, inasmuch as ye are partakers of Christ's sufferings; that, when his glory shall be revealed, ye may be glad also with exceeding joy. —1 Pet. 4:13

Reliability, see Faithfulness, Integrity, Veracity

RELIGION; see also Piety, Heresy

Fear God, and keep his commandments: for this is the whole duty of man. —Eccl. 12:13

What doth the Lord require of thee, but to do justly, and to love mercy, and to walk humbly with thy God? —Mic. 6:8

Love is the fulfilling of the law.
—Rom. 13:10

If any man among you seem to be religious, and bridleth not his tongue, but deceiveth his own heart, this man's religion is in vain.
—Jas. 1:26

Pure religion and undefiled before God and the Father is this, To visit the fatherless and widows in their affliction, and to keep himself unspotted from the world.
—Jas. 1:27

REMISSION

Thou art a God ready to pardon, gracious and merciful.—Neh. 9:17

Blessed is he whose transgression is forgiven, whose sin is covered.
—Psa. 32:1

Thou hast forgiven the iniquity of thy people, thou hast covered all their sin. —Psa. 85:2

Thou, Lord, art good, and ready to forgive; and plenteous in mercy unto all them that call upon thee.
—Psa. 86:5

Bless the Lord, O my soul, and forget not all his benefits: Who forgiveth all thine iniquities; who healeth all thy diseases.
—PSA. 103:2, 3

There is forgiveness with thee
—PSA. 130:4

Though your sins be as scarlet, they shall be as white as snow; though they be red like crimson, they shall be as wool.   —ISA. 1:18

Thine iniquity is taken away, and thy sin purged.   —ISA. 6:7

I have blotted out, as a thick cloud, thy transgressions, and, as a cloud, thy sins.   —ISA. 44:22

Let the wicked forsake his way, and the unrighteous man his thoughts: and let him return unto the Lord, and he will have mercy upon him; and to our God, for he will abundantly pardon.—ISA. 55:7

I will forgive their iniquity, and I will remember their sin no more.
—JER. 31:34

I will pardon all their iniquities.
—JER. 33:8

To the Lord our God belong mercies and forgiveness.—DAN. 9:9

Who is a God like unto thee, that pardoneth iniquity, and passeth by the transgression of the remnant of his heritage? he retained not his anger for ever, because he delighteth in mercy.   —MIC. 7:18

Forgive us our debts, as we forgive our debtors.   —MATT. 6:12

The Son of man hath power on earth to forgive sins. —MATT. 9:8

This is my blood of the new testament, which is shed for many for the remission of sins.
—MATT. 26:28

John did baptize in the wilderness, and preach the baptism of repentance for the remission of sins.
—MARK 1:4

When Jesus saw their faith, he said . . . thy sins be forgiven thee.
—MARK 2:5

Behold the Lamb of God, which taketh away the sin of the world.
—JOHN 1:29

Repent, and be baptized every one of you in the name of Jesus Christ for the remission of sins.
—ACTS 2:38

Repent ye therefore, and be converted, that your sins may be blotted out.   —ACTS 3:19

Through his name whosoever believeth in him shall receive remission of sins.   —ACTS 10:43

Christ Jesus: Whom God hath set forth to be a propitiation through faith in his blood, to declare his righteousness for the remission of sins that are past, through the forbearance of God. —ROM. 3:24, 25

In whom we have redemption through his blood, the forgiveness of sins, according to the riches of his grace.   —EPH. 1:7

Even as Christ forgave you, so also do ye.   —COL. 3:13

Their sins and iniquities will I remember no more. Now where remission of these is, there is no more offering for sin.
—HEB. 10:17, 18

If we confess our sins, he is faithful and just to forgive us our sins, and to cleanse us from all unrighteousness.   —1 JOHN 1:9

REMORSE; see also REPENTANCE

My life is spent with grief, and my years with sighing: my strength faileth because of my iniquity, and my bones are consumed.
—Psa. 31:10

The Lord is nigh unto them that are of a broken heart; and saveth such as be of a contrite spirit.
—Psa. 34:18

I will declare mine iniquity; I will be sorry for my sins. —Psa. 38:18

Lord, be merciful unto me: heal my soul; for I have sinned against thee.
—Psa. 41:4

Have mercy upon me, O God, according to thy lovingkindness: according unto the multitude of thy tender mercies blot out my transgressions.
—Psa. 51:1

My sin is ever before me.
—Psa. 51:3

Against thee, thee only, have I sinned, and done this evil in thy sight.
—Psa. 51:4

The sacrifices of God are a broken spirit: a broken and a contrite heart, O God, thou wilt not despise.
—Psa. 51:17

My heart was grieved, and I was pricked in my reins. —Psa. 73:21

I remembered God, and was troubled.
—Psa. 77:3

Woe is me! for I am undone; because I am a man of unclean lips, and I dwell in the midst of a people of unclean lips.
—Isa. 6:5

I dwell . . . with him also that is of a contrite and humble spirit, to revive the spirit of the humble, and to revive the heart of the contrite ones.
—Isa. 57:15

We lie down in our shame, and our confusion covereth us: for we have sinned against the Lord our God.
—Jer. 3:25

Behold, O Lord; for I am in distress: my bowels are troubled; mine heart is turned within me; for I have grievously rebelled.
—Lam. 1:20

Our transgressions and our sins be upon us, and we pine away in them.
—Ezek. 33:10

We have sinned, we have done wickedly.
—Dan. 9:5

There shall be weeping and gnashing of teeth, when ye shall see Abraham, and Isaac, and Jacob, and all the prophets, in the kingdom of God, and you yourselves thrust out.
—Luke 13:28

I have sinned against heaven, and before thee, And am no more worthy to be called thy son.
—Luke 15:18, 19

God be merciful to me a sinner.
—Luke 18:13

Peter went out, and wept bitterly.
—Luke 22:62

Godly sorrow worketh repentance to salvation not to be repented of.
—2 Cor. 7:10

If our heart condemn us, God is greater than our heart, and knoweth all things.
—1 John 3:20

RENUNCIATION; see also Absti- nence, Temperance, Celibacy

Remove thy foot from evil.
—Prov. 4:27

Let the wicked forsake his way, and the unrighteous man his thoughts.
—Isa. 55:7

If thy right hand offend thee, cut it off, and cast it from thee.
—MATT. 5:30

If thou wilt be perfect, go and sell that thou hast, and give to the poor, and thou shalt have treasure in heaven: and come and follow me.
—MATT. 19:20

Whosoever will come after me, let him deny himself, and take up his cross, and follow me.
—MARK 8:34

Lo, we have left all, and have followed thee.   —MARK 10:28

There is no man that hath left house, or parents, or brethren, or wife, or children, for the kingdom of God's sake, Who shall not receive manifold more in this present time, and in the world to come life everlasting.   —LUKE 18:29, 30

He must increase, but I must decrease.   —JOHN 3:30

He that loveth his life shall lose it.   —JOHN 12:25

Our old man is crucified with him, that the body of sin might be destroyed.   —ROM. 6:6

Be not conformed to this world.
—ROM. 12:2

Make no provision for the flesh, to fulfil the lusts thereof.
—ROM. 13:14

Even Christ pleased not himself.
—ROM. 15:3

I keep under my body, and bring it into subjection: lest that by any means, when I have preached to others, I myself should be a castaway.   —1 COR. 9:27

He died for all, that they which live should not henceforth live unto themselves, but unto him that died for them.   —2 COR. 5:15

They that are Christ's have crucified the flesh with the affections and lusts.   —GAL. 5:24

Set your affections on things above, not on things on the earth.
—COL. 3:2

Mortify . . . your members which are upon the earth.
—COL. 3:5

Put off the old man. —COL. 3:9

Flee . . . youthful lusts.
—2 TIM. 2:4

Denying ungodliness and worldly lusts, we should live soberly, righteously, and godly, in this present world.   —TIT. 2:12

Abstain from fleshly lusts, which war against the soul.—1 PET. 2:11

Love not the world, neither the things that are in the world.
—1 JOHN 2:15

Repayment, see RETRIBUTION, REWARD, RETALIATION

REPENTANCE; see also REMORSE, CONFESSION, REFORMATION, IMPENITENCE

If my people . . . shall humble themselves, and pray, and seek my face, and turn from their wicked ways; then will I hear from heaven, and will forgive their sin.
—2 CHRON. 7:14

The Lord your God is gracious and merciful, and will not turn away his face from you, if ye return unto him.   —2 CHRON. 30:9

Lord, be merciful unto me: heal my soul; for I have sinned against thee.   —PSA. 41:4

Let the wicked forsake his way, and the unrighteous man his thoughts; and let him return unto the Lord, and he will have mercy upon him; and to our God, for he will abundantly pardon.—Isa. 55:7

Repent, and turn yourselves from your idols; and turn away your faces from all your abominations. —Ezek. 14:6

Repent, and turn yourselves from all your transgressions; so iniquity shall not be your ruin.
—Ezek. 18:30

Come, and let us return unto the Lord: for he hath torn, and he will heal us; he hath smitten, and he will bind us up. —Hos. 6:1

It is time to seek the Lord, till he come and rain righteousness upon you. —Hos. 10:12

Turn thou to thy God: keep mercy and judgment, and wait on thy God continually. —Hos. 12:6

Turn to the Lord: say unto him, Take away all iniquity, and receive us graciously. —Hos. 14:1

Turn ye even to me with all your heart, and with fasting, and with weeping, and with mourning.
—Joel 2:12

Rend your heart, and not your garments, and turn unto the Lord your God: for he is gracious and merciful, slow to anger, and of great kindness, and repenteth him of the evil. —Joel 2:13

Let man and beast be covered with sackcloth, and cry mightily unto God. —Jon. 3:8

Turn ye unto me, saith the Lord of hosts, and I will turn unto you, saith the Lord of hosts.—Zech. 1:3

Bring forth . . . fruits meet for repentance. —Matt. 3:8

Repent: for the kingdom of heaven is at hand. —Matt. 4:17

John did baptize in the wilderness, and preach the baptism of repentance for the remission of sins.
—Mark 1:4

The time is fulfilled, and the kingdom of God is at hand: repent ye, and believe the gospel.
—Mark 1:15

I came not to call the righteous, but sinners to repentance.
—Mark 2:17

Except ye repent, ye shall all likewise perish. —Luke 13:3

Joy shall be in heaven over one sinner that repenteth, more than over ninety and nine just persons, which need no repentance.
—Luke 15:7

I will arise and go to my father, and will say unto him, Father, I have sinned against heaven, and before thee. —Luke 15:18

God be merciful to me a sinner.
—Luke 18:13

Repentance and remission of sins should be preached in his name among all nations. —Luke 24:47

Repent, and be baptized every one of you in the name of Jesus Christ for the remission of sins.
—Acts 2:38

Repent ye therefore, and be converted, that your sins may be blotted out. —Acts 3:19

Repent therefore of this thy wickedness, and pray God, if perhaps the thought of thine heart may be forgiven thee. —Acts 8:22

The times of this ignorance God winked at; but now commandeth all men everywhere to repent.
—ACTS 17:30

Repent and turn to God, and do works meet for repentance.
—ACTS 26:20

Despiseth thou the riches of his goodness and forbearance and long-suffering; not knowing that the goodness of God leadeth thee to repentance? —ROM. 2:4

Godly sorrow worketh repentance to salvation not to be repented of. —2 COR. 7:10

Remember therefore from whence thou art fallen, and repent. —REV. 2:5

As many as I love, I rebuke and chasten: be zealous therefore, and repent. —REV. 3:19

Reproach, see DISHONOUR, REPROOF, SCORN, CENSURE

REPROOF

Let the righteous smite me; it shall be a kindness: and let him reprove me; it shall be an excellent oil, which shall not break my head.
—PSA. 141:5

The law is light; and reproofs of instruction are the way of life.
—PROV. 6:23

He that reproveth a scorner getteth to himself shame: and he that rebuketh a wicked man getteth himself a blot. —PROV. 9:7

Reprove not a scorner, lest he hate thee: rebuke a wise man, and he will love thee. —PROV. 9:8

He is in the way of life that keepeth instruction: but he that refuseth reproof erreth.
—PROV. 10:17

Whoso loveth instruction loveth knowledge: but he that hateth reproof is brutish. —PROV. 12:1

Poverty and shame shall be to him that refuseth instruction: but he that regardeth reproof shall be honoured. —PROV. 13:18

A fool despiseth his father's instruction: but he that regardeth reproof is prudent. —PROV. 15:5

Correction is grievous unto him that forsaketh the way: and he that hateth reproof shall die.
—PROV. 15:10

A scorner loveth not one that reproveth him: neither will he go unto the wise. —PROV. 15:12

The ear that heareth the reproof of life abideth among the wise.
—PROV. 15:31

He that refuseth instruction despiseth his own soul: but he that heareth reproof getteth understanding. —PROV. 15:32

A reproof entereth more into a wise man than an hundred stripes into a fool. —PROV. 17:10

Smite a scorner, and the simple will beware: and reprove one that hath understanding, and he will understand knowledge.
—PROV. 19:25

As an earring of gold, and an ornament of fine gold, so is a wise reprover upon an obedient ear.
—PROV. 24:12

Open rebuke is better than secret love. —PROV. 27:5

He that rebuketh a man afterwards shall find more favour than he that flattereth with the tongue.
—PROV. 28:23

The rod and reproof give wisdom. —Prov. 29:15

It is better to hear the rebuke of the wise, than for a man to hear the song of fools. —Eccl. 7:5

They hate him that rebuketh in the gate, and they abhor him that speaketh uprightly. —Amos 5:10

If thy brother shall trespass against thee, go and tell him his fault between thee and him alone: if he shall hear thee, thou hast gained thy brother. —Matt. 18:15

If thy brother trespass against thee, rebuke him; and if he repent, forgive him. —Luke 17:3

Have no fellowship with the unfruitful works of darkness, but rather reprove them. —Eph. 5:11

All things that are reproved are made manifest by the light: for whatsoever doth make manifest is light. —Eph. 5:13

Preach the word; be instant in season, out of season; reprove, rebuke, exhort with all longsuffering and doctrine. —2 Tim. 4:2

Rebuke them sharply, that they may be sound in the faith.
—Tit. 1:13

My son, despise not thou the chastening of the Lord, nor faint when thou art rebuked of him.
—Heb. 12:5

As many as I love, I rebuke and chasten. —Rev. 3:19

Requirement, see Duty, Want

Requital, see Retaliation, Retribution, Reward

Resentment, see Anger, Hatred

RESIGNATION; see also Patience, Meekness

Let him do to me as seemeth good unto him. —2 Sam. 15:26

Naked came I out of my mother's womb, naked shall I return thither: the Lord gave, and the Lord hath taken away; blessed be the name of the Lord. —Job 1:21

Though he slay me, yet will I trust in him. —Job 13:15

He knoweth the way I take: when he hath tried me, I shall come forth as gold. —Job 23:10

Surely it is meet to be said unto God, I have borne chastisement, I will not offend any more.
—Job 34:31

Be still, and know that I am God.
—Psa. 46:10

It is good for me that I have been afflicted; that I might learn thy statutes. —Psa. 119:7

I know, O Lord, that thy judgments are right, and that thou in faithfulness hast afflicted me.
—Psa. 119:75

Teach me to do thy will; for thou art my God. —Psa. 143:10

My son, despise not the chastening of the Lord; neither be weary of his correction. —Prov. 3:11

The spirit of a man will sustain his infirmity; but a wounded spirit who can bear? —Prov. 18:14

Wherefore doth a living man complain, a man for the punishment of his sins? —Lam. 3:39

I will bear the indignation of the Lord, because I have sinned against him. —Mic. 7:9

Thy will be done. —Matt. 6:10

If it be possible, let this cup pass from me: nevertheless not as I will, but as thou wilt.
—MATT. 26:39

Be it unto me according to thy word. —LUKE 1:38

The cup which my Father hath given me, shall I not drink it?
—JOHN 18:11

Do all things without murmurings and disputings. —PHIL. 2:14

I have learned, in whatsoever state I am, therewith to be content.
—PHIL. 4:11

Watch thou in all things, endure afflictions. —2 TIM. 4:5

Be content with such things as ye have. —HEB. 13:5

Despise not thou the chastening of the Lord, nor faint when thou art rebuked of him. —HEB. 12:5

Submit yourselves therefore to God. —JAS. 4:7

We ought to say, If the Lord will, we shall live, and do this, or that.
—JAS. 4:15

What glory is it, if, when ye be buffeted for your faults, ye shall take it patiently? but if, when ye do well, and suffer for it, ye take it patiently, this is acceptable with God. —1 PET. 2:20

Let them that suffer according to the will of God commit the keeping of their souls to him in well doing, as unto a faithful Creator.
—1 PET. 4:19

RESOLUTION; see also CONSTANCY, INDECISION

All the Lord speaketh, that I must do. —NUM. 23:26

Cleave unto the Lord your God.
—JOSH. 23:8

As for me and my house, we will serve the Lord. —JOSH. 24:15

Turn not aside from following the Lord, but serve the Lord with all your heart. —1 SAM. 12:20

How long halt ye between two opinions? if the Lord be God, follow him: but if Baal, then follow him. —1 KIN. 18:21

The righteous . . . shall hold on his way. —JOB 17:9

I am purposed. —PSA. 17:3

I will dwell in the house of the Lord for ever. —PSA. 23:6

Wait on the Lord, and keep his way. —PSA. 37:34

Let thine eyes look right on, and let thine eyelids look straight before thee. —PROV. 4:25

Ponder the path of thy feet, and let all thy ways be established.
—PROV. 4:26

Turn not to the right hand nor to the left. —PROV. 4:27

The Lord God will help me; therefore shall I not be confounded: therefore have I set my face like a flint, and I know that I shall not be ashamed. —ISA. 50:7

Whither the spirit was to go, they went; and they turned not when they went. —EZEK. 1:12

Multitudes, multitudes in the valley of decision: for the day of the Lord is near in the valley of decision. —JOEL 3:14

The light of the body is the eye; if therefore thine eye be single, thy whole body shall be full of light.
—MATT. 6:22

Lord, I will follow thee whithersoever thou goest. —LUKE 9:57

I will arise and go to my father. —LUKE 15:18

I am resolved what to do. —LUKE 16:4

With purpose of heart . . . cleave unto the Lord. —ACTS 11:23

I am persuaded, that neither death, nor life, nor angels, nor principalities, nor powers, nor things present, nor things to come, Nor height, nor depth, nor any other creature, shall be able to separate us from the love of God, which is in Christ Jesus our Lord. —ROM. 8:38, 39

I determined not to know any thing among you, save Jesus Christ, and him crucified. —1 COR. 2:2

Be ye stedfast, unmoveable, always abounding in the work of the Lord. —1 COR. 15:58

Watch ye, stand fast in the faith, quit you like men, be strong. —1 COR. 16:13

Stand fast therefore in the liberty wherewith Christ hath made us free. —GAL. 5:1

Be no more children, tossed to and fro, and carried about with every wind of doctrine, by the sleight of men, and cunning craftiness, whereby they lie in wait to deceive. —EPH. 4:14

Take unto you the whole armour of God, that ye may be able to withstand in the evil day, and having done all, to stand. —EPH. 6:13

Stand fast in one spirit, with one mind striving together for the faith of the gospel. —PHIL. 1:27

This one thing I do, forgetting those things which are behind . . . I press toward the mark. —PHIL. 3:13, 14

Stand fast in the Lord. —PHIL. 4:1

Stand fast, and hold the traditions which ye have been taught. —2 THESS. 2:15

Hold fast the form of sound words. —2 TIM. 1:13

Be strong in the grace that is in Christ Jesus. —2 TIM. 2:1

Endure hardness, as a good soldier of Jesus Christ. —2 TIM. 2:3

We ought to give the more earnest heed to the things which we have heard, lest at any time we should let them slip. —HEB. 2:1

Hold fast the confidence and the rejoicing of the hope firm unto the end. —HEB. 3:6

Let us hold fast the profession of our faith without wavering. —HEB. 10:23

Cast not away . . . your confidence, which hath great recompence of reward. —HEB. 10:35

Let us run with patience the race that is set before us. —HEB. 12:1

Gird up the loins of your mind, be sober, and hope to the end for the grace that is to be brought unto you at the revelation of Jesus Christ. —1 PET. 1:13

Resist stedfast in the faith. —1 PET. 5:9

Give diligence to make your calling and election sure.—2 PET. 1:10

Keep yourselves in the love of God. —JUDE 1:21

Hold that fast which thou hast, that no man take thy crown.
—REV. 3:11

He that overcometh shall inherit all things; and I will be his God, and he shall be my son.—REV. 21:7

RESPONSIBILITY; see also DUTY

Am I my brother's keeper?
—GEN. 4:9

Every man shall be put to death for his own sin. —DEUT. 24:16

Be it indeed that I have erred, mine error remaineth with myself.
—JOB 19:4

Every one shall die for his own iniquity. —JER. 31:30

It is impossible but that offences will come: but woe unto him, through whom they come!
—LUKE 17:1

If ye were blind, ye should have no sin: but now ye say, We see; therefore your sin remaineth.
—JOHN 9:41

If I had not come and spoken unto them they had not had sin; but now they have no cloke for their sin. —JOHN 15:22

Every one of us shall give account of himself to God.
—ROM. 4:12

Let us not therefore judge one another any more: but judge this rather, that no man put a stumblingblock or an occasion to fall in his brother's way. —ROM. 14:13

We then that are strong ought to bear the infirmities of the weak, and not to please ourselves.
—ROM. 15:1

A little leaven leaveneth the whole lump. —1 COR. 5:6

When ye sin so against the brethren, and wound their weak conscience, ye sin against Christ.
—1 COR. 8:12

Work out your own salvation with fear and trembling.
—PHIL. 2:12

Keep that which is committed to thy trust. —1 TIM. 6:20

How shall we escape, if we neglect so great salvation. —HEB. 2:3

Let no man say when he is tempted, I am tempted of God: for God cannot be tempted with evil, neither tempteth he any man.
—JAS. 1:13

Restraint, see SELF-CONTROL, AB-STINENCE, TEMPERANCE

RETALIATION

Thou shalt not avenge, nor bear any grudge against the children of thy people. —LEV. 19:18

To me belongeth vengeance, and recompence. —DEUT. 32:35

Jealousy is the rage of a man: therefore he will not spare in the day of vengeance. —PROV. 6:34

Say not thou, I will recompense evil; but wait on the Lord, and he shall save thee. —PROV. 20:22

Say not, I will do so to him as he hath done to me: I will render to the man according to his work.
—PROV. 24:29

Resist not evil. —MATT. 5:39

Whosoever shall smite thee on thy right cheek, turn to him the other also. —MATT. 5:39

Bless them that curse you, do good to them that hate you, and pray for them which despitefully use you, and persecute you.
—MATT. 5:44

Judge not, that ye be not judged. For with what judgment ye judge, ye shall be judged; and with what measure ye mete, it shall be measured to you again. —MATT. 7:1, 2

Recompense to no man evil for evil. —ROM. 12:17

Avenge not yourselves, but rather give place unto wrath: for it is written, Vengeance is mine; I will repay, saith the Lord.—ROM. 12:19

If thine enemy hunger, feed him; if he thirst, give him drink: for in so doing thou shalt heap coals of fire on his head. —ROM. 12:20

See that none render evil for evil unto any man; but ever follow that which is good. —1 THESS. 5:15

Not rendering evil for evil, or railing for railing: but contrariwise blessing. —1 PET. 3:9

RETRIBUTION; see also REWARD

Be sure your sin will find you out. —NUM. 32:23

They that plow iniquity, and sow wickedness, reap the same.
—JOB 4:8

God will not cast away a perfect man, neither will he help the evil doers. —JOB 8:20

If I be wicked, woe unto me.
—JOB 10:15

The eyes of the wicked shall fail, and they shall not escape, and their hope shall be as the giving up of the ghost. —JOB 11:20

The light of the wicked shall be put out, and the spark of his fire shall not shine. —JOB 18:15

How oft is the candle of the wicked put out! and how oft cometh their destruction upon them!
—JOB 21:17

The ungodly shall not stand in the judgment, nor sinners in the congregation of the righteous.
—PSA. 1:5

The Lord knoweth the way of the righteous: but the way of the ungodly shall perish. —PSA. 1:6

Many sorrows shall be to the wicked. —PSA. 32:10

Evildoers shall be cut off: but those that wait upon the Lord, they shall inherit the earth. —PSA. 37:1

In the hand of the Lord there is a cup, and the wine is old; it is full of mixture; and he poureth out the same: but the dregs thereof, all the wicked of the earth shall wring them out, and drink them.
—PSA. 75:8

Fools because of their transgression, and because of their iniquities, are afflicted. —PSA. 107:17

The Lord preserveth all them that love him: but the wicked will he destroy. —PSA. 145:20

The Lord lifteth up the meek: he casteth the wicked down to the ground. —PSA. 147:6

The Lord will not suffer the soul of the righteous to famish: but he casteth away the substance of the wicked. —PROV. 10:3

Blessings are upon the head of the just: but violence covereth the mouth of the wicked. —PROV. 10:6

The memory of the just is blessed: but the name of the wicked shall rot. —PROV. 10:7

The fear of the wicked, it shall come upon him: but the desire of the righteous shall be granted.
—PROV. 10:24

As the whirlwind passeth, so is the wicked no more: but the righteous is an everlasting foundation.
—Prov. 10:25

The fear of the Lord prolongeth days: but the years of the wicked shall be shortened. —Prov. 10:27

The hope of the righteous shall be gladness: but the expectation of the wicked shall perish.—Prov. 10:28

The way of the Lord is strength to the upright: but destruction shall be to the workers of iniquity.
—Prov. 10:29

The righteous shall never be removed: but the wicked shall not inhabit the earth. —Prov. 10:30

The integrity of the upright shall guide them: but the perverseness of transgressors shall destroy them.
—Prov. 11:3

The righteousness of the perfect shall direct his way: but the wicked shall fall by his own wickedness.
—Prov. 11:5

The righteousness of the upright shall deliver them: but transgressors shall be taken in their own naughtiness. —Prov. 11:6

When a wicked man dieth, his expectation shall perish: and the hope of unjust men perisheth.
—Prov. 11:7

As righteousness tendeth to life: so he that pursueth evil pursueth it to his own death. —Prov. 11:19

Though hand join in hand, the wicked shall not be unpunished: but the seed of the righteous shall be delivered. —Prov. 11:21

The desire of the righteous is only good: but the expectation of the wicked is wrath. —Prov. 11:23

Behold, the righteous shall be recompensed in the earth: much more the wicked and the sinner.
—Prov. 11:31

A good man obtaineth favour of the Lord: but a man of wicked devices will he condemn.
—Prov. 12:2

A man shall not be established by wickedness: but the root of the righteous shall not be moved.
—Prov. 12:3

The wicked are overthrown, and are not: but the house of the righteous shall stand. —Prov. 12:7

A man shall eat good by the fruit of his mouth: but the soul of the transgressors shall eat violence.
—Prov. 13:2

Righteousness keepeth him that is upright in the way: but wickedness overthroweth the sinner.
—Prov. 13:6

The light of the righteous rejoiceth: but the lamp of the wicked shall be put out. —Prov. 13:9

The way of transgressors is hard.
—Prov. 13:15

Evil pursueth sinners: but to the righteous good shall be repayed.
—Prov. 13:21

The righteous eateth to the satifying of his soul: but the belly of the wicked shall want. —Prov. 13:25

There is a way which seemeth right unto a man, but the end thereof are the ways of death.
—Prov. 14:12

He that keepeth the commandment keepeth his own soul; but he that despiseth his ways shall die.
—Prov. 19:16

It is joy to the just to do judgment: but destruction shall be to the workers of iniquity. —Prov. 21:15

There shall be no reward to the evil man; the candle of the wicked shall be put out.   —Prov. 24:20

The great God that formed all things both rewardeth the fool, and rewardeth transgressors.
                        —Prov. 26:10

Happy is the man that feareth alway: but he that hardeneth his heart shall fall into mischief.
                        —Prov. 28:14

Whoso walketh uprightly shall be saved: but he that is perverse in his ways shall fall at once.
                        —Prov. 28:18

When the wicked are multiplied, transgression increaseth: but the righteous shall see their fall.
                        —Prov. 29:16

God giveth to a man that is good in his sight wisdom, and knowledge, and joy: but to the sinner he giveth travail, to gather and to heap up, that he may give to him that is good before God.   —Ecc. 2:26

Be not over much wicked, neither be thou foolish: why shouldest thou die before thy time? —Eccl. 7:17

Woe unto the wicked! it shall be ill with him: for the reward of his hands shall be given him.
                        —Isa. 3:11

I will punish the world for their evil, and the wicked for their iniquity; and I will cause the arrogancy of the proud to cease, and will lay low the haughtiness of the terrible.   —Isa. 13:11

There is no peace, saith the Lord, unto the wicked.   —Isa. 48:22

According to their deeds, accordingly he will repay, fury to his adversaries, recompense to his enemies.   —Isa. 59:18

Wherefore doth a living man complain, a man for the punishment of his sins?   —Lam. 3:39

I will do unto them after their way, and according to their deserts will I judge them.   —Ezek. 7:27

Thus saith the Lord God, I will even deal with thee as thou hast done.   —Ezek. 16:59

The ways of the Lord are right, and the just shall walk in them: but the transgressors shall fall therein.
                        —Hos. 14:9

Whosoever hath, to him shall be given, and he shall have more abundance: but whosoever hath not, from him shall be taken away even that he hath.   —Matt. 13:12

Whosoever will save his life shall lose it: but whosoever will lose his life for my sake, the same shall save it.   —Luke 9:24

If ye live after the flesh, ye shall die: but if ye through the Spirit do mortify the deeds of the body, ye shall live.   —Rom. 8:13

Whatsoever a man soweth, that shall he also reap.   —Gal. 6:7

He that soweth to his flesh shall of the flesh reap corruption; but he that soweth to the Spirit shall of the Spirit reap life everlasting.
                        —Gal. 6:8

He that doeth wrong shall receive for the wrong which he hath done: and there is no respect of persons.
                        —Col. 3:25

How shall we escape, if we neglect so great salvation.
—HEB. 2:3

Vengeance belongeth unto me, I will recompense, saith the Lord.
—HEB. 10:30

Revelation, see SCRIPTURE

Revenge, see RETALIATION

REVERENCE; see also WORSHIP, IRREVERENCE

The place whereon thou standest is holy ground. —EX. 3:5

Ye shall keep my sabbaths, and reverence my sanctuary.
—LEV. 19:30

I fell down before the Lord.
—DEUT. 9:18

What doth the Lord thy God require of thee, but to fear the Lord thy God, to walk in all his ways, and to love him, and to serve the Lord thy God with all thy heart and with all thy soul. —DEUT. 10:12

Thou shalt fear the Lord thy God; him thou shalt serve, and to him shalt thou cleave, and swear by his name. —DEUT. 10:20

Fear the Lord, and serve him in sincerity and in truth.
—JOSH. 24:14

Them that honour me I will honour, and they that despise me shall be lightly esteemed.
—1 SAM. 2:30

Fear the Lord, and serve him in truth with all your heart: for consider how great things he hath done for you. —1 SAM. 12:24

Let the fear of the Lord be upon you; take heed and do it: for there is no iniquity with the Lord our God. —2 CHRON. 19:7

The fear of the Lord, that is wisdom; and to depart from evil is understanding. —JOB 28:28

Men do therefore fear him: he respecteth not any that are wise of heart. —JOB 37:24

Stand in awe, and sin not: commune with your own heart upon your bed, and be still. —PSA. 4:4

He honoureth them that fear the Lord. —PSA. 15:4

The fear of the Lord is clean, enduring forever. —PSA. 19:9

What man is he that feareth the Lord? him shall he teach in the way that he shall choose. —PSA. 25:12

The secret of the Lord is with them that fear him; and he will shew them his covenant.
—PSA. 25:14

Let all the earth fear the Lord: let all the inhabitants of the world stand in awe of him. —PSA. 33:8

The eye of the Lord is upon them that fear him, upon them that hope in his mercy. —PSA. 33:18

His salvation is nigh them that fear him. —PSA. 85:9

God is greatly to be feared in the assembly of the saints, and to be had in reverence of all them that are about him. —PSA. 89:7

O come, let us worship and bow down; let us kneel before the Lord our maker. —PSA. 95:6

The mercy of the Lord is from everlasting to everlasting upon them that fear him. —PSA. 103:17

Holy and reverend is his name.
—PSA. 111:9

The fear of the Lord is the beginning of wisdom. —PSA. 111:10

Ye that fear the Lord, trust in the Lord.   —Psa. 115:11

My heart standeth in awe of thy word.   —Psa. 119:161

Blessed is every one that feareth the Lord; that walketh in his ways.   —Psa. 128:1

He will fulfil the desire of them that fear him: he also will hear their cry, and will save them.   —Psa. 145:19

The fear of the Lord is the beginning of knowledge.   —Prov. 1:7

Fear the Lord and depart from evil.   —Prov. 3:7

The fear of the Lord is to hate evil.   —Prov. 3:13

He that walketh in his uprightness feareth the Lord: but he that is perverse in his ways despiseth him.   —Prov. 14:2

In the fear of the Lord is strong confidence.   —Prov. 14:26

The fear of the Lord is a fountain of life, to depart from the snares of death.   —Prov. 14:27

The fear of the Lord tendeth to life: and he that hath it shall abide satisfied; he shall not be visited with evil.   —Prov. 19:23

Fear God, and keep his commandments: for this is the whole duty of man.   —Eccl. 12:13

Who is among you that feareth the Lord . . . let him trust in the name of the Lord, and stay upon his God.   —Isa. 50:10

Wherewith shall I come before the Lord, and bow myself before the high God?   —Mic. 6:6

The Lord is in his holy temple: let all the earth keep silence before him.   —Hab. 2:20

Be silent, O all flesh, before the Lord: for he is raised up out of his holy habitation.   —Zech. 2:13

He that feareth him, and worketh righteousness, is accepted with him.   —Acts 10:35

I bow my knees unto the Father of our Lord Jesus Christ.   —Eph. 3:14

At the name of Jesus every knee should bow.   —Phil. 2:10

We have had fathers of our flesh which corrected us, and we gave them reverence: shall we not much rather be in subjection unto the Father of spirits, and live?   —Heb. 12:9

Let us have grace, whereby we may serve God acceptably with reverence and godly fear.   —Heb. 12:28

REWARD; see also Retribution

If thou wilt walk in my ways, to keep my statutes and my commandments . . . then I will lengthen thy days.   —1 Kin. 3:14

For the work of a man shall he render unto him, and cause every man to find according to his ways.   —Job 34:11

Thou, Lord, wilt bless the righteous.   —Psa. 5:12

Those that wait upon the Lord, they shall inherit the earth.   —Psa. 37:1

Delight thyself also in the Lord; and he shall give thee the desires of thine heart.   —Psa. 37:4

The Lord knoweth the days of the upright: and their inheritance shall be for ever.   —Psa. 37:18

The righteous shall inherit the earth.   —Psa. 37:29

Wait on the Lord, and keep his way, and he shall exalt thee to inherit the land. —Psa. 37:34

Mark the perfect man, and behold the upright: for the end of that man is peace. —Psa. 37:37

Unto thee, O Lord, belongeth mercy: for thou renderest to every man according to his work.
—Psa. 62:12

No good thing will he withhold from them that walk uprightly.
—Psa. 84:11

The Lord preserveth all them that love him. —Psa. 145:20

My son, forget not my law; but let thine heart keep my commandments: For length of days, and long life, and peace, shall they add to thee. —Prov. 3:1, 2

Blessings are upon the head of the just. —Prov. 10:6

The desire of the righteous shall be granted. —Prov. 10:24

Behold, the righteous shall be recompensed in the earth.
—Prov. 11:31

The recompense of a man's hands shall he render unto him.
—Prov. 12:14

To the righteous good shall be repayed. —Prov. 13:21

He that followeth after righteousness and mercy findeth life, righteousness, and honour.
—Prov. 21:21

Shall not he render to every man according to his works?
—Prov. 24:12

He that putteth his trust in the Lord shall be made fat.
—Prov. 28:25

God giveth to a man that is good in his sight wisdom, and knowledge, and joy. —Eccl. 2:26

Cast thy bread upon the waters: for thou shalt find it after many days. —Eccl. 11:1

Say ye to the righteous, that it shall be well with him: for they shall eat the fruit of their doings.
—Isa. 3:10

If thou draw out thy soul to the hungry, and satisfy the afflicted soul; then shall thy light rise in obscurity, and thy darkness be as the noon day. —Isa. 58:10

According to their deeds, accordingly he will repay. —Isa. 59:18

I the Lord search the heart, I try the reins, even to give every man according to his ways and according to the fruit of his doings.
—Jer. 17:10

Thus saith the Lord God, I will even deal with thee as thou hast done. —Ezek. 16:59

Blessed are the poor in spirit: for theirs is the kingdom of heaven. Blessed are they that mourn: for they shall be comforted. Blessed are the meek: for they shall inherit the earth. Blessed are they which do hunger and thirst after righteousness: for they shall be filled. Blessed are the merciful: for they shall obtain mercy. Blessed are the pure in heart: for they shall see God. Blessed are the peacemakers: for they shall be called the children of God. Blessed are they which are persecuted for righteousness' sake: for theirs is the kingdom of heaven.
—Matt. 5:3–12

If ye love them which love you, what reward have ye?
—MATT. 5:46

Whosoever . . . shall confess me before men, him will I confess also before my Father which is in heaven. —MATT. 10:32

Whosoever shall give to drink unto one of these little ones a cup of cold water only in the name of a disciple, verily I say unto you, he shall in no wise lose his reward.
—MATT. 10:42

Whosoever hath, to him shall be given, and he shall have more abundance. —MATT. 13:12

He shall reward every man according to his works.
—MATT. 16:27

Well done, thou good and faithful servant: thou hast been faithful over a few things, I will make thee ruler over many things: enter thou into the joy of thy Lord.
—MATT. 25:21

Come, ye blessed of my Father, inherit the kingdom prepared for you from the foundation of the world: For I was an hungred, and ye gave me meat: I was thirsty, and ye gave me drink: I was a stranger, and ye took me in.
—MATT. 25:34, 35

Whosoever shall give you a cup of water to drink in my name . . . verily I say unto you, he shall not lose his reward. —MARK 9:41

Go thy way, sell whatsoever thou hast, and give to the poor, and thou shalt have treasure in heaven.
—MARK 10:21

Blessed are ye, when men shall hate you . . . for the Son of man's sake. Rejoice ye in that day, and leap for joy: for, behold, your reward is great in heaven.
—LUKE 6:22, 23

Love ye your enemies, and do good, and lend, hoping for nothing again; and your reward shall be great. —LUKE 6:35

Glory, honour, and peace, to every man that worketh good.
—ROM. 2:10

The gift of God is eternal life through Jesus Christ our Lord.
—ROM. 6:23

Eye hath not seen, nor ear heard, neither have entered into the heart of man, the things which God hath prepared for them that love him.
—1 COR. 2:9

Every man shall receive his own reward according to his own labour.
—1 COR. 3:8

He which soweth sparingly shall reap also sparingly; and he which soweth bountifully shall reap bountifully. —2 COR. 9:6

Whatsoever a man soweth, that shall he also reap. —GAL. 6:7

He that soweth to the Spirit shall of the Spirit reap life everlasting.
—GAL. 6:8

Let us not be weary in well doing: for in due season we shall reap, if we faint not. —GAL. 6:9

Whatsoever good things any man doeth, the same shall he receive of the Lord. —EPH. 6:8

Of the Lord ye shall receive the reward of the inheritance: for ye serve the Lord Jesus. —COL. 3:24

Godliness is profitable unto all things, having promise of the life that now is, and of that which is to come. —1 TIM. 4:8

If we suffer, we shall also reign with him. —2 TIM. 2:12

Henceforth there is laid up for me a crown of righteousness, which the Lord, the righteous judge, shall give me at that day. —2 TIM. 4:8

We are made partakers of Christ, if we hold the beginning of our confidence stedfast unto the end. —HEB. 3:14

Be not slothful, but followers of them who through faith and patience inherit the promise. —HEB. 6:12

Cast not away therefore your confidence, which hath great recompense of reward. —HEB. 10:35

Ye have need of patience, that, after ye have done the will of God, ye might receive the promise. —HEB. 10:36

Blessed is the man that endureth temptation: for when he is tried, he shall receive the crown of life. —JAS. 1:12

Whoso looketh into the perfect law of liberty, and continueth therein, he being not a forgetful hearer, but a doer of the work, this man shall be blessed in his deed. —JAS. 1:25

Be thou faithful unto death, and I will give thee a crown of life. —REV. 2:10

Behold, I come quickly; and my reward is with me, to give every man according as his work shall be. —REV. 22:12

Riches, see WEALTH

Right, see GOODNESS, RIGHTEOUSNESS, JUSTICE

RIGHTEOUSNESS; see also GOODNESS, INTEGRITY, PERFECTION, REWARD

He withdraweth not his eyes from the righteous. —JOB 36:7

Blessed is the man that walketh not in the counsel of the ungodly, nor standeth in the way of sinners, nor sitteth in the seat of the scornful. But his delight is in the law of the Lord; and in his law doth he meditate day and night. —PSA. 1:1, 2

Lord, who shall abide in thy tabernacle? who shall dwell in thy holy hill? He that walketh uprightly, and worketh righteousness, and speaketh the truth in his heart. —PSA. 15:1, 2

Blessed is the man unto whom the Lord imputeth not iniquity, and in whose spirit there is no guile. —PSA. 32:2

The mouth of the righteous speaketh wisdom, and his tongue talketh judgment. —PSA. 37:30

The righteous shall be glad in the Lord, and shall trust in him; and all the upright in heart shall glory. —PSA. 64:10

Light is sown for the righteous, and gladness for the upright in heart. PSA. 97:11

Blessed are they that keep judgment, and he that doeth righteousness at all times. —PSA. 106:3

Unto the upright there ariseth light in the darkness: he is gracious, and full of compassion, and righteous. —PSA. 112:4

Blessed are the undefiled in the way, who walk in the law of the Lord. —PSA. 119:1

Walk in the way of good men, and keep the paths of the righteous. —PROV. 2:20

The Lord will not suffer the soul of the righteous to famish. —PROV. 10:3

The desire of the righteous is only good. —PROV. 11:23

The fruit of the righteous is a tree of life; and he that winneth souls is wise. —PROV. 11:30

In the way of righteousness is life; and in the pathway thereof there is no death. —PROV. 12:28

Righteousness keepeth him that is upright in the way.—PROV. 13:6

He that followeth after righteousness and mercy findeth life, righteousness, and honour. —PROV. 21:21

The work of righteousness shall be peace; and the effect of righteousness quietness and assurance for ever. —ISA. 32:17

Sow to yourselves in righteousness, reap in mercy. —HOS. 10:12

Seek righteousness. —ZEPH. 2:3

Blessed are they which do hunger and thirst after righteousness: for they shall be filled. —MATT. 5:6

Blessed are the pure in heart: for they shall see God. —MATT. 5:8

Ye are the light of the world. —MATT. 5:14

A good man out of the good treasure of his heart bringeth forth that which is good. —LUKE 6:45

He that doeth truth cometh to the light, that his deeds may be made manifest, that they are wrought in God. —JOHN 3:21

Herein do I exercise myself, to have always a conscience void of offence toward God, and toward men. —ACTS 24:16

Yield your members servants to righteousness unto holiness. —ROM. 6:19

They that are after the flesh do mind the things of the flesh: but they that are after the Spirit, the things of the Spirit. —ROM. 8:5

To be spiritually minded is life and peace. —ROM. 8:6

As many as are led by the Spirit of God, they are the sons of God. —ROM. 8:14

Awake to righteousness, and sin not. —1 COR. 15:34

If any man be in Christ, he is a new creature: old things are passed away; behold, all things are become new. —2 COR. 5:17

Let us cleanse ourselves from all filthiness of the flesh and spirit, perfecting holiness in the fear of God. —2 COR. 7:1

The fruit of the spirit is love, joy, peace, longsuffering, gentleness, goodness, faith, Meekness, temperance. —GAL. 5:22, 23

If we live in the Spirit, let us also walk in the Spirit. —GAL. 5:25

Put on the new man, which after God is created in righteousness and true holiness. —EPH. 4:24

The fruit of the Spirit is in all goodness and righteousness and truth. —EPH. 5:9

Be blameless and harmless, the sons of God, without rebuke, in the midst of a crooked and perverse nation, among whom ye shine as lights in the world. —PHIL. 2:15

Whatsoever things are true, whatsoever things are honest, whatsoever things are just, whatsoever things are pure, whatsoever things are lovely, whatsoever things are of good report; if there be any virtue, and if there be any praise, think on these things. —PHIL. 4:8

Put on the new man, which is renewed in knowledge after the image of him that created him.
—COL. 3:10

Walk worthy of God.
—1 THESS. 2:12

God hath not called us into uncleanliness, but unto holiness.
—1 THESS. 4:7

Ye are all the children of light, and the children of the day: we are not of the night, nor of the darkness. 1 THESS. 5:5

Prove all things; hold fast that which is good. —1 THESS. 5:21

Abstain from all appearance of evil. —1 THESS. 5:22

Keep thyself pure.
—1 TIM. 5:22

Godliness with contentment is great gain. —1 TIM. 6:6

Flee also youthful lusts: but follow righteousness, faith, charity, peace, with them that call on the Lord out of a pure heart.
—2 TIM. 2:22

Unto the pure all things are pure.
—TIT. 1:15

Denying ungodliness and worldly lusts, we should live soberly, righteously, and godly, in this present world. —TIT. 2:12

Pure religion and undefiled before God and the Father is this, To visit the fatherless and widows in their affliction, and to keep himself unspotted from the world.
—JAS. 1:27

The wisdom that is from above is first pure, then peaceable, gentle, and easy to be intreated, full of mercy and good fruits, without partiality, and without hypocrisy.
—JAS. 3:17

The fruit of righteousness is sown in peace of them that make peace.
—JAS. 3:18

He that will love life, and see good days, let him refrain his tongue from evil, and his lips that they speak no guile. Let him eschew evil, and do good; let him seek peace, and ensue it.
—1 PET. 3:10, 11

Add to your faith virtue; and to virtue knowledge; And to knowledge temperance; and to temperance patience; and to patience godliness; And to godliness brotherly kindness; and to brotherly kindness charity. —2 PET. 1:5–7

Every one that doeth righteousness is born of him. —1 JOHN 2:29

If our heart condemn us not, then have we confidence toward God.
—1 JOHN 3:21

Follow not that which is evil, but that which is good. —3 JOHN 1:11

Rivalry, see CONTENTION

S

SACRIFICE; see also REDEMPTION, SUFFERING, RENUNCIATION

Hath the Lord as great delight in burnt offerings and sacrifices, as in obeying the voice of the Lord?
—1 SAM. 15:22

Offer the sacrifices of righteousness.
—PSA. 4:5

The sacrifices of God are a broken heart.
—PSA. 51:17

To do justice and judgment is more acceptable to the Lord than sacrifice.
—PROV. 21:3

To what purpose is the multitude of your sacrifices unto me?
—ISA. 1:11

I desired mercy, and not sacrifice.
—HOS. 6:6

If thy right hand offend thee, cut it off, and cast it from thee.
—MATT. 5:30

Go ye and learn what that meaneth, I will have mercy and not sacrifice.
—MATT. 9:13

He that loseth his life for my sake shall find it.
—MATT. 10:39

If thou wilt be perfect, go and sell that thou hast, and give to the poor, and thou shalt have treasure in heaven: and come and follow me.
—MATT. 19:20

Are ye able to drink of the cup that I shall drink of, and to be baptized with the baptism that I am baptized with?
—MATT. 20:22

To love him with all the heart . . . is more than all whole burnt offerings and sacrifices.
—MARK 12:33

Of a truth I say unto you, that this poor widow hath cast in more than they all: For all these have of their abundance cast in unto the offerings of God: but she of her penury hath cast in all the living that she had.
—LUKE 21:3, 4

He that loveth his life shall lose it.
—JOHN 12:25

Greater love hath no man than this, that a man lay down his life for his friends.
—JOHN 15:13

Our old man is crucified with him, that the body of sin might be destroyed.
—ROM. 6:6

Present your bodies a living sacrifice, holy, acceptable unto God, which is your reasonable service.
—ROM. 12:1

We then that are strong ought to bear the infirmities of the weak, and not to please ourselves.
—ROM. 15:1

Even Christ pleased not himself.
—ROM. 15:3

Though I give my body to be burned, and have not charity, it profiteth me nothing.

—1 COR. 13:3

We which live are always delivered unto death for Jesus' sake, that the life also of Jesus might be made manifest in our mortal flesh.

—2 COR. 4:11

I will very gladly spend and be spent for you; though the more abundantly I love you, the less I be loved.   —2 COR. 12:15

I am crucified with Christ.

—GAL. 2:20

God forbid that I should glory, save in the cross of our Lord Jesus Christ, by whom the world is crucified unto me, and I unto the world.

—GAL. 6:14

Sacrifice and offering thou wouldest not, but a body hast thou prepared me.   —HEB. 10:5

Offer up spiritual sacrifices.

—1 PET. 2:5

Hereby perceive we the love of God, because he laid down his life for us: and we ought to lay down our lives for the brethren.

—1 JOHN 3:16

Sacrilege, see IRREVERENCE

SADNESS; see also SORROW

Why is thy countenance sad, seeing thou art not sick? this is nothing else but sorrow of heart.

—NEH. 2:2

O my God, my soul is cast down within me: therefore will I remember thee.   —PSA. 42:6

Why art thou cast down, O my soul? and why art thou disquieted within me? hope thou in God.

—PSA. 43:5

Trouble and anguish have taken hold on me: yet thy commandments are my delights.   —PSA. 119:143

He healeth the broken in heart, and bindeth up their wounds.

—PSA. 147:3

Heaviness in the heart of man maketh it stoop: but a good word maketh it glad.   —PROV. 12:25

Hope deferred maketh the heart sick: but when the desire cometh, it is a tree of life.   —PROV. 13:12

A merry heart doeth good like a medicine: but a broken spirit drieth the bones.   —PROV. 17:22

Sorrow is better than laughter: for by the sadness of the countenance the heart is made better.

—ECCL. 7:3

Give unto them . . . the garment of praise for the spirit of heaviness.

—ISA. 61:3

He hath filled me with bitterness, he hath made me drunken with wormwood.   —LAM. 3:15

Remembering mine affliction and my misery, the wormwood and the gall. My soul hath them still in remembrance, and is humbled in me.

—LAM. 3:19,20

When my soul fainted within me I remembered the Lord.—JON. 2:7

Safety, see PROTECTION

SALVATION; see also REDEMPTION, RECONCILIATION, REMISSION, JUSTIFICATION, REGENERATION

Salvation belongeth unto the Lord.   —PSA. 3:8

He that is our God is the God of salvation; and unto God the Lord belong the issues from death.

—PSA. 68:20

Great is thy mercy toward me: and thou hast delivered my soul from the lowest hell. —Psa. 86:13

The Lord hath made known his salvation: his righteousness hath he openly shewed in the sight of the heathen. —Psa. 98:2

My righteousness is near; my salvation is gone forth, and mine arms shall judge the people; the isles shall wait upon me, and on mine arm shall they trust. —Isa. 51:5

The Lord hath made bare his holy arm in the eyes of all the nations; and all the ends of the earth shall see the salvation of our God. —Isa. 52:10

Ho, every one that thirsteth, come ye to the waters, and he that hath no money; come ye, buy, and eat; yea, come, buy wine and milk without money and without price. —Isa. 55:1

Incline your ear, and come unto me: hear, and your soul shall live. —Isa. 55:3

Keep ye judgment, and do justice: for my salvation is near to come, and my righteousness to be revealed. —Isa. 56:1

And it shall come to pass, that whosoever shall call on the name of the Lord shall be delivered. —Joel 2:32

Seek ye me, and ye shall live. —Amos 5:4

Unto you that fear my name shall the sun of righteousness arise with healing in his wings. —Mal. 4:2

She shall bring forth a son, and thou shalt call his name Jesus: for he shall save his people from their sins. —Matt. 1:21

Except ye be converted, and become as little children, ye shall not enter into the kingdom of God. —Matt. 18:3

All flesh shall see the salvation of God. —Luke 3:6

The Son of man is come to seek and to save that which was lost. —Luke 19:10

For God so loved the world, that he gave his only begotten Son, that whosoever believeth in him should not perish, but have everlasting life. —John 3:16

God sent not his Son into the world to condemn the world; but that the world through him might be saved. —John 3:17

Whosoever drinketh of the water that I shall give him shall never thirst; but the water that I shall give him shall be in him a well of water springing up into everlasting life. —John 4:14

He that heareth my word, and believeth on him that sent me, hath everlasting life, and shall not come into condemnation; but is passed from death unto life. —John 5:24

He that believeth on me hath everlasting life. —John 5:47

I am the bread of life: he that cometh to me shall never hunger; and he that believeth on me shall never thirst. —John 6:35

I am the resurrectioin and the life: he that believeth in me, though he were dead, yet shall he live. —John 11:25

These are written, that ye might believe that Jesus is the Christ, the Son of God; and that believing ye might have life through his name. —John 20:31

Neither is there salvation in any other: for there is none other name under heaven given among men, whereby we must be saved.

—ACTS 4:12

Whosoever among you feareth God, to you is the word of this salvation sent.   —ACTS 13:26

So hath the Lord commanded us, saying, I have set thee to be a light of the Gentiles, that thou shouldest be for salvation unto the ends of the earth.   —ACTS 13:47

We believe that through the grace of the Lord Jesus Christ we shall be saved.   —ACTS 14:11

What must I do to be saved?

—ACTS 14:30

Believe on the Lord Jesus Christ, and thou shalt be saved, and thy house.   —ACTS 14:31

I am not ashamed of the gospel of Christ: for it is the power of God unto salvation to every one that believeth.   —ROM. 1:16

The just shall live by faith.

—ROM. 1:17

Being justified by faith, we have peace with God through our Lord Jesus Christ: by whom also we have access by faith into his grace wherein we stand, and rejoice in hope of the glory of God.

—ROM. 5:1, 2

If thou shalt confess with thy mouth the Lord Jesus, and shalt believe in thine heart that God hath raised him from the dead, thou shalt be saved.   —ROM. 10:9

With the heart man believeth unto righteousness; and with the mouth confession is made unto salvation.   —ROM. 10:10

Whosoever shall call upon the name of the Lord shall be saved.

—ROM. 10:13

The preaching of the cross is to them that perish, foolishness; but unto us which are saved, it is the power of God.   —1 COR. 1:18

Godly sorrow worketh repentance to salvation not to be repented of.   —2 COR. 7:10

Ye are all the children of God by faith in Christ Jesus. —GAL. 3:26

By grace are ye saved through faith; and that not of yourselves; it is the gift of God.   —EPH. 2:8

Work out your own salvation with fear and trembling.

—PHIL. 2:12

Let us, who are of the day, be sober, putting on the breastplate of faith and love; and for an helmet, the hope of salvation.

—1 THESS. 5:8

God hath not appointed us to wrath, but to obtain salvation by our Lord Jesus Christ.

—1 THESS. 5:9

Christ Jesus came into the world to save sinners; of whom I am chief.   —1 TIM. 1:15

We trust in the living God, who is the Saviour of all men, specially of those that believe. —1 TIM. 4:10

The grace of God that bringeth salvation hath appeared to all men.

—TIT. 2:11

Not by works of righteousness which we have done, but according to his mercy he saved us, by the washing of regeneration, and renewing of the Holy Ghost. —TIT. 3:5

How shall we escape, if we neglect so great salvation. —HEB. 2:3

Being made perfect, he became the author of eternal salvation unto all them that obey him. —HEB. 5:9

He is able also to save them to the uttermost that come unto God by him, seeing he ever liveth to make intercession for them.
—HEB. 7:25

Lay apart all filthiness and superfluity of naughtiness, and receive with meekness the engrafted word, which is able to save your souls.
—JAS. 1:21

In this was manifested the love of God toward us, because that God sent his only begotten Son into the world, that we might live through him.   —1 JOHN 4:9

Sanctification, see PURIFICATION, REMISSION

Sanctimony, see HYPOCRISY, SELF-RIGHTEOUSNESS

Satisfaction, see CONTENTMENT

Scandal, see GOSSIP, SLANDER

SCORN; see also PRIDE

Wherefore hast thou despised the commandment of the Lord, to do evil in his sight? —2 SAM. 12:9

He that is ready to slip with his feet is as a lamp despised in the thought of him that is at ease.
—JOB 12:5

Blessed is the man that walketh not in the counsel of the ungodly, nor standeth in the way of sinners, nor sitteth in the seat of the scornful.   —PSA. 1:1

Let the lying lips be put to silence; which speak grievous things proudly and contemptuously against the righteous.   —PSA. 31:18

Our soul is exceedingly filled with the scorning of those that are at ease, and with the contempt of the proud.   —PSA. 123:4

The fear of the Lord is the beginning of knowledge: but fools despise wisdom and instruction.
—PROV. 1:7

How long, ye simple ones, will ye love simplicity? and the scorners delight in their scorning, and fools hate knowledge?   —PROV. 1:22

Surely he scorneth the scorners: but he giveth grace unto the lowly.
—PROV. 3:34

Reprove not a scorner, lest he hate thee: rebuke a wise man, and he will love thee.   —PROV. 9:8

If thou be wise, thou shalt be wise for thyself: but if thou scornest, thou alone shall bear it.
—PROV. 9:12

He that is void of wisdom despiseth his neighbour.
—PROV. 11:12

A wise son heareth his father's instruction: but a scorner heareth not rebuke.   —PROV. 13:1

A scorner seeketh wisdom, and findeth it not.   —PROV. 14:6

Fools make a mock at sin.
—PROV. 14:9

He that despiseth his neighbour sinneth.   —PROV. 14:21

A scorner loveth not one that reproveth him: neither will he go unto the wise.   —PROV. 15:12

Whoso mocketh the poor reproacheth his Maker; and he that is glad at calamities shall not be unpunished.   —PROV. 17:5

Judgments are prepared for scorners, and stripes for the back of fools. —Prov. 19:29

When the scorner is punished, the simple is made wise.
—Prov. 21:11

Proud and haughty scorner is his name, who dealeth in proud wrath. —Prov. 19:24

Cast out the scorner, and contention shall go out; yea, strife and reproach shall cease.—Prov. 22:10

The thought of foolishness is sin: and the scorner is an abomination to men. —Prov. 24:9

Shall the axe boast itself against him that heweth therewith? or shall the saw magnify itself against him that shaketh it? as if the rod should shake itself against them that lift it up, or as if the staff should lift up itself, as if it were no wood.
—Isa. 10:15

Hear the word of the Lord, ye scornful men. —Isa. 28:14

Physician, heal thyself.
—Luke 4:23

He that despiseth you despiseth me; and he that despiseth me despiseth him that sent me.
—Luke 10:16

He . . . that despiseth, despiseth not man, but God. —Thess. 4:8

SCRIPTURE; see also Law

Moses wrote all the words of the Lord. —Ex. 24:4

Man doth not live by bread only, but by every word that proceedeth out of the mouth of the Lord doth man live. —Deut. 8:3

The secret things belong unto the Lord our God: but those things which are revealed belong unto us

and to our children for ever, that we may do all the words of this law. —Deut. 29:29

This book of the law shall not depart out of thy mouth; but thou shalt meditate therein day and night, that thou mayest observe to do according to all that is written therein. —Josh. 1:8

Lay up his words in thine heart.
—Job 22:22

I have esteemed the words of his mouth more than my necessary food. —Job 23:12

The words of the Lord are pure words: as silver tried in a furnace of earth, purified seven times.
—Psa. 12:6

The word of the Lord is right.
—Psa. 33:4

O send out thy light and thy truth: let them lead me; let them bring me unto thy holy hill, and to thy tabernacles. —Psa. 43:3

I will hear what God the Lord will speak. —Psa. 85:8

Wherewithal shall a young man cleanse his way? by taking heed thereto according to thy word.
—Psa. 119:9

Thy word have I hid in mine heart, that I might not sin against thee. —Psa. 119:11

I have rejoiced in the way of thy testimonies, as much as in all riches.
—Psa. 119:14

I will delight myself in thy statutes: I will not forget thy word.
—Psa. 119:16

Thy testimonies also are my delight and my counsellors.
—Psa. 119:24

This is my comfort in my affliction: for thy word hath quickened me.   —PSA. 119:50

I will meditate in thy precepts.   —PSA. 119:78

For ever, O Lord, thy word is settled in heaven.   —PSA. 119:89

How sweet are thy words unto my taste! yea, sweeter than honey to my mouth!   —PSA. 119:103

Thy word is a lamp unto my feet, and a light unto my path.
                    —PSA. 119:105

The entrance of thy words giveth light; it giveth understanding to the simple.   —PSA. 119:130

Thy word is very pure: therefore thy servant loveth it.
                    —PSA. 119:140

Thy word is true from the beginning: and every one of thy righteous judgments endureth for ever.
                    —PSA. 119:160

The commandment is a lamp; and the law is light; and reproofs of instruction are the way of life.
                    —PROV. 6:23

Every word of God is pure.
                    —PROV. 30:5

Seek ye out of the book of the Lord, and read.   —ISA. 34:16

The grass withereth, the flower fadeth: but the word of our God shall stand for ever.   —ISA. 40:8

Hear ye, and give ear; be not proud: for the Lord hath spoken.
                    —JER. 13:15

Thy words were found, and I did eat them; and thy word was unto me the joy and rejoicing of mine heart.   —JER. 15:16

O earth, earth, earth, hear the word of the Lord.   —JER. 22:29

I will shew thee that which is noted in the scripture of truth.
                    —DAN. 10:21

Whosoever heareth these sayings of mine, and doeth them, I will liken him unto a wise man, which built his house upon a rock.
                    —MATT. 7:24

He that hath ears to hear, let him hear.   —MATT. 11:15

Ye do err, not knowing the scriptures, nor the power of God.
                    —MATT. 22:29

Repent ye, and believe the gospel.
                    —MARK 1:15

Heaven and earth shall pass away, but my words shall not pass away.   —MARK 13:31

Blessed are they that hear the word of God and keep it.
                    —LUKE 11:28

Search the scriptures; for in them ye think ye have eternal life: and they are they which testify of me.
                    —JOHN 5:39

The words that I speak unto you, they are spirit, and they are life.
                    —JOHN 6:63

If ye continue in my word, then are ye my disciples indeed; And ye shall know the truth, and the truth shall make you free.
                    —JOHN 8:31, 32

The scripture cannot be broken.
                    —JOHN 10:35

Thy word is truth.—JOHN 17:17

These are written, that ye might believe that Jesus is the Christ, the Son of God; and that believing ye might have life through his name.
                    —JOHN 20:31

What saith the scripture?
—Rom. 4:3

Faith cometh by hearing, and hearing by the word of God.
—Rom. 10:17

Whatsoever things were written aforetime were written for our learning, that we through patience and comfort of the scriptures might have hope. —Rom. 15:4

Take the helmet of salvation, and the sword of the Spirit, which is the word of God. —Eph. 6:17

The word of life. —Phil. 2:16

Let the word of Christ dwell in you richly in all wisdom.
—Col. 3:16

Stand fast, and hold the traditions which ye have been taught, whether by word, or our epistle.
—2 Thess. 2:15

Hold fast the form of sound words, which thou hast heard of me. —2 Tim. 1:13

Study to shew thyself approved unto God, a workman that needeth not to be ashamed, rightly dividing the word of truth. —2 Tim. 2:15

All scripture is given by inspiration of God, and is profitable for doctrine, for reproof, for correction, for instruction in righteousness: That the man of God may be perfect, throughly furnished unto all good works. —2 Tim. 3:16, 17

We ought to give the more earnest heed to the things which we have heard, lest at any time we should let them slip. —Heb. 2:1

The word of God is quick, and powerful, and sharper than any two-edged sword. —Heb. 4:12

Receive with meekness the engrafted word, which is able to save your souls. —Jas. 1:21

Be ye doers of the word, and not hearers only, deceiving your own selves. —Jas. 1:22

As newborn babes, desire the sincere milk of the word, that ye may grow thereby. —1 Pet. 2:2

The prophecy came not in old time by the will of man: but holy men of God spake as they were moved by the Holy Ghost.
—2 Pet. 1:21

Be mindful of the words which were spoken before by the holy prophets, and of the commandment of us the apostles of the Lord and Saviour. —2 Pet. 3:2

These things write we unto you, that your joy may be full.
—1 John 1:4

Secrecy, see Concealment

Security, see Protection

SELF-CONTROL; see also Meekness, Patience, Abstinence, Temperance, Chastity, Celibacy

Be ye not as the horse, or as the mule, which have no understanding: whose mouth must be held in with bit and bridle. —Psa. 32:9

I will keep my mouth with a bridle, while the wicked is before me. —Psa. 39:1

Set a watch, O Lord, before my mouth; keep the door of my lips.
—Psa. 141:3

In the multitude of words there wanteth not sin: but he that refraineth his lips is wise. —Prov. 10:19

A fool's wrath is presently known: but a prudent man covereth shame. —PROV. 12:16

He that keepeth his mouth keepeth his life: but he that openeth wide his lips shall have destruction. —PROV. 13:3

He that is slow to wrath is of great understanding.—PROV. 14:29

He that is slow to anger is better than the mighty; and he that ruleth his spirit than he that taketh a city. —PROV. 16:32

Whoso keepeth his mouth and his tongue keepeth his soul from troubles. —PROV. 21:23

He that hath no rule over his own spirit is like a city that is broken down, and without walls. —PROV. 25:28

Mortify the deeds of the body. —ROM. 8:13

All things are lawful unto me, but all things are not expedient. —1 COR. 6:12

Every man that striveth for the mastery is temperate in all things. —1 COR. 9:25

Charity . . . is not easily provoked. —1 COR. 13:4, 5

Take unto you the whole armour of God, that ye may be able to stand in the evil day, and having done all, to stand. —EPH. 6:11

Ye have not yet resisted unto blood, striving against sin. —HEB. 12:3

Be swift to hear, slow to speak, slow to wrath. —JAS. 1:19

If any man offend not in word, the same is a perfect man, and able also to bridle the whole body. —JAS. 3:2

Resist stedfast in the faith. —1 PET. 5:9

He that overcometh shall inherit all things; and I will be his God, and he shall be my son.—REV. 21:7

Self-denial, see RENUNCIATION, SACRIFICE, ABSTINENCE, TEMPERANCE, CHASTITY, CELIBACY

Self-exaltation, see BOASTING, CONCEIT, PRIDE

Self-indulgence, see LICENTIOUSNESS, PLEASURE

SELFISHNESS; see also PARSIMONY, UNSELFISHNESS

Am I my brother's keeper? —GEN. 4:9

All that a man hath will he give for his life. —JOB 2:4

He that is first in his own cause seemeth just; but his neighbour cometh and searcheth him. —PROV. 18:17

The poor useth intreaties; but the rich answereth roughly. —PROV. 18:23

He that giveth unto the poor shall not lack: but he that hideth his eyes shall have many a curse. —PROV. 28:27

I was a stranger, and ye took me not in. —MATT. 25:43

If ye do good to them which do good to you, what thank have ye? —LUKE 6:33

Ye entered not in yourselves, and them that were entering in ye hindered. —LUKE 11:52

Charity . . . seeketh not her own. —1 COR. 13:4, 5

Let no man seek his own. —1 COR. 10:24

Not that we are sufficient of ourselves to think any thing as of ourselves; but our sufficiency is of God.
—2 Cor. 3:5

He died for all, that they which live should not henceforth live unto themselves, but unto him which died for them, and rose again.
—2 Cor. 5:15

Look not every man on his own things, but every man also on the things of others. —Phil. 2:4

Men shall be lovers of their own selves. —2 Tim. 3:2

Whoso hath this world's good, and seeth his brother have need, and shutteth up his bowels of compassion from him, how dwelleth the love of God in him? —1 John 3:17

Self-restraint, see Self-control, Abstinence, Temperance, Patience

SELF-RIGHTEOUSNESS; see also Hypocrisy, Bigotry, Conceit

Wherefore . . . lift ye up yourselves above the congregation of the Lord? —Num. 16:3

If I justify myself, mine own mouth shall condemn me.
—Job 9:20

Thinketh thou this to be right, that thou saidst, My righteousness is more than God's? —Job 35:2

The way of a fool is right in his own eyes: but he that hearkeneth unto counsel is wise.—Prov. 12:15

There is a way which seemeth right unto a man, but the end thereof are the ways of death.
—Prov. 14:12

All the ways of a man are clean in his own eyes; but the Lord weigheth the spirits. —Prov. 16:2

Most men will proclaim every one his own goodness: but a faithful man who can find?—Prov. 20:6

Every way of a man is right in his own eyes: but the Lord pondereth the hearts. —Prov. 21:2

Whoso boasteth himself of a false gift is like clouds and wind without rain. —Prov. 25:14

He that trusteth in his own heart is a fool: but whoso walketh wisely, he shall be delivered.
—Prov. 28:26

There is a generation that are pure in their own eyes, and yet is not washed from their filthiness.
—Prov. 30:12

Woe unto them that are wise in their own eyes, and prudent in their own sight! —Isa. 5:21

Which say, Stand by thyself, come not near to me; for I am holier than thou. These are a smoke in my nose, a fire that burneth all the day. —Isa. 65:5

Take heed and beware of the leaven of the Pharisees and of the Sadducees. —Matt. 16:6

Ye are they which justify yourselves before men; but God knoweth your hearts. —Luke 16:15

God, I thank thee, that I am not as other men are. —Luke 18:9

They being ignorant of God's righteousness, and going about to establish their own righteousness, have not submitted themselves unto the righteousness of God.
—Rom. 10:3

Let him that thinketh he standeth take heed lest he fall.
—1 COR. 10:12

We should not trust in ourselves,
but in God.   —2 COR. 1:9

Not that we are sufficient of ourselves to think any thing of ourselves; but our sufficiency is of
God.   —2 COR. 3:5

He that glorieth, let him glory
in the Lord.   —2 COR. 10:17

Not he that commendeth himself is approved, but whom the
Lord commendeth. —2 COR. 10:18

If a man think himself to be
something, when he is nothing, he
deceiveth himself.   —GAL. 6:3

Self-sacrifice, see SACRIFICE, RE-
NUNCIATION

Sensuality, see ADULTERY, LICEN-
TIOUSNESS, LUST

Serenity, see PEACE

Seriousness, see SOBRIETY, SIN-
CERITY

SERVICE; see also MINISTRY,
HELP, GIVING, WORKS

Trust in the Lord, and do good.
—PSA. 37:3

Withhold not good from them to
whom it is due, when it is in the
power of thine hand to do it.
—PROV. 3:27

The liberal soul shall be made
fat: and he that watereth shall also
be watered himself. —PROV. 11:9

He that winneth souls is wise.
—PROV. 11:30

Heaviness in the heart of man
maketh it stoop: but a good word
maketh it glad.   —PROV. 12:25

He that hath mercy on the poor,
happy is he.   —PROV. 14:21

Whatsoever thy hand findeth to
do, do it with thy might.
—ECCL. 9:10

Cast thy bread upon the waters:
for thou shalt find it after many
days.   —ECCL. 11:1

In the morning sow thy seed, and
in the evening withhold not thine
hand.   —ECCL. 11:6

Relieve the oppressed, judge the
fatherless, plead for the widow.
—ISA. 1:17

Here am I; send me.   —ISA. 6:8

Blessed are ye that sow beside all
waters.   —ISA. 32:20

If thou draw out thy soul to the
hungry, and satisfy the afflicted
soul; then shall thy light rise in obscurity, and thy darkness be as the
noon day.   —ISA. 58:10

Whosoever shall give to drink
unto one of these little ones a cup
of cold water only in the name of
a disciple, verily I say unto you, he
shall in no wise lose his reward.
—MATT. 10:42

Whoso shall receive one such little child in my name receiveth me.
—MATT. 18:5

If thou wilt be perfect, go and
sell that thou hast, and give to the
poor, and thou shalt have treasure
in heaven: and come and follow me.
—MATT. 19:21

Come, ye blessed of my Father,
inherit the kingdom prepared for
you from the foundation of the
world: For I was an hungred, and
ye gave me meat: I was thirsty, and
ye gave me drink: I was a stranger,
and ye took me in: Naked, and ye
clothed me: I was sick, and ye
visited me: I was in prison, and ye
came unto me. —MATT. 25:34–36

Inasmuch as ye have done it unto one of the least of these my brethren, ye have done it unto me. —MATT. 25:40

Serve him, without fear, In holiness and righteousness before him, all the days of our life.
—LUKE 1:74, 75

Wist ye not that I must be about my Father's business?—LUKE 2:49

As ye would that men should do to you, do ye also to them likewise.
—LUKE 6:31

Love ye your enemies, and do good, and lend, hoping for nothing again; and your reward shall be great, and ye shall be the children of the Highest: for he is kind unto the unthankful and to the evil.
—LUKE 6:35

The harvest is great, but the labourers are few: pray ye therefore the Lord of the harvest, that he should send forth labourers into his harvest. —LUKE 10:1

He that reapeth receiveth wages, and gathereth fruit unto life eternal: that both he that soweth and he that reapeth may rejoice together.
—JOHN 4:36

I must work the works of him that sent me, while it is day.
—JOHN 9:4

Feed my lambs. —JOHN 21:15

Jesus . . . went about doing good. —ACTS 10:38

So labouring ye ought to support the weak. —ACTS 20:35

By patient continuance in well doing seek for glory and honour and immortality. —ROM. 2:7

Glory, honour, and peace, to every man that worketh good.
—ROM. 2:10

Present your bodies a living sacrifice, holy, acceptable unto God, which is your reasonable service.
—ROM. 12:1

Be kindly affectioned one to another with brotherly love; in honour preferring one another; Not slothful in business; fervent in spirit; serving the Lord. —ROM. 12:10, 11

Rejoice with them that do rejoice, and weep with them that weep.
—ROM. 12:15

We then that are strong ought to bear the infirmities of the weak, and not to please ourselves.
—ROM. 15:1

Let every one of us please his neighbour for his good to edification. —ROM. 15:2

I have planted, Apollos watered; but God gave the increase.
—1 COR. 3:6

We are labourers together with God. —1 COR. 3:9

Ye know that your labour is not in vain in the Lord. —1 COR. 15:58

Wherefore we labour, that . . . we may be accepted of him.
—2 COR. 5:9

He which soweth bountifully shall reap also bountifully.
—2 COR. 9:6

God is able to make all grace abound toward you; that ye, always having all sufficiency in all things, may abound to every good work. —2 COR. 9:8

We should remember the poor.
—GAL. 2:10

By love serve one another.
—GAL. 5:13

Bear ye one another's burdens, and so fulfil the law of Christ.
—GAL. 6:2

Let us not be weary in well doing: for in due season we shall reap, if we faint not.   —GAL. 6:9

As we have therefore opportunity, let us do good unto all men.
—GAL. 6:10

We are his workmanship, created in Christ Jesus unto good works.
—EPH. 2:10

As the servants of Christ, doing the will of God from the heart; With good will doing service, as to the Lord, and not to men: Knowing that whatsoever good thing any man doeth, the same shall he receive of the Lord.   —EPH. 6:6–8

Walk worthy of the Lord unto all pleasing, being fruitful in every good work.   —COL. 1:10

Whatsoever ye do in word or deed, do all in the name of the Lord Jesus.   —COL. 3:17

Whatsoever ye do, do it heartily, as to the Lord, and not unto men; Knowing that of the Lord ye shall receive the reward of the inheritance: for ye serve the Lord Christ.
—COL. 3:23, 24

Comfort yourselves together, and edify one another. —1 THESS. 5:11

Comfort the feebleminded, support the weak, be patient toward all men.   —1 THESS. 5:14

Be not weary in well doing.
—2 THESS. 3:13

Charge them . . . That they do good, that they be rich in good works, ready to distribute, willing to communicate; Laying up in store for themselves a good foundation against the time to come, that they may lay hold on eternal life.
—1 TIM. 6:17–19

Be a vessel unto honour, sanctified, and meet for the master's use, and prepared unto every good work.
—2 TIM. 2:21

Be perfect, throughly furnished unto all good works. —2 TIM. 3:17

Be careful to maintain good works.   —TIT. 3:8

Thy benefit should not be as it were of necessity, but willingly.
—PHIL. 1:4

God is not unrighteous to forget your work and labour of love, which ye have shewed toward his name, in that ye have ministered to the saints, and do minister.
—HEB. 6:10

Let us consider one another to provoke unto love and good works.
—HEB. 10:24

Lift up the hands which hang down, and the feeble knees.
—HEB. 12:12

Remember them that are in bonds, as bound with them; and them which suffer adversity, as being yourselves also in the body.
—HEB. 13:3

To do good and to communicate forget not: for with such sacrifices God is well pleased.
—HEB. 13:16

Make you perfect in every good work to do his will. —HEB. 13:21

Pure religion and undefiled before God and the Father is this, To visit the fatherless and widows in their affliction, and to keep himself unspotted from the world.
—JAS. 1:27

If a brother or sister be naked, and destitute of daily food, And one of you say unto them, Depart in peace, be ye warmed and filled; notwithstanding ye give them not those things which are needful to the body; what doth it profit?
—JAS. 2:15, 16

With well doing ye may put to silence the ignorance of foolish men.
—1 PET. 2:15

As every man hath received the gift, even so minister the same one to another, as good stewards of the manifold grace of God.
—1 PET. 4:10

Let us not love in word, neither in tongue; but in deed and in truth.
—1 JOHN 3:18

Shame, see DISHONOUR, REMORSE

Shortcoming, see IMPERFECTION, WANT

Sickness, see AFFLICTION, INFIRMITY, HEALING

SIN; see also EVIL, IMPERFECTION, REMISSION, RETRIBUTION

Be sure your sin will find you out.
—NUM. 32:23

How many are mine iniquities and sins? make me to know my transgression and my sin.
—JOB 13:23

My sin is ever before me.
—PSA. 51:3

Behold, I was shapen in iniquity; and in sin did my mother conceive me.
—PSA. 51:5

O God, thou knowest my foolishness; and my sins are not hid from thee.
—PSA. 69:5

If thou, Lord, shouldest mark iniquities, O Lord, who shall stand?
—PSA. 130:3

His own iniquities shall take the wicked himself, and he shall be holden with the cords of his sins.
—PROV. 5:23

He that sinneth against me wrongeth his own soul.
—PROV. 8:36

Wickedness overthroweth the sinner.
—PROV. 13:6

The way of transgressors is hard.
—PROV. 13:15

Evil pursueth sinners.
—PROV. 13:21

Fools make a mock of sin.
—PROV. 14:9

As he thinketh in his heart, so is he.
—PROV. 23:7

The thought of foolishness is sin.
—PROV. 24:9

In the transgression of the evil man there is a snare. —PROV. 29:6

Suffer not thy mouth to cause thy flesh to sin.
—ECCL. 5:8

One sinner destroyeth much good.
—ECCL. 9:18

All we like sheep have gone astray; we have turned every one to his own way.
—ISA. 53:6

Your iniquities have separated between you and your God.
—ISA. 59:2

We have sinned, and have committed iniquity, and have done wickedly, and have rebelled, even by departing from thy precepts and from thy judgments. —DAN. 9:5

The ways of the Lord are right, and the just shall walk in them: but the transgressors shall fall therein. —Hos. 14:9

Forgive us our sins. —Luke 11:4

God be merciful to me a sinner. —Luke 18:13

He that is without sin among you, let him first cast a stone. —John 8:7

Whosoever committeth sin is the servant of sin. —John 8:34

If I had not come and spoken unto them, they had not had sin. —John 15:22

All have sinned, and come short of the glory of God. —Rom. 3:23

Where no law is, there is no transgression. —Rom. 4:15

Wherefore, as by one man sin entered into the world, and death by sin; and so death passed upon all men, for that all have sinned. —Rom. 5:12

Sin is not imputed when there is no law. —Rom. 5:13

When ye were the servants of sin, ye were free from righteousness. —Rom. 6:20

The wages of sin is death. —Rom. 6:23

When we were in the flesh, the motions of sins, which were by the law, did work in our members to bring forth fruit unto death. —Rom. 7:5

I had not known sin, but by the law. —Rom. 7:7

Was then that which is good made death unto me? God forbid. But sin, that it might appear sin, working death in me by that which

is good; that sin by the commandment might become exceedingly sinful. —Rom. 7:13

There is nothing unclean of itself: but to him that esteemeth any thing to be unclean, to him it is unclean. —Rom. 14:14

Whatsoever is not of faith is sin. —Rom. 14:23

The scripture hath concluded all under sin. —Gal. 3:22

Unto the pure all things are pure. —Tit. 1:15

The sin that doth so easily beset us. —Heb. 12:1

When lust hath conceived, it bringeth forth sin: and sin, when it is finished, bringeth forth death. —Jas. 1:15

Whosoever shall keep the whole law, and yet offend in one point, he is guilty of all. —Jas. 2:10

To him that knoweth to do good, and doeth it not, to him it is sin. —Jas. 4:17

If we say that we have no sin, we deceive ourselves, and the truth is not in us. —1 John 1:8

Sin is transgression of the law. —1 John 3:4

Whosoever abideth in him sinneth not: whosoever sinneth hath not seen him, neither known him. —1 John 3:6

He that committeth sin is of the devil. —1 John 3:8

Whosoever is born of God doth not commit sin; for his seed remaineth in him: and he cannot commit sin, because he is born of God. — 1 John 3:9

All unrighteousness is sin.

—1 JOHN 5:17

SINCERITY; see also INTEGRITY, VERACITY

Fear the Lord, and serve him in sincerity and in truth.

—JOSH. 24:14

Serve the Lord with all your heart. —1 SAM. 12:20

My lips shall not speak wickedness, nor my tongue utter deceit.

—JOB 27:4

My words shall be of the uprightness of my heart: and my lips shall utter knowledge clearly.

—JOB 33:3

Lord, who shall abide in thy tabernacle? who shall dwell in thy holy hill? He that walketh uprightly, and worketh righteousness, and speaketh the truth in his heart.

—PSA. 15:1 ,2

Thou desirest truth in the inward parts. —PSA. 51:6

They that deal truly are his delight. —PROV. 12:22

He that walketh righteously, and speaketh uprightly . . . shall dwell on high. —ISA. 33:15, 16

Not every one that saith to me, Lord, Lord, shall enter into the kingdom of heaven; but he that doeth the will of my Father which is in heaven. —MATT. 7:21

They say, and do not.

—MATT. 23:3

Why call ye me, Lord, Lord, and do not the things which I say?

—LUKE 6:46

If it were not so, I would have told you. —JOHN 14:2

Let love be without dissimulation. —ROM. 12:9

Let us walk honestly, as in the day. —ROM. 13:13

Let us keep the feast . . . with the unleavened bread of sincerity.

—1 COR. 5:8

Whether therefore ye eat, or drink, or whatsoever ye do, do all to the glory of God.

—1 COR. 10:31

Though I speak with the tongues of men and of angels, and have not charity, I am become as sounding brass, or a tinkling cymbal.

—1 COR. 13:1

Grace be with all them that love our Lord Jesus Christ in sincerity.

—EPH. 6:24

This I pray, that . . . ye may approve things that are excellent; that ye may be sincere and without offence till the day of Christ.

—PHIL. 1:9, 10

Whatsoever ye do, do it heartily, as to the Lord, and not unto men.

—COL. 3:23

They profess that they know God; but in works they deny him.

—TIT. 1:16

Be ye doers of the word, and not hearers only, deceiving your own selves. —JAS. 1:22

Laying aside all malice, and all guile, and hypocrisies, and envies, and all evil speakings, As newborn babes, desire the sincere milk of the word, that ye may grow thereby.

—1 PET. 2:1, 2

If we say that we have fellowship with him, and walk in the darkness, we lie, and do not the truth.

—1 JOHN 1:6

He that saith, I know him, and keepeth not his commandments, is a liar, and the truth is not in him.
—1 JOHN 2:4

If a man say, I love God, and hateth his brother, he is a liar.
—1 JOHN 4:20

Sinlessness, see PERFECTION, RIGHTEOUSNESS

Sinner, see SIN, EVIL

Skepticism, see UNBELIEF, INFIDELITY

SLANDER

Thou shalt not raise a false report: put not thine hand with the wicked to be an unrighteous witness.
—EX. 23:1

Lord, who shall abide in thy tabernacle? . . . He that backbiteth not with his tongue, nor doeth evil to his neighbour, nor taketh up a reproach against his neighbour.
—PSA. 15:1, 3

Hide me from the secret counsel of the wicked; from the insurrection of the workers of iniquity: Who whet their tongue like a sword, and bend their bows to shoot their arrows, even bitter words.
—PSA. 64:2, 3

Whoso privily slandereth his neighbour, him will I cut off.
—PSA. 101:5

Deliver my soul, O Lord, from lying lips, and from a deceitful tongue.
—PSA. 120:2

He that hideth hatred with lying lips, and he that uttereth a slander, is a fool.
—PROV. 10:18

An hypocrite with his mouth destroyeth his neighbour.
—PROV. 11:9

There is that speaketh like the piercings of a sword: but the tongue of the wise is health.
—PROV. 12:18

A true witness delivereth souls: but a deceitful witness speaketh lies.
—PROV. 14:25

A froward man soweth strife: and a whisperer separateth chief friends.
—PROV. 16:28

A wicked doer giveth heed to false lips; and a liar giveth ear to a naughty tongue.
—PROV. 17:4

He that covereth a transgression seeketh love; but he that repeateth a matter separateth very friends.
—PROV. 17:9

The words of a talebearer are as wounds, and they go down into the innermost parts of the belly.
—PROV. 18:8

The north wind driveth away rain: so doth an angry countenance a backbiting tongue.—PROV. 25:23

A lying tongue hateth those that are afflicted by it; and a flattering mouth worketh ruin.
—PROV. 26:28

Surely the serpent will bite without enchantment; and a babbler is no better.
—ECCL. 10:11

Curse not the king, no not in thy thought; and curse not the rich in thy bedchamber: for a bird of the air shall carry the voice, and that which hath wings shall tell the matter.
—ECCL. 10:20

Blessed are ye, when men shall revile you, and persecute you, and shall say all manner of evil against you falsely, for my sake.
—MATT. 5:11

Do violence to no man, neither accuse any falsely.   —LUKE 3:14

Let all bitterness . . . and evil speaking, be put away from you, with all malice.   —EPH. 4:31

Speak evil of no man.

—TIT. 3:2

The tongue can no man tame; it is an unruly evil, full of deadly poison.   —JAS. 3:8

Speak not evil one of another.

—JAS. 4:11

He that speaketh evil of his brother, and judgeth his brother, speaketh evil of the law, and judgeth the law.   —JAS. 4:11

Sloth, see IDLENESS

SOBRIETY; see also ABSTINENCE, TEMPERANCE

Speak forth the words of truth and soberness.   —ACTS 26:25

I say, through the grace given unto me, to every man that is among you, not to think of himself more highly than he ought to think; but to think soberly, according as God hath dealt to every man the measure of faith.   —ROM. 12:3

Let us watch and be sober.

—1 THESS. 5:6

Let us, who are of the day, be sober.   —1 THESS. 5:8

A bishop then must be . . . vigilant, sober, of good behaviour.

—1 TIM. 3:2

A bishop must be . . . sober, just, holy, temperate.—TIT. 1:7, 8

Aged men be sober, grave, temperate, sound in faith, in charity, in temperance.   —TIT. 2:2

Teach the young women to be sober.   —TIT. 2:4

Young men likewise exhort to be sober minded.   —TIT. 2:6

Denying ungodliness and worldly lusts, we should live soberly, righteously, and godly, in this present world.   —TIT. 2:12

Be sober, and hope to the end for the grace that is to be brought unto you.   —1 PET. 1:13

The end of all things is at hand: be ye therefore sober, and watch unto prayer.   —1 PET. 4:7

Be sober, be vigilant.

—1 PET. 5:8

Solace, see COMFORT

Solemnity, see SOBRIETY

Solicitude, see ANXIETY

SORROW; see also SADNESS, REMORSE, COMFORT

Those which mourn may be exalted to safety.   —JOB 5:11

Mine eyes poureth out tears unto God.   —JOB 16:20

My harp is tuned to mourning.

—JOB 30:31

The Lord hath heard the voice of my weeping.   —PSA. 6:8

Weeping may endure for a night, but joy cometh in the morning.

—PSA. 30:5

Many sorrows shall be to the wicked.   —PSA. 32:10

I am poor and sorrowful: let thy salvation, O God, set me up on high.   —PSA. 69:29

They that sow in tears shall reap in joy.   —PSA. 126:5

He that goeth forth and weepeth, bearing precious seed, shall doubtless come again with rejoicing, bringing his sheaves with him.

—PSA. 126:6

He healeth the broken in heart, and bindeth up their wounds.

—Psa. 147:3

Even in laughter the heart is sorrowful; and the end of that mirth is heaviness.   —Prov. 14:13

A merry heart maketh a cheerful countenance: but by sorrow of the heart, the spirit is broken.

—Prov. 15:13

A time to mourn, and a time to dance.   —Eccl. 3:4

It is better to go to the house of mourning, than to the house of feasting.   —Eccl. 7:2

Sorrow is better than laughter: for by the sadness of the countenance the heart is made better.

—Eccl. 7:3

The heart of the wise is in the house of mourning; but the heart of fools is in the house of mirth.

—Eccl. 7:4

The Lord God will wipe away tears from off all faces.—Isa. 25:8

Thou shalt weep no more: he will be very gracious unto thee at the voice of thy cry.   —Isa. 30:19

The redeemed of the Lord shall return . . . and sorrow and mourning shall flee away.   —Isa. 51:11

Surely he hath borne our griefs, and carried our sorrows.

—Isa. 53:4

The Lord shall be thine everlasting light, and the days of thy mourning shall be ended.

—Isa. 60:20

He hath sent me . . . to comfort all that mourn . . . to give unto them beauty for ashes, the oil of joy for mourning, the garment of praise for the spirit of heaviness.

—Isa. 61:1–3

Weep ye not for the dead, neither bemoan him: but weep sore for him that goeth away.   —Jer. 22:10

I will turn their mourning into joy, and will comfort them.

—Jer. 31:13

Blessed are they that mourn: for they shall be comforted.

—Matt. 5:4

Blessed are ye that weep now: for ye shall laugh.   —Luke 6:21

Jesus wept.   —John 11:35

Ye shall weep and lament, but the world will rejoice; and ye shall be sorrowful, but your sorrow shall be turned into joy.   —John 16:20

Rejoice with them that do rejoice, and weep with them that weep.

—Rom. 12:15

Godly sorrow worketh repentance to salvation not to be repented of.

—2 Cor. 7:10

I would not have you to be ignorant, brethren, concerning them which are asleep, that ye sorrow not, even as others which have no hope.   —1 Thess. 4:13

God shall wipe away all tears from their eyes.   —Rev. 7:17

SPIRIT, SOUL; see also Heart

Man became a living soul.

—Gen. 2:7

There is a spirit in man: and the inspiration of the Almighty giveth them understanding.   —Job 32:8

Return, O Lord, deliver my soul.

—Psa. 6:4

Thou wilt not leave my soul in hell.   —Psa. 16:10

Your heart shall live for ever.
—Psa. 22:26

Unto thee, O Lord, do I lift up my soul. —Psa. 25:1

Into thine hand I commit my spirit. —Psa. 31:5

The Lord redeemeth the soul of his servants. —Psa. 34:22

My soul shall be joyful in the Lord. —Psa. 35:9

As the hart panteth after the water brooks, so panteth my soul after thee, O God. —Psa. 42:1

Create in me a clean heart, O God; and renew a right spirit within me. —Psa. 51:10

The Lord shall preserve thee from all evil: he shall preserve thy soul. —Psa. 121:7

The spirit of man will sustain his infirmity. —Prov. 18:14

He that keepeth the commandments keepeth his own soul.
—Prov. 19:16

The spirit of man is the candle of the Lord. —Prov. 20:27

Who knoweth the spirit of man that goeth upward, and the spirit of the beast that goeth downward to the earth? —Eccl. 3:21

There is no man that hath power over the spirit to retain the spirit.
—Eccl. 8:8

Then shall the dust return to the earth as it was: and the spirit shall return unto God who gave it.
—Eccl. 12:7

Make you a new heart and a new spirit: for why will ye die?
—Ezek. 18:31

With my soul have I desired thee in the night; yea, with my spirit within me will I seek thee early.
—Isa. 29:9

Fear not them which kill the body, but are not able to kill the soul. —Matt. 10:28

The spirit indeed is willing, but the flesh is weak. —Matt. 26:41

What shall it profit a man, if he shall gain the whole world, and lose his own soul? —Mark 8:36

When Jesus had cried with a loud voice, he said, Father, into thy hands I commend my spirit: and having said thus, he gave up the ghost. —Luke 23:46

A spirit hath not flesh and bones, as ye see me have. —Luke 24:39

God is a Spirit: and they that worship him must worship him in spirit and in truth. —John 4:24

It is the spirit that quickeneth; the flesh profiteth nothing.
—John 6:63

What man knoweth the things of a man, save the spirit of man which is in him? —1 Cor. 2:11

Glorify God in your body, and in your spirit, which are God's.
—1 Cor. 6:20

My spirit prayeth, but my understanding is unfruitful.
—1 Cor. 14:14

There is a natural body, and there is a spiritual body. —1 Cor. 15:44

The first Adam was made a living soul; the last Adam was made a quickening spirit. —1 Cor. 15:45

Flesh and blood cannot inherit the kingdom of God.
—1 Cor. 15:50

Though our outward man perish, yet the inward man is renewed day by day. —2 Cor. 4:7

We know that if our earthly house of this tabernacle were dissolved, we have a building of God, an house not made with hands, eternal in the heavens.—2 Cor. 5:1

I pray God your whole spirit and soul and body be preserved blameless unto the coming of our Lord Jesus Christ. —1 Thess. 5:23

As the body without the spirit is dead, so faith without works is dead also. —Jas. 2:26

The hidden man of the heart.
—1 Pet. 3:4

Stedfastness, see Constancy, Faithfulness

Stinginess, see Parsimony

Stranger, see Hospitality

STRENGTH; see also Ability, Omnipotence

Be strong, and quit yourselves like men. —1 Sam. 4:9

How are the mighty fallen!
—2 Sam. 1:19

In thine hand it is to make great, and to give strength unto all.
—Chron. 29:12

The joy of the Lord is your strength. —Neh. 8:10

The righteous also shall hold on his way, and he that hath clean hands shall be stronger and stronger. —Job 17:9

O Lord, my strength, and my redeemer. —Psa. 19:14

The Lord is the strength of my life. —Psa. 27:1

The God of Israel is he that giveth strength and power unto his people. —Psa. 68:35

Blessed is the man whose strength is in thee. —Psa. 84:5

The race is not to the swift, or the battle to the strong. —Eccl. 9:11

Strengthen ye the weak hands, and confirm the feeble knees.
—Isa. 35:3

He giveth power to the faint; and to them that have no might he increaseth strength. —Isa. 40:29

They that wait on the Lord shall renew their strength; they shall mount up with wings as eagles; they shall run, and not be weary; and they shall walk, and not faint.
—Isa. 40:31

The people that do know their God shall be strong, and do exploits. —Dan. 11:32

The Lord God is my strength.
—Hab. 3:19

The floods came, and the winds blew, and beat upon that house; and it fell not: for it was founded upon a rock. —Matt. 7:25

Tarry ye . . . until ye be endued with power from on high.
—Luke 24:49

In all these things we are more than conquerors through him that loved us. —Rom. 8:37

The foolishness of God is wiser than men; and the weakness of God is stronger than men.—1 Cor. 1:25

God hath chosen the weak things of this world to confound the things that are mighty. —1 Cor. 1:27

Watch ye, stand fast in the faith, quit you like men, be strong.
—1 Cor. 16:13

My grace is sufficient for thee: for my strength is made perfect in weakness. —2 Cor. 12:9

Be strong in the Lord, and in the power of his might. —EPH. 6:10

I can do all things through Christ which strengtheneth me.
—PHIL. 4:13

Walk worthy of the Lord unto all pleasing . . . Strengthened with all might, according to his glorious power, unto all patience and long-suffering with joyfulness.
—COL. 1:10, 11

His working . . . worketh in me mightily. —COL. 1:29

God hath not given us the spirit of fear; but of power, and of love, and of a sound mind. —2 TIM 1:7

Strife, see CONTENTION, WAR

Stupidity, see FOLLY, FOOL, IGNORANCE, INCOMPREHENSION

Submission, see RESIGNATION, PATIENCE, MEEKNESS, OBEDIENCE

Success, see ACCOMPLISHMENT

SUFFERING; see also AFFLICTION, PERSECUTION, SORROW, COMFORT

For thy sake we are killed all the day long; we are counted as sheep for the slaughter. —PSA. 44:22

Like as a woman with child, that draweth near the time of her delivery, is in pain, and crieth out in her pangs; so have we been in thy sight, O Lord. —ISA. 26:17

He was wounded for our transgressions, he was bruised for our iniquities. —ISA. 53:5

Ye shall be hated of all men for my name's sake: but he that endureth to the end shall be saved.
—MATT. 10:22

Are ye able to drink of the cup that I shall drink of, and to be baptized with the baptism that I am baptized with? —MATT. 20:22

I will shew him how great things he must suffer for my name's sake.
—ACTS 9:16

If children, then heirs; heirs of God, and joint-heirs with Christ; if so be that we suffer with him that we may be also glorified together.
—ROM. 8:17

I reckon that the sufferings of this present time are not worthy to be compared with the glory which shall be revealed in us. —ROM. 8:18

Being reviled, we bless; being persecuted, we suffer it. —1 COR. 4:12

Charity suffereth long.
—1 COR. 13:4

As ye are partakers of the sufferings, so shall ye be also of the consolation. —2 COR. 1:7

I will take pleasure in infirmities, in reproaches, in necessities, in persecutions, in distresses for Christ's sake: for when I am weak, then am I strong. —2 COR. 12:10

Unto you it is given in the behalf of Christ, not only to believe on him, but also to suffer for his sake.
—PHIL. 1:29

If we suffer, we shall also reign with him. —2 TIM. 2:12

Christ also suffered for us, leaving us an example, that ye should follow his steps. —1 PET. 2:21

If ye suffer for righteousness' sake, happy are ye. —1 PET. 3:14

It is better, if the will of God be so, that ye suffer for well doing, than for evil doing. —1 PET. 3:17

Rejoice, inasmuch as ye are partakers of Christ's sufferings; that, when his glory shall be revealed, ye may be glad also with exceeding joy.
—1 PET. 4:13

If any man suffer as a Christian, let him not be ashamed; but let him glorify God on this behalf.

—1 PET. 4:16

Let them that suffer according to the will of God commit the keeping of their souls to him in well doing, as unto a faithful Creator.

—1 PET. 4:19

The God of all grace, who hath called us unto his eternal glory by Christ Jesus, after that ye have suffered a while, make you perfect, stablish, strengthen, settle you.

—1 PET. 5:10

Fear none of those things which thou shalt suffer. —REV. 2:10

There shall be no more death, neither sorrow, nor crying, neither shall there be any more pain.

—REV. 21:4

Sufficiency, see PLENTY, CONTENTMENT

Superficiality, see HYPOCRISY, SELF-RIGHTEOUSNESS, HALFHEARTEDNESS

Supplication, see PRAYER

Surrender, see RESIGNATION

Swearing, see IRREVERENCE, VOW

Sycophancy, see FLATTERY

Sympathy, see COMFORT, MERCY

T

Talebearing, see GOSSIP

TALENT; see also CALLING

Unto one he gave five talents, to another two, and to another one; to every man according to his several ability. —MATT. 25:15

Having then gifts differing differently according to the grace that is given to us. —ROM. 12:6

There are diversities of gifts, but the same Spirit. —1 COR. 12:4

Covet earnestly the best gifts.
—1 COR. 12:31

He gave some, apostles; and some, prophets; and some, evangelists; and some, pastors and teachers. —EPH. 4:1

Neglect not the gift that is in thee.
—1 TIM. 4:14

As every man hath received the gift, even so minister the same one to another. —1 PET. 4:10

If any man minister, let him do it as of the ability which God giveth.
—1 PET. 4:11

Task, see DUTY, SERVICE, INDUSTRY, WORKS

Teaching, see INSTRUCTION

TEMPERANCE; see also ABSTINENCE, INTOXICATION

When thou sittest to eat with a ruler, consider diligently what is before thee: And put a knife to thy throat, if thou be a man given to appetite. —PROV. 23:1, 2

The drunkard and glutton shall come to poverty. —PROV. 23:21

Hast thou found honey? eat so much as is sufficient for thee, lest thou be filled therewith, and vomit it. —PROV. 25:16

Give me neither poverty nor riches; feed me with food convenient for me: Lest I be full, and deny thee, and say, Who is the Lord? or lest I be poor, and steal, and take the name of my God in vain.
—PROV. 30:8, 9

Be not righteous over much; neither make thyself over wise: why shouldst thou destroy thyself?
—ECCL. 7:16

Put ye on the Lord Jesus Christ, and make not provision for the flesh, to fulfil the lusts thereof.
—ROM. 13:14

Every man that striveth for the mastery is temperate in all things.
—1 COR. 9:25

I keep under my body, and bring it into subjection: lest that by any means, when I have preached to others, I myself should be a castaway. —1 COR. 9:27

The fruit of the Spirit is . . . temperance. —GAL. 5:22, 23

Be not drunk with wine, wherein is excess. —EPH. 5:18

Deacons be grave, not double-tongued, not given to much wine.
—1 Tim. 3:8

A bishop must be . . . sober, just, holy, temperate. —Tit. 1:7, 8

Add to your faith virtue; and to virtue knowledge; And to knowledge temperance. —2 Pet. 1:5, 6

TEMPTATION; see also Meekness, Patience, Abstinence, Temperance, Chastity, Celibacy

If sinners entice thee, consent thou not. —Prov. 1:10

Can a man take fire in his bosom, and his clothes not be burned?
—Prov. 6:27

Stolen waters are sweet, and bread eaten in secret is pleasant.
—Prov. 9:17

The righteous is more excellent than his neighbour: but the way of the wicked seduceth them.
—Prov. 12:26

The fear of the Lord is a fountain of life, to depart from the snares of death. —Prov. 13:14

A violent man enticeth his neighbour, and leadeth him into the way that is not good. —Prov. 16:29

Whoso causeth the righteous to go astray in an evil way, he shall fall himself into his own pit.
—Prov. 28:10

Watch and pray, that ye enter not into temptation. —Matt. 26:41

The spirit indeed is willing, but the flesh is weak. —Matt. 26:41

Lead us not into temptation; but deliver us from evil. —Luke 11:14

Why sleep ye? rise and pray, lest ye enter into temptation.
—Luke 22:46

Be not overcome of evil, but overcome evil with good.
—Rom. 12:21

Let him that thinketh he standeth take heed lest he fall.
—1 Cor. 10:12

God is faithful, who will not suffer you to be tempted above that ye are able; but will with the temptation also make a way to escape, that ye may be able to bear it.
—1 Cor. 10:13

Take unto you the whole armour of God, that ye may be able to withstand in the evil day, and having done all, to stand. —Eph. 6:11

They that will be rich fall into temptation and a snare, and into many foolish and hurtful lusts, which drown men in destruction and perdition. —1 Tim. 6:9

In that he himself hath suffered being tempted, he is able to succour them that are tempted. —Heb. 2:18

Ye have not resisted unto blood, striving against sin. —Heb. 12:3

Count it all joy when ye fall into divers temptations; Knowing this, that the trying of your faith worketh patience. —Jas. 1:2, 3

Blessed is the man that endureth temptation: for when he is tried, he shall receive the crown of life.
—Jas. 1:12

Let no man say when he is tempted, I am tempted of God: for God cannot be tempted with evil, neither tempteth he any man.
—Jas. 1:13

Every man is tempted, when he is drawn away of his own lust, and enticed. —Jas. 1:14

Resist the devil, and he will flee from you. —JAS. 4:7

Be vigilant; because your adversary the devil, as a roaring lion, walketh about, seeking whom he may devour. —1 PET. 5:8

Resist stedfast in the faith.
—1 PET. 5:9

The Lord knoweth how to deliver the godly out of temptations.
—2 PET. 2:9

Beware lest ye also, being led away with the error of the wicked, fall from your own stedfastness.
—2 PET. 3:17

Because thou hast kept the word of my patience, I also will keep thee from the hour of temptation.
—REV. 3:10

He that overcometh shall inherit all things; and I will be his God, and he shall be my son.
—REV. 21:7

Tenacity, see CONSTANCY, RESOLUTION

Tenderness, see KINDNESS

Test, see PROOF, CHASTENING, TEMPTATION

Testimony, see LAW, SCRIPTURE

THANKSGIVING; see also PRAISE

I will sing unto the Lord, because he hath dealt bountifully with me. —PSA. 13:6

Sing unto the Lord, O ye saints of his, and give thanks at the remembrance of his holiness.
—PSA. 30:4

O Lord my God, I will give thanks unto thee for ever.
—PSA. 30:12

Offer unto God thanksgiving; and pay thy vows unto the most High.
—PSA. 50:14

I will praise the name of God with a song, and will magnify him with thanksgiving. —PSA. 69:30

Unto thee, O God, do we give thanks, unto thee do we give thanks: for that thy name is near thy wondrous works declare.
—PSA. 75:1

We thy people and sheep of thy pasture will give thee thanks for ever: we will shew forth thy praises to all generations. —PSA. 79:13

It is a good thing to give thanks unto the Lord, and to sing praises unto thy name, O most High.
—PSA. 92:1

Let us come before his presence with thanksgiving, and make a joyful noise unto him with psalms.
—PSA. 95:2

Enter into his gates with thanksgiving, and into his courts with praise: be thankful unto him, and bless his name. —PSA. 100:4

O give thanks unto the Lord; call upon his name: make known his deeds among the people.
—PSA. 105:1

O give thanks unto the Lord, for he is good, for his mercy endureth for ever. —PSA. 107:1

Oh that men would praise the Lord for his goodness, and for his wonderful works to the children of men! —PSA. 107:8

Sacrifice the sacrifices of thanksgiving, and declare his works with rejoicing. —PSA. 107:22

I will offer unto thee the sacrifice of thanksgiving, and will call upon the name of the Lord.
—PSA. 116:17

Accept, I beseech thee, the free-will offerings of my mouth, O Lord, and teach me thy judgments. —PSA. 119:108

Thanks be to God, which giveth us the victory through our Lord Jesus Christ.   —1 COR. 15:57

Thanks be unto God for his unspeakable gift.   —2 COR. 9:15

In every thing by prayer and supplication with thanksgiving let your requests be made known unto God.   —PHIL. 4:6

We give thanks to God and the Father of our Lord Jesus Christ. —COL. 1:3

Let the peace of God rule in your hearts, to the which also ye are called in one body; and be ye thankful.   —COL. 3:15

Whatsoever ye do in word or deed, do all in the name of the Lord Jesus, giving thanks to God and the Father by him.   —COL. 3:17

Continue in prayer, and watch in the same with thanksgiving. —COL. 4:2

In every thing give thanks. —1 THESS. 5:18

I exhort therefore, that, first of all, supplications, prayers, intercessions, and giving of thanks, be made for all men.   —1 TIM. 2:1

Every creature of God is good, and nothing to be refused, if it be received with thanksgiving. —1 TIM. 4:4

Let us offer the sacrifice of praise to God continually, that is, the fruit of our lips giving thanks to his name.   —HEB. 13:5

Thirst, see DESIRE

THRIFT

A gracious woman retaineth honour: and strong men retain riches. —PROV. 11:16

The slothful man roasteth not that which he took in hunting: but the substance of a diligent man is precious.   —PROV. 12:27

A good man leaveth an inheritance to his children's children: and the wealth of the sinner is laid up for the just.   —PROV. 13:22

He that loveth pleasure shall be a poor man: he that loveth wine and oil shall not be rich. —PROV. 21:17

There is treasure to be desired and oil in the dwelling of the wise; but a foolish man spendeth it up. —PROV. 21:20

The ants are a people not strong, yet they prepare their meat in summer.   —PROV. 30:25

Let him that stole steal no more: but rather let him labour, working with his hands the thing which is good, that he may have to give to him that needeth.   —EPH. 4:28

Time, see AGE, ETERNITY, IMPERMANENCE, OPPORTUNITY

Timidity, see MEEKNESS, HUMILITY, COURAGE

Toil, see INDUSTRY

TOLERANCE; see also CHARITY, FORGIVENESS

He that is void of wisdom despiseth his neighbour: but a man of understanding holdeth his peace. —PROV. 11:12

The rich and poor meet together: the Lord is the maker of them all. —PROV. 22:2

Love your enemies.—Matt. 5:44

Judge not, that ye be not judged.
—Matt. 7:1

Why beholdest thou the mote that is in thy brother's eye, but considerest not the beam that is in thine own eye?   —Matt. 7:3

First cast out the beam out of thine own eye; and then shalt thou see clearly to cast out the mote out of thy brother's eye. —Matt. 7:5

He that is not against us is on our part.   —Mark 9:40

If ye love them which love you, what thank have ye? for sinners also love those that love them.
—Luke 6:32

He that is without sin among you, let him first cast a stone.
—John 8:7

God hath shewed me that I should not call any man common or unclean.   —Acts 10:28

God is no respecter of persons.
—Acts 10:34

Wherein thou judgest another, thou condemnest thyself; for thou that judgest doest the same things.
—Rom. 2:1

Who makest thee to differ from another? and what hast thou that thou didst not receive?
—1 Cor. 4:7

Charity suffereth long, and is kind . . . is not easily provoked . . . Beareth all things, believeth all things, hopeth all things, endureth all things.   —1 Cor. 13:4, 5, 7

If a man be overtaken in a fault, ye which are spiritual, restore such an one in the spirit of meekness; considering thyself, lest thou also be tempted.   —Gal. 6:1

Put on . . . bowels of mercies, kindness, humbleness of mind, meekness, longsuffering; Forbearing one another, and forgiving one another.   —Col. 3:12, 13

Be patient toward all men.
—1 Thess. 5:14

Speak evil of no man. —Tit. 3:2

Honour all men. —1 Pet. 2:17

Torment, see Suffering, Sorrow

Trade, see Commerce

Training, see Instruction

Tranquillity, see Peace

Transformation, see Conversion, Reformation, Regeneration

Transgression, see Sin, Retribution

Transience, see Impermanence

Trial, see Proof, Affliction, Suffering, Chastening, Temptation

Tribulation, see Affliction, Suffering, Sorrow, Persecution

Tribute, see Duty, Praise

TROUBLE; see also Affliction, Suffering, Sorrow, Persecution

Man is born unto trouble, as the sparks fly upward.   —Job 5:7

Man that is born of a woman is of few days, and full of trouble.
—Job 14:1

The Lord also will be a refuge for the oppressed, a refuge in times of trouble.   —Psa. 9:9

Have mercy upon me, O Lord, for I am in trouble. —Psa. 31:9

God is our refuge and strength, a very present help in trouble.
—Psa. 46:1

Call upon me in the day of trouble: I will deliver thee, and thou shalt glorify me. —Psa. 50:15

Thou hast been my defence and refuge in the day of my trouble. —Psa. 59:16

Thou, which hast shewed me great and sore trouble, shalt quicken me again, and shalt bring me up again from the depths of the earth. —Psa. 71:20

In the day of my trouble I sought the Lord. —Psa. 77:2

I will be with him in trouble; I will deliver him, and honour him. —Psa. 91:15

Trouble and anguish have taken hold on me: yet thy commandments are my delights. —Psa. 119:143

Though I walk in the midst of trouble, thou wilt revive me. —Psa. 138:7

The wicked is snared by the transgression of his lips: but the just shall come out of trouble. —Prov. 12:13

The Lord is good, a strong hold in the day of trouble; and he knoweth them that trust in him. —Nah. 1:7

Let not your heart be troubled: ye believe in God, believe also in me. —John 14:1

We are troubled on every side, yet not distressed. —2 Cor. 4:8

Trust, see Faith

TRUTH; see also Veracity, Falsehood

Send out thy light and thy truth: let them lead me. —Psa. 43:3

Behold, thou desirest truth in the inward parts. —Psa. 51:6

Thy mercy is great unto the heavens, and thy truth unto the clouds. —Psa. 57:10

Mercy and truth are met together; righteousness and peace have kissed each other. —Psa. 85:10

The Lord is good; his mercy is everlasting; and his truth endureth to all generations. —Psa. 100:5

Thy mercy is great above the heavens: and thy truth reacheth unto the clouds. —Psa. 108:4

I have chosen the way of truth. —Psa. 119:30

Let not mercy and truth forsake thee: bind them about thy neck; write them upon the table of thine heart. —Prov. 3:3

They that deal truly are his delight. —Prov. 12:22

Buy the truth, and sell it not. —Prov. 23:23

Truth is fallen in the street, and equity cannot enter. —Isa. 59:14

O Lord, are not thine eyes upon the truth? —Jer. 5:3

Grace and truth came by Jesus Christ. —John 1:17

If ye continue in my word, then are ye my disciples indeed; And ye shall know the truth, and the truth shall make you free. —John 8:31, 32

I am the way, the truth, and the life. —John 14:6

Howbeit when he, the Spirit of truth, is come, he will guide you into all truth. —John 16:13

Thy word is truth. —John 17:17

To this end was I born, and for this cause came I into the world, that I should bear witness unto the truth. —JOHN 18:37

Every one that is of the truth heareth my voice. —JOHN 18:37

Charity . . . rejoiceth in the truth. —1 COR. 13:4, 6

Stand therefore, having your loins girt about with truth.
—EPH. 6:14

Whatsoever things are true . . . think on these things. —PHIL. 4:8

He that saith, I know him, and keepeth not his commandments, is a liar, and the truth is not in him.
—1 JOHN 2:4

U

UNBELIEF; see also INFIDELITY

The fool hath said in his heart, There is no God.   —PSA. 14:1

Harden not your heart, as in the provocation, and as in the day of temptation in the wilderness.
    —PSA. 95:8

If ye will not believe, surely ye shall not be established.—ISA. 7:9

He is despised and rejected of men: a man of sorrows, and acquainted with grief: and we hid as it were our faces from him; he was despised, and we esteemed him not.
    —ISA. 53:3

I have loved you, saith the Lord. Yet ye say, Wherein hast thou loved us?   —MAL. 1:2

This people's heart is waxed gross, and their ears are dull of hearing, and their eyes they have closed; lest at any time they should see with their eyes, and hear with their ears, and should understand with their heart, and should be converted, and I should heal them.
    —MATT. 13:15

Why are ye so fearful? how is it that ye have no faith? —MARK 4:40

A prophet is not without honour, but in his own country, and among his own kin, and in his own house.
    —MARK 6:4

Lord, I believe: help thou mine unbelief.   —MARK 9:24

He that believeth and is baptized shall be saved; but he that believeth not shall be damned.
    —MARK 16:16

He that heareth you heareth me; and he that despiseth you despiseth me; and he that despiseth me despiseth him that sent me.
    —LUKE 10:16

O Jerusalem, Jerusalem, which killest the prophets, and stonest them that are sent unto thee; how often would I have gathered thy children together, as a hen doth gather her brood under her wings, and ye would not! —LUKE 13:34

If they hear not Moses and the prophets, neither will they be persuaded, though one rose from the dead.   —LUKE 16:31

Increase our faith. —LUKE 17:5

When the Son of man cometh, shall he find faith on the earth?
    —LUKE 18:8

Art thou the Christ? tell us. And he said unto them, If I tell you, ye will not believe.   —LUKE 22:67

O fools, and slow of heart to believe all that the prophets have spoken.   —LUKE 24:25

He was in the world, and the world was made by him, and the world knew him not. —JOHN 1:10

He came unto his own and his own received him not.—JOHN 1:11

We speak that we do know, and testify that we have seen; and ye receive not our witness.

—JOHN 3:11

If I have told you earthly things, and ye believe not, how shall ye believe, if I tell you of heavenly things? —JOHN 3:12

He that believeth on him is not condemned: but he that believeth not is condemned already, because he hath not believed in the name of the only begotten Son of God.

—JOHN 3:18

He that believeth on the Son hath everlasting life: and he that believeth not the Son shall not see life; but the wrath of God abideth on him. —JOHN 3:36

Except ye see signs and wonders, ye will not believe. —JOHN 4:48

Ye have not his word abiding in you: for whom he hath sent, him ye believe not. —JOHN 5:38

Ye will not come to me, that ye might have life. —JOHN 5:40

I am come in my Father's name, and ye receive me not: if another shall come in his own name, him ye will receive. —JOHN 5:43

How can ye believe, which receive honour one of another, and seek not the honour that cometh from God only? —JOHN 5:44

Had ye believed Moses, ye would have believed me: for he wrote of me. But if ye believe not his writings, how shall ye believe my words? —JOHN 5:46, 47

If ye believe not that I am he, ye shall die in your sins.

—JOHN 8:24

Because I tell you the truth, ye believe me not. —JOHN 8:45

If I say the truth, why do ye not believe me? —JOHN 8:46

He that is of God heareth God's words: ye therefore hear them not, because ye are not of God.

—JOHN 8:47

I told you, and ye believed not: the works that I do in my Father's name, they bear witness of me.

—JOHN 10:25

If I do not the works of my Father, believe me not. But if I do, though ye believe not me, believe the works: that ye may know, and believe, that the Father is in me, and I in him. —JOHN 10:37

If any man hear my words, and believe not, I judge him not: for I came not to judge the world, but to save the world. —JOHN 12:47

He that rejecteth me, and receiveth not my words, hath one that judgeth him: the word that I have spoken, the same shall judge him in the last day. —JOHN 12:48

Be not faithless, but believing.

—JOHN 20:27

How then shall they call on him in whom they have not believed? and how shall they believe in him of whom they have not heard?

—ROM. 10:14

Whatsoever is not of faith is sin.

—ROM. 14:23

The preaching of the cross is to them that perish foolishness; but unto us which are saved it is the power of God. —1 COR. 1:18

The natural man receiveth not the things of the Spirit of God: for they are foolishness unto him: neither can he know them, because they are spiritually discerned.
—1 Cor. 2:14

Be ye not unequally yoked together with unbelievers.
—2 Cor. 6:14

I obtained mercy, because I did it ignorantly in unbelief.
—1 Tim. 1:13

If we believe not, yet he abideth faithful: he cannot deny himself.
—2 Tim. 2:13

Take heed, brethren, lest there be in any of you an evil heart of unbelief, in departing from the living God. —Heb. 3:12

They could not enter in because of unbelief. —Heb. 3:19

Let us labour therefore to enter into that rest, lest any man fall after the example of unbelief.
—Heb. 4:11

Without faith it is impossible to please him: for he that cometh to God must believe that he is, and that he is a rewarder of them that diligently seek him. —Heb. 11:6

Who is a liar but he that denieth that Jesus is the Christ?
—1 John 2:22

Whosoever denieth the Son, the same hath not the Father.
—1 John 2:23

He that believeth on the Son of God hath the witness in himself: he that believeth not God hath made him a liar; because he believeth not the record that God gave of his Son. —1 John 5:10

Uncertainty, see Indecision, Instability, Unbelief

Uncharitableness, see Hatred, Enmity, Injustice, Judgment, Malice, Retaliation

UNDERSTANDING; see also Knowledge, Wisdom, Incomprehension

O that they were wise, that they understood this, that they would consider their latter end!
—Deut. 32:29

Give therefore thy servant an understanding heart . . . that I may discern between good and bad.
—1 Kin. 3:9

I have given thee a wise and understanding heart. —1 Kin. 3:12

Behold, the fear of the Lord, that is wisdom; and to depart from evil is understanding. —Job 28:28

Be ye not as the horse, or as the mule, which have no understanding.
—Psa. 32:9

A good understanding have all they that do his commandments.
—Psa. 111:10

The entrance of thy words giveth light; it giveth understanding unto the simple. —Psa. 119:130

Incline thine ear unto wisdom, and apply thine heart to understanding. —Prov. 2:2

If thou criest after knowledge, and liftest up thy voice for understanding: If thou seekest her as silver and searchest for her as for hid treasures: Then shalt thou understand the fear of the Lord, and find the knowledge of God.
—Prov. 2:3–5

Happy is the man . . . that getteth understanding. —PROV. 3:13

Hear, ye children, the instruction of a father, and attend to understanding. —PROV. 4:1

Get wisdom, get understanding: forget it not. —PROV. 4:5

Wisdom is the principal thing; therefore get wisdom: and with all thy getting get understanding.
—PROV. 4:7

O ye simple, understand wisdom: and ye fools, be ye of an understanding heart. —PROV. 8:5

Forsake the foolish, and live; and go in the way of understanding.
—PROV. 9:6

The fear of the Lord is the beginning of wisdom: and the knowledge of the holy is understanding.
—PROV. 9:10

In the lips of him that hath understanding wisdom is found.
—PROV. 10:13

A man of understanding hath wisdom. —PROV. 10:23

The wisdom of the prudent is to understand his way. —PROV. 14:8

Wisdom resteth in the heart of him that hath understanding.
—PROV. 14:33

The heart of him that hath understanding seeketh knowledge.
—PROV. 15:14

Folly is joy to him that is destitute of wisdom: but a man of understanding walketh uprightly.
—PROV. 15:21

Understanding is a wellspring of life unto him that hath it.
—PROV. 16:22

A fool hath no delight in understanding, but that his heart may discover itself. —PROV. 18:2

He that keepeth understanding shall find good. —PROV. 19:8

The man that wandereth out of the way of understanding shall remain in the congregation of the dead. —PROV. 21:16

Buy the truth, and sell it not; also wisdom, and instruction, and understanding. —PROV. 23:23

I will pray with the spirit, and I will pray with the understanding also: and I will sing with the spirit, and I will sing with the understanding also. —1 COR. 14:15

Be not children in understanding: howbeit in malice be ye children, but in understanding be men.
—1 COR. 14:20

Through faith we understand.
—HEB. 11:3

Unfairness, see INJUSTICE

Unfaithfulness, see DECEIT, INFIDELITY, INSTABILITY

Ungodliness, see EVIL, SIN

Unhappiness, see SADNESS, SORROW, REMORSE, DESPAIR

Unity, see HARMONY, BROTHERHOOD

Unrighteousness, see EVIL, SIN, IMPERFECTION

UNSELFISHNESS; see also CHARITY, GIVING HELP, SERVICE

Not as I will, but as thou wilt.
—MATT. 26:39

I seek not mine own will, but the will of the Father which hath sent me. —JOHN 5:30

Greater love hath no man than this, that a man lay down his life for his friends.　—JOHN 15:13

We then that are strong ought to bear the infirmities of the weak, and not to please ourselves.
　　　　　—ROM. 15:1

Even Christ pleased not himself.
　　　　　—ROM. 15:1

Let every one of us please his neighbour for his good to edification.　—ROM. 15:2

Though I be free from all men, yet have I made myself servant unto all, that I might gain the more.
　　　　　—1 COR. 9:19

Let no man seek his own, but every man another's wealth.
　　　　　—1 COR. 10:24

Charity . . . seeketh not her own.
　　　　　—1 COR. 13:4, 5

Not that we are sufficient of ourselves to think any thing of ourselves; but our sufficiency is of God.
　　　　　—2 COR. 3:5

He died for all, that they which live should not henceforth live unto themselves, but unto him which died for them, and rose again.
　　　　　—2 COR. 5:15

Though he was rich, yet for your sakes he became poor, that ye through his poverty might be rich.
　　　　　—2 COR. 8:9

I will very gladly spend and be spent for you.　—2 COR. 12:15

Let nothing be done through strife or vainglory; but in lowliness of mind let each esteem other better than themselves.　—PHIL. 2:3

Look not every man on his own things, but every man also on things of others.　—PHIL. 2:4

If ye fulfil the royal law according to the scripture, Thou shalt love thy neighbour as thyself, ye do well.
　　　　　—JAS. 2:8

Hereby perceive we the love of God, because he laid down his life for us: and we ought to lay down our lives for the brethren.
　　　　　—1 JOHN 3:16

Untruthfulness, see FALSEHOOD

Uprightness, see INTEGRITY, RIGHTEOUSNESS

V

Vanity, see BOASTING, CONCEIT, PRIDE

Veneration, see REVERENCE

Vengeance, see RETALIATION

VERACITY; see also INTEGRITY, SINCERITY, FALSEHOOD

Tell me nothing but that which is true in the name of the Lord.
—1 KIN. 22:16

My lips shall not speak wickedness, nor my tongue utter deceit.
—JOB 27:4

Lord, who shall abide in thy tabernacle? who shall dwell in thy holy hill? He that walketh uprightly, and worketh righteousness, and speaketh the truth in his heart.
—PSA. 15:1, 2

He that speaketh truth sheweth forth righteousness. —PROV. 12:17

The lip of truth shall be established for ever: but a lying tongue is but for a moment. —PROV. 12:19

Lying lips are abomination to the Lord: but they that deal truly are his delight. —PROV. 12:22

A righteous man hateth lying.
—PROV. 13:5

Righteous lips are the delight of kings; and they love him that speaketh right. —PROV. 16:13

Speak ye every man the truth to his neighbour. —ZECH. 8:16

Putting away lying, speak every man truth with his neighbour.
—EPH. 4:25

Vexation, see ANGER, AFFLICTION, TROUBLE

Vice, see EVIL, SIN, IMPERFECTION

VIGILANCE

Take heed to yourselves, that your heart be not deceived, and ye turn aside. —DEUT. 11:16

I watch, and am as a sparrow alone upon the house top.
—PSA. 102:7

My soul waiteth for the Lord more than they that watch for the morning. —PSA. 130:6

Blessed is the man that heareth me, watching daily at my gates, waiting at the posts of my doors.
—PROV. 8:34

The watchman said, The morning cometh, and also the night.
—ISA. 21:12

Watch the way, make thy loins strong, fortify thy power mightily.
—NAH. 2:1

I will stand upon my watch, and set me upon the tower, and will watch to see what he will say unto me. —HAB. 2:1

Watch therefore: for ye know not what hour your Lord doth come. —MATT. 24:42

If the goodman of the house had known in what watch the thief would come, he would have watched, and would not have suffered his house to be broken up. —MATT. 24:43

What, could ye not watch with me one hour? —MATT. 26:40

Watch and pray. —MATT. 26:41

Take ye heed, watch and pray: for ye know not when the time is. —MARK 13:33

What I say unto you I say unto all, Watch. —MARK 13:37

Let your loins be girded about, and your lights burning; And ye yourselves like unto men that wait for their lord. —LUKE 12:35, 36

Blessed are those servants, whom the lord when he cometh shall find watching. —LUKE 12:37

Be ye therefore ready also: for the Son of man cometh at an hour when ye think not. —LUKE 12:40

Why sleep ye? rise and pray, lest ye enter into temptation. —LUKE 22:46

Now it is high time to awake out of sleep: for now is our salvation nearer than when we believed. —ROM. 13:11

Watch ye, stand fast in the faith, quit you like men, be strong. —1 COR. 16:13

Continue in prayer, and watch in the same with thanksgiving. —COL. 4:2

Let us not sleep, as do others; but let us watch and be sober. —1 THESS. 5:6

Watch thou in all things. —2 TIM. 4:5

We ought to give the more earnest heed to the things which we have heard, lest at any time we should let them slip. —HEB. 2:1

The end of all things is at hand: be ye therefore sober, and watch unto prayer. —1 PET. 4:7

Be sober, be vigilant; because your adversary the devil, as a roaring lion, walketh about, seeking whom he may devour. —1 PET. 5:8

Look to yourselves, that we lose not those things which we have wrought. —2 JOHN 1:8

Be watchful, and strengthen the things which remain. —REV. 3:2

Blessed is he that watcheth. —REV. 16:15

Vigor, see STRENGTH

Vindictiveness, see RETALIATION

Violence, see MALICE

Virtue, see CHASTITY, GOODNESS, RIGHTEOUSNESS, INTEGRITY

Visitation, see AFFLICTION, TROUBLE, RETRIBUTION

Vocation, see CALLING, MINISTRY, ORDINATION

VOW

If a man vow a vow unto the Lord, or swear an oath to bind his soul with a bond; he shall not break his word, he shall do according to all that proceedeth out of his mouth. —NUM. 30:2

When thou shalt vow a vow unto the Lord thy God, thou shalt not slack to pay it: for the Lord thy God will surely require it of thee. —DEUT. 23:21

That which is gone out of thy lips thou shalt keep and perform. —DEUT. 23:23

Pay thy vows unto the most High. —PSA. 50:14

I have sworn, and I will perform it. —PSA. 119:106

When thou vowest a vow unto God, defer not to pay it.
—ECCL. 5:4

Better is it that thou shouldest not vow, than that thou shouldest vow and not pay. —ECCL. 5:5

Thou shalt not forswear thyself, but shalt perform unto the Lord thine oaths. —MATT. 5:33

Swear not, neither by heaven, neither by the earth, neither by any other oath: but let your yea be yea; and your nay, nay. —JAS. 5:12

W

WANT; see also IMPERFECTION, POVERTY, DESIRE

The Lord is my shepherd; I shall not want. —PSA. 23:1

There is no lack to them that fear him. —PSA. 34:9

They that seek the Lord shall not want any good thing. —PSA. 34:10

He will regard the prayer of the destitute. —PSA. 102:17

There is that maketh himself rich, yet hath nothing. —PROV. 13:7

He that giveth to the poor shall not lack. —PROV. 28:27

My people are destroyed for lack of knowledge. —HOS. 4:6

Your Father knoweth what things ye have need of, before ye ask him. —MATT. 6:8

They that be whole need not a physician, but they that are sick. —MATT. 9:12

Everywhere and in all things I am instructed both to be full and to be hungry, both to abound and to suffer need. —PHIL. 4:12

My God shall supply all your need according to his riches in glory by Christ Jesus. —PHIL. 4:19

Let patience have her perfect work, that ye may be perfect and entire, wanting nothing. —JAS. 1:4

If any of you lack wisdom, let him ask of God. —JAS. 1:5

WAR; see also CONTENTION

How are the mighty fallen in the midst of battle! —2 SAM. 1:25

The battle is not yours but God's. —2 CHRON. 20:15

Scatter thou the people that delight in war. —PSA. 68:30

He maketh wars to cease unto the end of the earth. —PSA. 46:9

I am for peace: but when I speak, they are for war. —PSA. 120:7

Every purpose is established by counsel: and with good advice make war. —PROV. 20:18

By wise counsel thou shalt make thy war: and in multitude of counsellors there is safety. —PROV. 24:6

Wisdom is better than weapons of war. —ECCL. 9:18

They shall beat their swords into plowshares, and their spears into pruninghooks. —ISA. 2:4

Woe to them that . . . trust in chariots, because they are many; and in horsemen, because they are very strong. —ISA. 31:1

Thou art my battle axe and weapons of war: for with these will I break in pieces the nations.

—JER. 51:20

The mighty . . . are gone down to hell with their weapons of war.
—Ezek. 32:27

I will break the bow and the sword and the battle out of the earth. —Hos. 2:18

Beat your plowshares into swords, and your pruninghooks into spears.
—Joel 3:10

Ye shall hear of wars and rumours of wars. —Matt. 24:6

All they that take the sword shall perish with the sword.
—Matt. 26:52

Love your enemies. —Luke 6:27

No man that warreth entangleth himself with the affairs of this life; that he may please him who hath chosen him to be a soldier.
—2 Tim. 2:4

Whence came wars and fightings among you? —Jas. 4:1

Ye fight and war, yet ye have not, because ye ask not. —Jas. 4:2

He that killeth with the sword must be killed with the sword.
—Rev. 13:10

Watchfulness, see Vigilance

Wavering, see Indecision

Weakness, see Infirmity

WEALTH; see also Avarice, Poverty

Beware that thou forget not the Lord thy God . . . when thou hast eaten and art full, and hast built goodly houses, and dwelt therein.
—Deut. 8:11, 12

Thou shalt remember the Lord thy God: for it is he that giveth thee power to get wealth.
—Deut. 8:18

The Lord maketh poor, and maketh rich: he bringeth low, and lifteth up. —1 Sam. 2:7

The rich man shall lie down, but he shall not be gathered: he openeth his eyes, and he is not.—Job 27:19

If I have made gold my hope, or have said to the fine gold, Thou art my confidence; If I rejoiced because my wealth was great, and because mine hand had gotten much; This also were an iniquity to be punished by the judge: for I should have denied the God that is above.
—Job 31:24–28

A little that a righteous man hath is better than the riches of many wicked. —Psa. 37:16

Be not thou afraid when one is made rich, when the glory of his house is increased; For when he dieth he shall carry nothing away: his glory shall not descend after him. —Psa. 49:16, 17

Behold, these are the ungodly, who prosper in the world; they increase in riches. —Psa. 73:12

Riches profit not in the day of wrath. —Prov. 11:4

He that trusteth in his riches shall fall. —Prov. 11:28

There is that maketh himself rich, yet hath nothing: there is that maketh himself poor, yet hath great riches. —Prov. 13:7

Better is little with the fear of the Lord than great treasure and trouble therewith. —Prov. 15:16

Better is a little with righteousness than great revenues without right. —Prov. 16:8

The poor useth intreaties; but the rich answereth roughly.

—Prov. 18:23

Wealth maketh many friends; but the poor is separated from his neighbour. —Prov. 19:4

The getting of treasures by a lying tongue is a vanity tossed to and fro of them that seek death.

—Prov. 21:6

Labour not to be rich.

—Prov. 23:4

Wilt thou set thine eyes upon that which is not? for riches certainly make themselves wings; they fly away as an eagle toward heaven.

—Prov. 23:5

He that by usury and unjust gain increaseth his substance, he shall gather it for him that will pity the poor. —Prov. 28:8

The rich man is wise in his own conceit; but the poor that hath understanding searcheth him out.

—Prov. 28:11

A faithful man shall abound with blessings: but he that maketh haste to be rich shall not be innocent.

—Prov. 28:20

He that hasteth to be rich hath an evil eye, and considereth not that poverty shall come upon him.

—Prov. 28:22

Give me neither poverty nor riches; feed me with food convenient for me: Lest I be full, and deny thee, and say, Who is the Lord? or lest I be poor, and steal, and take the name of my God in vain. —Prov. 30:8, 9

The profit of the earth is for all: the king himself is served by the field. —Eccl. 5:9

He that loveth silver shall not be satisfied with silver; nor he that loveth abundance with increase.

—Eccl. 5:10

When goods increase, they are increased that eat them: and what good is there to the owners thereof, saving the beholding of them with their eyes? —Eccl. 5:11

The sleep of a labouring man is sweet, whether he eat little or much: but the abundance of the rich will not suffer him to sleep.—Eccl. 5:12

There is a sore evil which I have seen under the sun, namely, riches kept for the owners thereof to their hurt. —Eccl. 5:13

As he came forth of his mother's womb, naked shall he return to go as he came, and shall take nothing of his labour, which he may carry away in his hand. —Eccl. 5:15

What profit hath he that hath laboured for the wind?

—Eccl. 5:16

There is an evil which I have seen under the sun, and it is common among men: A man to whom God hath given riches, wealth, and honour, so that he wanteth nothing for his soul of all that he desireth, yet God giveth him not power to eat thereof, but a stranger eateth it: this is vanity, and it is an evil disease. —Eccl. 6:1, 2

A feast is made for laughter, and wine maketh merry: but money answereth all things.—Eccl. 10:19

Woe unto them that join house to house, that lay field to field, till there be no place, that they may be placed alone in the midst of the earth. —Isa. 5:8

Let not the rich man glory in his riches.   —JER. 9:23

As the partridge sitteth on eggs, and hatcheth them not: so he that getteth riches, and not by right, shall leave them in the midst of his days, and at the end shall be a fool.
                —JER. 17:11

Woe unto him that buildeth his house by unrighteousness, and his chambers by wrong; that useth his neighbour's service without wages, and giveth him not for his work.
                —JER. 22:13

Neither their silver nor their gold shall be able to deliver them in the day of the Lord's wrath.
                —ZEPH. 1:18

Lay not up for yourselves treasures upon earth, where moth and rust doth corrupt, and where thieves break through and steal: But lay up for yourselves treasures in heaven.
                —MATT. 6:19, 20

Where your treasure is, there will your heart be also.   —MATT. 6:21

What is a man profited, if he shall gain the whole world, and lose his own soul?   —MATT. 16:26

It is easier for a camel to go through the eye of a needle, than for a rich man to enter into the kingdom of God.   —MATT. 19:24

The cares of this world, and the deceitfulness of riches, and the lusts of other things entering in choke the word, and it becometh unfruitful.
                —MARK 4:19

Woe unto you that are rich! for ye have received your consolation. Woe unto you that are full! for ye shall hunger.   —LUKE 6:24

A man's life consisteth not in the abundance of the things which he possesseth.   —LUKE 12:15

Ye cannot serve God and mammon.   —LUKE 16:13

We brought nothing into this world, and it is certain we can carry nothing out.   —1 TIM. 6:7

They that will be rich fall into temptation and a snare, and into many foolish and hurtful lusts, which drown men in destruction and perdition.   —1 TIM. 6:9

The love of money is the root of all evil.   —1 TIM. 6:10

Charge them that are rich in this world, that they be not highminded, nor trust in uncertain riches, but in the living God, who giveth us richly all things to enjoy.
                —1 TIM. 6:17

Go to now, ye rich men, weep and howl for your miseries that shall come upon you. Your riches are corrupted and your garments are motheaten. Your gold and silver is cankered; and the rust of them shall be a witness against you, and shall eat your flesh as it were fire . . . Behold, the hire of the labourers who have reaped down your fields, which is of you kept back by fraud, crieth: and the cries of them which have reaped are entered into the ears of the Lord. —JAS. 5:1–5

Whoso hath this world's good, and seeth his brother have need, and shutteth up his bowels of compassion from him, how dwelleth the love of God in him?
                —1 JOHN 3:17

Weeping, see SORROW

Welcome, see HOSPITALITY

Wickedness, see EVIL, SIN, IMPER-
FECTION, RETRIBUTION

Wife, see MARRIAGE

Will, see RESOLUTION, SELF-CON-
TROL

WISDOM; see also PRUDENCE,
KNOWLEDGE, UNDERSTANDING, IN-
STRUCTION, COUNSEL, IGNORANCE

Vain man would be wise, though
man be born like a wild ass's colt.
—JOB 11:2

With the ancient is wisdom; and
in length of days understanding.
—JOB 12:12

Behold the fear of the Lord, that
is wisdom; and to depart from evil
is understanding. —JOB 28:28

Behold, thou desirest truth in the
inward parts: and in the hidden part
thou shalt make me to know wisdom. —PSA. 51:6

A wise man will hear, and will increase learning; and a man of
understanding shall attain unto wise
counsels. —PROV. 1:5

Wisdom crieth without; she
uttereth her voice in the streets.
—PROV. 1:20

Incline thine ear unto wisdom,
and apply thine heart to understanding. —PROV. 2:2

The Lord giveth wisdom: out of
his mouth cometh knowledge and
understanding. —PROV. 1:6

He layeth up sound wisdom for
the righteous: he is a buckler to
them that walk uprightly.
—PROV. 2:7

Happy is the man that findeth
wisdom, and the man that getteth
understanding. —PROV. 3:13

Keep sound wisdom and discretion. —PROV. 3:21

Get wisdom, get understanding;
forget it not. —PROV. 4:5

Wisdom is the principal thing;
therefore get wisdom: and with all
thy getting get understanding.
—PROV. 4:7

Say unto wisdom, Thou art my
sister; and call understanding thy
kinswoman. —PROV. 7:4

O ye simple, understand wisdom:
and, ye fools, be ye of an understanding heart. —PROV. 8:5

Wisdom is better than rubies; and
all things that may be desired are
not to be compared to it.
—PROV. 8:11

I wisdom dwell with prudence,
and find out knowledge of witty inventions. —PROV. 8:12

Give instruction to a wise man,
and he will be yet wiser: teach a
just man, and he will increase in
learning. —PROV. 9:9

The fear of the Lord is the beginning of wisdom: and the knowledge of the holy is understanding.
—PROV. 9:10

If thou be wise, thou shalt be
wise for thyself: but if thou scornest, thou alone shalt bear it.
—PROV. 9:12

The wise in heart will receive
commandments: but a prating fool
shall fall. —PROV. 10:8

In the lips of him that hath
understanding wisdom is found.
—PROV. 10:13

Wise men lay up knowledge: but
the mouth of the foolish is near
destruction. —PROV. 10:14

The lips of the righteous feed
many; but fools die for want of wisdom. —PROV. 10:21

A man of understanding hath wisdom. —Prov. 10:23

A man shall be commended according to his wisdom.
—Prov. 12:8

The law of the wise is a fountain of life, to depart from the snares of death. —Prov. 13:14

A scorner seeketh wisdom, and findeth it not: but knowledge is easy unto him that understandeth.
—Prov. 14:6

The wisdom of the prudent is to understand his way: but the folly of fools is deceit. —Prov. 14:8

Wisdom resteth in the heart of him that hath understanding.
—Prov. 14:33

The lips of the wise disperse knowledge. —Prov. 15:7

The fear of the Lord is the instruction of wisdom. —Prov. 15:33

How much better is it to get wisdom than gold! and to get understanding rather to be chosen than silver! —Prov. 16:16

The wise in heart shall be called prudent: and the sweetness of the lips increaseth learning.
—Prov. 16:21

The heart of the wise teacheth his mouth, and addeth learning to his lips. —Prov. 16:23

Wisdom is before him that hath understanding. —Prov. 17:24

The heart of the prudent getteth knowledge; and the ear of the wise seeketh knowledge. —Prov. 18:15

He that getteth wisdom loveth his own soul: he that keepeth understanding shall find good.
—Prov. 19:18

There is treasure to be deserved and oil in the dwelling of the wise; but a foolish man spendeth it up.
—Prov. 21:20

Buy the truth, and sell it not; also wisdom, and instruction, and understanding. —Prov. 23:12

Through wisdom is an house builded; and by understanding it is established. —Prov. 24:3

A wise man is strong; yea, a man of knowledge increaseth strength.
—Prov. 24:5

Wisdom is too high for a fool: he openeth not his mouth in the gate.
—Prov. 24:7

Whoso keepeth the law is a wise son. —Prov. 28:5

In much wisdom is much grief: and he that increaseth knowledge increaseth sorrow. —Eccl. 1:18

God giveth to a man that is good in his sight wisdom, and knowledge, and joy. —Eccl. 2:26

Wisdom is a defence, and money is a defence; but the excellency of knowledge is, that wisdom giveth life to them that have it.
—Eccl. 7:12

Be not righteous over much; neither make thyself over wise: why shouldest thou destroy thyself?
—Eccl. 7:16

A man's wisdom maketh his face to shine. —Eccl. 8:1

A wise man's heart discerneth both time and judgment.
—Eccl. 8:5

Wisdom is better than strength.
—Eccl. 9:16

The words of wise men are heard in quiet more than the cry of him that ruleth among fools.

—Eccl. 9:17

Wisdom is better than weapons of war. —Eccl. 9:18

The words of a wise man's mouth are gracious. —Eccl. 10:12

Wisdom and knowledge shall be the stability of thy times, and strength of salvation. —Isa. 33:6

Let not the wise man glory in his wisdom. —Jer. 9:23

Wisdom is justified of her children. —Matt. 11:19

I would have you wise unto that which is good, and simple concerning evil. —Rom. 16:19

If any man among you seemeth to be wise in this world, let him become a fool, that he may be wise.

—1 Cor. 3:18

Walk circumspectly, not as fools, but as wise. —Eph. 5:15

Let the word of Christ dwell in you richly in all wisdom.

—Col. 3:10

Woe, see Sorrow, Affliction, Trouble

WONDER

That thy name is near thy wondrous works declare. —Psa. 75:1

Declare his glory among the heathen, his wonders among all people. —Psa. 96:3

Oh that men would praise the Lord for his goodness, and for his wonderful works to the children of men! —Psa. 107:8

Open thou mine eyes, that I may behold wondrous things out of thy law. —Psa. 119:18

I will praise thee; for I am fearfully and wonderfully made.

—Psa. 139:14

Marvellous are thy works; and that my soul knoweth right well.

—Psa. 139:14

There be three things which are too wonderful for me, yea, four which I know not: The way of an eagle in the air; the way of a serpent upon a rock; the way of a ship in the midst of the sea; and the way of a man with a maid.

—Prov. 30:18, 19

His name shall be called Wonderful. —Isa. 9:6

All the inhabitants of the isles shall be astonished at thee.

—Ezek. 27:35

How great are his signs! and how mighty are his wonders!

—Dan. 4:3

Many believed in his name, when they saw the miracles which he did.

—John 2:23

Jesus of Nazareth, a man approved of God among you by miracles and wonders and signs, which God did by him in the midst of you, as ye yourselves also know. —Acts 2:22

Word of God, see Scripture

Work, see Industry, Service, Works

WORKS; see also Service, Reward (*according to works*)

Even a child is known by his doings, whether his work be pure, and whether it be right.

—Prov. 20:11

Let your light so shine before men, that they may see your good works, and glorify your Father which is in heaven. —Matt. 5:16

Why call ye me, Lord, Lord, and do not the things which I say?
—Luke 6:46

Do works meet for repentance.
—Acts 26:20

A man is justified by faith without the deeds of the law.
—Rom. 3:28

A man is not justified by the works of the law, but by the faith of Jesus Christ. —Gal. 2:16

Be ye doers of the word, and not hearers only. —Jas. 1:22

Whoso looketh into the perfect law of liberty, and continueth therein, he being not a forgetful hearer, but a doer of the work, this man shall be blessed in his deed. —Jas. 1:25

What doth it profit, my brethren, though a man say he have faith, and have not works? —Jas. 2:14

Faith, if it hath not works, is dead. —Jas. 2:17

Shew me thy faith without thy works, and I will shew thee my faith by my works. —Jas. 2:18

As the body without the spirit is dead, so faith without works is dead also. —Jas. 2:20

By works a man is justified, and not by faith only. —Jas. 2:24

Let us not love in word, neither in tongue; but in deed.
—1 John 3:18

WORLDLINESS; see also Wealth, Pleasure, Lust

There is a way which seemeth right unto a man, but the end thereof are the ways of death.
—Prov. 14:12

A feast is made for laughter, and wine maketh merry: but money answereth all things.—Eccl. 10:19

Ye have sown much, and bring in little; ye eat, but ye have not enough; ye drink, but ye are not filled with drink; ye clothe you, but there is none warm; and he that earneth wages earneth wages to put it into a bag with holes.
—Hab. 1:6

No servant can serve two masters. —Luke 16:13

Where your treasure is, there will your heart be also. —Matt. 6:21

Take no thought for your life, what ye shall eat, or what ye shall drink; nor yet for your body, what ye shall put on. Is not life more than meat, and the body more than raiment? —Matt. 6:25

That which fell among thorns are they, which, when they have heard, go forth, and are choked with cares and riches and pleasures of this life, and bring no fruit to perfection.
—Luke 8:14

Be not conformed to this world: but be ye transformed by the renewing of your mind, that ye may prove what is the good, and acceptable, and perfect, will of God.
—Rom. 12:2

The wisdom of this world is foolishness with God.
—1 Cor. 3:19

The God of this world hath blinded the minds of them which believe not. —2 Cor. 4:4

Many walk . . . Whose end is destruction, whose God is their belly, and whose glory is in their shame, who mind earthly things.
—PHIL. 3:18, 19

Set your affections on things above, not on things on the earth.
—COL. 3:2

Mortify therefore your members which are upon the earth.
—COL. 3:5

Denying ungodliness and worldly lusts, we should live soberly, righteously, and godly, in this present world. —TIT. 2:12

Friendship of the world is enmity with God. —JAS. 4:4

Love not the world, neither the things that are in the world.
—1 JOHN 2:15

If any man love the world, the love of the Father is not in him.
—1 JOHN 2:15

All that is in the world, the lust of the flesh, and the lust of the eyes, and the pride of life, is not of the Father, but is of the world.
—1 JOHN 2:16

Worry, see ANXIETY

WORSHIP; see also PRAISE, PRAYER, THANKSGIVING

Worship the Lord in the beauty of holiness. —1 CHRON. 16:29

As for me, I will come into thy house in the multitude of thy mercy: and in thy fear will I worship toward thy holy temple.
—PSA. 5:7

We took sweet counsel together, and walked unto the house of God in company. —PSA. 55:14

All the earth shall worship thee, and shall sing unto thee; they shall sing to thy name. —PSA. 66:4

O come, let us worship and bow down: let us kneel before the Lord our maker. —PSA. 95:6

Worship him, all ye gods.
—PSA. 97:7

Exalt ye the Lord our God, and worship at his footstool; for he is holy. —PSA. 99:5

I was glad when they said unto me, Let us go into the house of the Lord. —PSA. 122:1

We will go into his tabernacles: we will worship at his footstool.
—PSA. 132:7

I will worship toward thy holy temple, and praise thy name for thy lovingkindness and for thy truth: for thou hast magnified thy word above all thy name. —PSA. 138:2

Come ye, and let us go up to the mountain of the Lord, to the House of the God of Jacob. —ISA. 2:3

Call a solemn assembly, gather the elders and all the inhabitants of the land into the house of the Lord your God, and cry unto the Lord.
—JOEL 1:14

The Lord is in his holy temple: let all the earth keep silence before him. —HAB. 2:20

Where two or three are gathered together in my name, there am I in the midst of them. —MATT. 18:20

Thou shalt worship the Lord thy God, and him only shalt thou serve.
—LUKE 4:8

God is a Spirit: and they that worship him must worship him in spirit and in truth. —JOHN 4:24

I bow my knees unto the Father of our Lord Jesus Christ.
—EPH. 3:14

At the name of Jesus every knee should bow. —PHIL. 2:10

Let all the angels of God worship him. —HEB. 1:6

All nations shall come and worship before thee. —REV. 15:4

Wrath, see ANGER

Wrong, see INJUSTICE, HARM, EVIL, SIN

Y

Yearning, see DESIRE

Z

ZEAL; see also CONSTANCY

Come with me, and see my zeal for the Lord. —2 KIN. 10:16

As the hart panteth after the water brooks, so panteth my soul after thee, O God. —PSA. 42:1

Sing unto the Lord, bless his name; shew forth his salvation from day to day. Declare his glory among the heathen, his wonders among all people. —PSA. 96:2, 3

With my whole heart have I sought thee. —PSA. 119:10

Whatsoever thy hand findeth to do, do it with thy might.
—ECCL. 9:10

Ye shall seek me, and find me, when ye shall search for me with all your heart. —JER. 29:13

Turn ye even to me with all your heart. —JON. 2:12

I must work the works of him that sent me, while it is day: the night cometh, when no man can work. —JOHN 9:14

With purpose of heart . . . cleave unto the Lord. —ACTS 11:23

By patient continuance in well doing seek for glory and honour and immortality. —ROM. 2:6

Not slothful in business; fervent in spirit; serving the Lord.
—ROM. 12:11

Forasmuch as ye are zealous of spiritual gifts, seek that ye may excel to the edifying of the church.
—1 COR. 14:12

Be ye stedfast, unmoveable, always abounding in the work of the Lord. —1 COR. 15:58

Wherefore we labour, that, whether present or absent, we may be accepted of him. —2 COR. 5:9

Let us not be weary in well doing: for in due season we shall reap, if we faint not. —GAL. 6:9

I press toward the mark for the prize of the high calling of God in Christ Jesus. —PHIL. 3:14

Whatsoever ye do, do it heartily, as to the Lord. —COL. 3:23

Be not weary in well doing.
—2 THESS. 3:13

The effectual fervent prayer of a righteous man availeth much.

—JAS. 5:16

See that ye love one another with a pure heart fervently.

—1 PET. 1:22

Above all things have fervent charity among yourselves.

—1 PET. 4:8

Earnestly contend for the faith which was once delivered unto the saints.

—JUDE 1:3

Subject Index

A

Abasement, see Humility, 94

Ability, 15; see also Strength, 220; Talent, 223

Absence, 15

Absolution, see Remission, 180; Forgiveness, 76

Abstinence, 16; see also Temperance, 223; Renunciation, 182; Intoxication, 113

Abuse, see Harm, 86; Malice, 130; Oppression, 142; Persecution, 151

Accomplishment, 16

Accord, see Harmony, 87

Accountability, see Responsibility, 189

Accusation, 16; see also Judgment, 116; Censure, 39

Acquittal, see Forgiveness, 76; Remission, 180

Action, see Industry, 106; Works, 244

Admonition, see Counsel, 55; Reproof, 185

Adoration, see Reverence, 193; Worship, 246; Praise, 158

Adulation, see Flattery, 74; Praise, 158

Adultery, 17

Adversity, see Affliction, 18; Trouble, 227

Advice, see Counsel, 55; Instruction, 111

Affection, see Love, 127

Affliction, 18; see also Sorrow, 217; Suffering, 221; Trouble, 227; Chastening, 41

Age, 20

Agreement, see Harmony, 87

Aid, see Help, 91; Service, 210; Giving, 79

Ailment, see Affliction, 18; Infirmity, 108; Healing, 89

Alms, see Giving, 79

Altruism, see Charity, 40; Giving, 79; Kindness, 119; Unselfishness, 233; Help, 91; Service, 210

Ambition, 21; see also Aspiration, 24; Pride, 163

Amusement, see Pleasure, 155

Anger, 22

Anguish, see Sorrow, 217; Suffering, 221

Animosity, see Anger, 22; Contention, 53; Enmity, 66; Hatred, 88; Malice, 130; Retaliation, 189

Anticipation, see Expectation, 69; Hope, 92

Anxiety, 23; see also Care, 38; Courage, 56

Apathy, see Halfheartedness, 86

Apostasy, see Backsliding, 27

Appearance, 24; see also Hypocrisy, 94

B

C

E

F

I

J

K

L

M

N

Q

R

S

W

Y

Z

A CATALOG OF SELECTED
DOVER BOOKS
IN ALL FIELDS OF INTEREST

A CATALOG OF SELECTED DOVER
BOOKS IN ALL FIELDS OF INTEREST

CONCERNING THE SPIRITUAL IN ART, Wassily Kandinsky. Pioneering work by father of abstract art. Thoughts on color theory, nature of art. Analysis of earlier masters. 12 illustrations. 80pp. of text. 5⅜ x 8½. 23411-8

ANIMALS: 1,419 Copyright-Free Illustrations of Mammals, Birds, Fish, Insects, etc., Jim Harter (ed.). Clear wood engravings present, in extremely lifelike poses, over 1,000 species of animals. One of the most extensive pictorial sourcebooks of its kind. Captions. Index. 284pp. 9 x 12. 23766-4

CELTIC ART: The Methods of Construction, George Bain. Simple geometric techniques for making Celtic interlacements, spirals, Kells-type initials, animals, humans, etc. Over 500 illustrations. 160pp. 9 x 12. (Available in U.S. only.) 22923-8

AN ATLAS OF ANATOMY FOR ARTISTS, Fritz Schider. Most thorough reference work on art anatomy in the world. Hundreds of illustrations, including selections from works by Vesalius, Leonardo, Goya, Ingres, Michelangelo, others. 593 illustrations. 192pp. 7⅛ x 10¼. 20241-0

CELTIC HAND STROKE-BY-STROKE (Irish Half-Uncial from "The Book of Kells"): An Arthur Baker Calligraphy Manual, Arthur Baker. Complete guide to creating each letter of the alphabet in distinctive Celtic manner. Covers hand position, strokes, pens, inks, paper, more. Illustrated. 48pp. 8¼ x 11. 24336-2

EASY ORIGAMI, John Montroll. Charming collection of 32 projects (hat, cup, pelican, piano, swan, many more) specially designed for the novice origami hobbyist. Clearly illustrated easy-to-follow instructions insure that even beginning papercrafters will achieve successful results. 48pp. 8¼ x 11. 27298-2

THE COMPLETE BOOK OF BIRDHOUSE CONSTRUCTION FOR WOODWORKERS, Scott D. Campbell. Detailed instructions, illustrations, tables. Also data on bird habitat and instinct patterns. Bibliography. 3 tables. 63 illustrations in 15 figures. 48pp. 5¼ x 8½. 24407-5

BLOOMINGDALE'S ILLUSTRATED 1886 CATALOG: Fashions, Dry Goods and Housewares, Bloomingdale Brothers. Famed merchants' extremely rare catalog depicting about 1,700 products: clothing, housewares, firearms, dry goods, jewelry, more. Invaluable for dating, identifying vintage items. Also, copyright-free graphics for artists, designers. Co-published with Henry Ford Museum & Greenfield Village. 160pp. 8¼ x 11. 25780-0

HISTORIC COSTUME IN PICTURES, Braun & Schneider. Over 1,450 costumed figures in clearly detailed engravings—from dawn of civilization to end of 19th century. Captions. Many folk costumes. 256pp. 8⅜ x 11¾. 23150-X

CATALOG OF DOVER BOOKS

THE BEST TALES OF HOFFMANN, E. T. A. Hoffmann. 10 of Hoffmann's most important stories: "Nutcracker and the King of Mice," "The Golden Flowerpot," etc. 458pp. 5⅜ x 8½. 21793-0

FROM FETISH TO GOD IN ANCIENT EGYPT, E. A. Wallis Budge. Rich detailed survey of Egyptian conception of "God" and gods, magic, cult of animals, Osiris, more. Also, superb English translations of hymns and legends. 240 illustrations. 545pp. 5⅜ x 8½. 25803-3

FRENCH STORIES/CONTES FRANÇAIS: A Dual-Language Book, Wallace Fowlie. Ten stories by French masters, Voltaire to Camus: "Micromegas" by Voltaire; "The Atheist's Mass" by Balzac; "Minuet" by de Maupassant; "The Guest" by Camus, six more. Excellent English translations on facing pages. Also French-English vocabulary list, exercises, more. 352pp. 5⅜ x 8½. 26443-2

CHICAGO AT THE TURN OF THE CENTURY IN PHOTOGRAPHS: 122 Historic Views from the Collections of the Chicago Historical Society, Larry A. Viskochil. Rare large-format prints offer detailed views of City Hall, State Street, the Loop, Hull House, Union Station, many other landmarks, circa 1904-1913. Introduction. Captions. Maps. 144pp. 9⅜ x 12¼. 24656-6

OLD BROOKLYN IN EARLY PHOTOGRAPHS, 1865-1929, William Lee Younger. Luna Park, Gravesend race track, construction of Grand Army Plaza, moving of Hotel Brighton, etc. 157 previously unpublished photographs. 165pp. 8⅞ x 11¾. 23587-4

THE MYTHS OF THE NORTH AMERICAN INDIANS, Lewis Spence. Rich anthology of the myths and legends of the Algonquins, Iroquois, Pawnees and Sioux, prefaced by an extensive historical and ethnological commentary. 36 illustrations. 480pp. 5⅜ x 8½. 25967-6

AN ENCYCLOPEDIA OF BATTLES: Accounts of Over 1,560 Battles from 1479 B.C. to the Present, David Eggenberger. Essential details of every major battle in recorded history from the first battle of Megiddo in 1479 B.C. to Grenada in 1984. List of Battle Maps. New Appendix covering the years 1967-1984. Index. 99 illustrations. 544pp. 6½ x 9¼. 24913-1

SAILING ALONE AROUND THE WORLD, Captain Joshua Slocum. First man to sail around the world, alone, in small boat. One of great feats of seamanship told in delightful manner. 67 illustrations. 294pp. 5⅜ x 8½. 20326-3

ANARCHISM AND OTHER ESSAYS, Emma Goldman. Powerful, penetrating, prophetic essays on direct action, role of minorities, prison reform, puritan hypocrisy, violence, etc. 271pp. 5⅜ x 8½. 22484-8

MYTHS OF THE HINDUS AND BUDDHISTS, Ananda K. Coomaraswamy and Sister Nivedita. Great stories of the epics; deeds of Krishna, Shiva, taken from puranas, Vedas, folk tales; etc. 32 illustrations. 400pp. 5⅜ x 8½. 21759-0

THE TRAUMA OF BIRTH, Otto Rank. Rank's controversial thesis that anxiety neurosis is caused by profound psychological trauma which occurs at birth. 256pp. 5⅜ x 8½. 27974-X

A THEOLOGICO-POLITICAL TREATISE, Benedict Spinoza. Also contains unfinished Political Treatise. Great classic on religious liberty, theory of government on common consent. R. Elwes translation. Total of 421pp. 5⅜ x 8½. 20249-6

MY BONDAGE AND MY FREEDOM, Frederick Douglass. Born a slave, Douglass became outspoken force in antislavery movement. The best of Douglass' autobiographies. Graphic description of slave life. 464pp. 5⅜ x 8½.　　22457-0

FOLLOWING THE EQUATOR: A Journey Around the World, Mark Twain. Fascinating humorous account of 1897 voyage to Hawaii, Australia, India, New Zealand, etc. Ironic, bemused reports on peoples, customs, climate, flora and fauna, politics, much more. 197 illustrations. 720pp. 5⅜ x 8½.　　26113-1

THE PEOPLE CALLED SHAKERS, Edward D. Andrews. Definitive study of Shakers: origins, beliefs, practices, dances, social organization, furniture and crafts, etc. 33 illustrations. 351pp. 5⅜ x 8½.　　21081-2

THE MYTHS OF GREECE AND ROME, H. A. Guerber. A classic of mythology, generously illustrated, long prized for its simple, graphic, accurate retelling of the principal myths of Greece and Rome, and for its commentary on their origins and significance. With 64 illustrations by Michelangelo, Raphael, Titian, Rubens, Canova, Bernini and others. 480pp. 5⅜ x 8½.　　27584-1

PSYCHOLOGY OF MUSIC, Carl E. Seashore. Classic work discusses music as a medium from psychological viewpoint. Clear treatment of physical acoustics, auditory apparatus, sound perception, development of musical skills, nature of musical feeling, host of other topics. 88 figures. 408pp. 5⅜ x 8½.　　21851-1

THE PHILOSOPHY OF HISTORY, Georg W. Hegel. Great classic of Western thought develops concept that history is not chance but rational process, the evolution of freedom. 457pp. 5⅜ x 8½.　　20112-0

THE BOOK OF TEA, Kakuzo Okakura. Minor classic of the Orient: entertaining, charming explanation, interpretation of traditional Japanese culture in terms of tea ceremony. 94pp. 5⅜ x 8½.　　20070-1

LIFE IN ANCIENT EGYPT, Adolf Erman. Fullest, most thorough, detailed older account with much not in more recent books, domestic life, religion, magic, medicine, commerce, much more. Many illustrations reproduce tomb paintings, carvings, hieroglyphs, etc. 597pp. 5⅜ x 8½.　　22632-8

SUNDIALS, Their Theory and Construction, Albert Waugh. Far and away the best, most thorough coverage of ideas, mathematics concerned, types, construction, adjusting anywhere. Simple, nontechnical treatment allows even children to build several of these dials. Over 100 illustrations. 230pp. 5⅜ x 8½.　　22947-5

THEORETICAL HYDRODYNAMICS, L. M. Milne-Thomson. Classic exposition of the mathematical theory of fluid motion, applicable to both hydrodynamics and aerodynamics. Over 600 exercises. 768pp. 6⅛ x 9¼.　　68970-0

SONGS OF EXPERIENCE: Facsimile Reproduction with 26 Plates in Full Color, William Blake. 26 full-color plates from a rare 1826 edition. Includes "The Tyger," "London," "Holy Thursday," and other poems. Printed text of poems. 48pp. 5¼ x 7.　　24636-1

OLD-TIME VIGNETTES IN FULL COLOR, Carol Belanger Grafton (ed.). Over 390 charming, often sentimental illustrations, selected from archives of Victorian graphics—pretty women posing, children playing, food, flowers, kittens and puppies, smiling cherubs, birds and butterflies, much more. All copyright-free. 48pp. 9¼ x 12¼.　　27269-9

CATALOG OF DOVER BOOKS

THE STORY OF THE TITANIC AS TOLD BY ITS SURVIVORS, Jack Winocour (ed.). What it was really like. Panic, despair, shocking inefficiency, and a little heroism. More thrilling than any fictional account. 26 illustrations. 320pp. 5⅜ x 8½. 20610-6

FAIRY AND FOLK TALES OF THE IRISH PEASANTRY, William Butler Yeats (ed.). Treasury of 64 tales from the twilight world of Celtic myth and legend: "The Soul Cages," "The Kildare Pooka," "King O'Toole and his Goose," many more. Introduction and Notes by W. B. Yeats. 352pp. 5⅜ x 8½. 26941-8

BUDDHIST MAHAYANA TEXTS, E. B. Cowell and others (eds.). Superb, accurate translations of basic documents in Mahayana Buddhism, highly important in history of religions. The Buddha-karita of Asvaghosha, Larger Sukhavativyuha, more. 448pp. 5⅜ x 8½. 25552-2

ONE TWO THREE . . . INFINITY: Facts and Speculations of Science, George Gamow. Great physicist's fascinating, readable overview of contemporary science: number theory, relativity, fourth dimension, entropy, genes, atomic structure, much more. 128 illustrations. Index. 352pp. 5⅜ x 8½. 25664-2

EXPERIMENTATION AND MEASUREMENT, W. J. Youden. Introductory manual explains laws of measurement in simple terms and offers tips for achieving accuracy and minimizing errors. Mathematics of measurement, use of instruments, experimenting with machines. 1994 edition. Foreword. Preface. Introduction. Epilogue. Selected Readings. Glossary. Index. Tables and figures. 128pp. 5⅜ x 8½. 40451-X

DALÍ ON MODERN ART: The Cuckolds of Antiquated Modern Art, Salvador Dalí. Influential painter skewers modern art and its practitioners. Outrageous evaluations of Picasso, Cézanne, Turner, more. 15 renderings of paintings discussed. 44 calligraphic decorations by Dalí. 96pp. 5⅜ x 8½. (Available in U.S. only.) 29220-7

ANTIQUE PLAYING CARDS: A Pictorial History, Henry René D'Allemagne. Over 900 elaborate, decorative images from rare playing cards (14th–20th centuries): Bacchus, death, dancing dogs, hunting scenes, royal coats of arms, players cheating, much more. 96pp. 9¼ x 12¼. 29265-7

MAKING FURNITURE MASTERPIECES: 30 Projects with Measured Drawings, Franklin H. Gottshall. Step-by-step instructions, illustrations for constructing handsome, useful pieces, among them a Sheraton desk, Chippendale chair, Spanish desk, Queen Anne table and a William and Mary dressing mirror. 224pp. 8⅛ x 11¼. 29338-6

THE FOSSIL BOOK: A Record of Prehistoric Life, Patricia V. Rich et al. Profusely illustrated definitive guide covers everything from single-celled organisms and dinosaurs to birds and mammals and the interplay between climate and man. Over 1,500 illustrations. 760pp. 7½ x 10⅞. 29371-8

Paperbound unless otherwise indicated. Available at your book dealer, online at **www.doverpublications.com**, or by writing to Dept. GI, Dover Publications, Inc., 31 East 2nd Street, Mineola, NY 11501. For current price information or for free catalogues (please indicate field of interest), write to Dover Publications or log on to **www.doverpublications.com** and see every Dover book in print. Dover publishes more than 500 books each year on science, elementary and advanced mathematics, biology, music, art, literary history, social sciences, and other areas.